Interpreting the
Old Testament

Interpreting the Old Testament

A Guide for Exegesis

Craig C. Broyles, Editor

Baker Academic
A Division of Baker Book House Co
Grand Rapids, Michigan 49516

Published by Baker Academic
a division of Baker Book House Company
P.O. Box 6287, Grand Rapids, MI 49516–6287

Printed in the United States of America

Library of Congress Cataloging-in-Publication Data

Interpreting the Old Testament : a guide for exegesis / Craig C. Broyles, editor.
    p.   cm.
Includes bibliographical references and index.
ISBN 0-8010-2271-1 (pbk.)
    1. Bible. O.T.—Criticism, interpretation, etc. I. Broyles, Craig C.
BS1171.2 .I585   2001
221.6′01—dc21

2001035581

For information about Baker Academic, visit our web site:
    www.bakerbooks.com/academic

Contents

Preface

CRAIG C. BROYLES

Each Sunday millions of us gather to hear about a two-thousand year-old book. We have filled libraries with interpretations and discussions of this foreign anthology. When I was writing a commentary on the Psalms a few years ago, my son Nathan, then three years old, opened the door to my study, sat on my lap, and looked at the books on the surrounding walls. He was just discovering the joy of books, and he asked, "Daddy, what are all these books about?" I said, "All these books are really about one book, the Bible." He paused and said, "Daddy, where is 'Jesus loves me' here?" I remembered all the nights we sang him to sleep with "Jesus loves me this I know for the Bible tells me so," and I wondered how many of these commentaries and scholarly monographs really explicate the love of God? And what about the commentary I was about to add to those shelves?

Here is yet another book about the Bible, this one about interpreting the great book. How can a volume on exegesis present a method that unfolds the revealed love of God? Before such a question I feel intimidated and overwhelmed, and so I should. No book on the Bible can do what the Bible alone can do. We can only hope to shed light on the Bible and send readers directly back to it.

All of us have grimaced at enough uninformed and ill-informed interpretations of the Bible that we know something must be done. Layreaders wonder at the meanings scholars infer from their historical reconstructions and their close literary readings. Scholars wonder at the meanings layreaders infer from their strings of proof texts. Many believers, lay and clergy alike, are either too busy or can't be bothered with exegesis that is too hard and too complicated. They insist the Bible speaks to them directly. Indeed, the simple love of Jesus and the essence of the gospel are plain enough. But the fact remains (and this is not a scholarly invention) that much of the Bible is complicated and hard to interpret. If we want our faith to reflect the depth and breadth of the Bible itself, then we must both mine its treasures and expand our horizons. For example, who does not more fully appreciate Isaiah's prophecy concerning Sennacherib's siege of Jerusalem ("Thus says the LORD concerning the king of Assyria: he shall not come into this city. . . . For I will defend this city to save it," Isa. 37:33–35) after seeing Sennacherib's palace wall relief (*ANEP* figs. 371–74) of his prior conquest of Lachish, one of Judah's fortified cities? We now hear the text and see with informed imagination how God miraculously comes to rescue his undeserving people from the most fearsome of empires.

This is not a book on the contents (the "what") of the Old Testament. Nor is it a book preoccupied with methodology. Rather it offers observations on the Bible, points us to resources to enhance study, and raises questions that help unlock the Bible's richness and depth. This volume also has the advantage that the different facets of Old Testament interpretation are treated by a variety of specialists from various countries and church backgrounds. My lead essay, "Interpreting the Old Testament: Principles and Steps," briefly considers the nature and function of the Bible to determine what tools and skills are appropriate for its study. It then surveys all the steps of exegesis, which are covered in detail in the following essays. In "Language and Text of the Old Testament" David Baker cautions us that Hebrew is not merely a code to be cracked but a language shaped within a culture ancient and foreign to our own. He also sets forth the principles of textual criticism that help us ascertain the "original" text. V. Philips Long ("Reading the Old Testament as Literature") details many of the features to be explored in literature. Few would deny that the Old Testament is literature, but many laypersons read its verses as though they were legal dogma or guarantees. Long enhances our literary sensitivities to both narrative and poetry. Because much of the Old Testament is literature that refers to and bears witness of historical figures and events, John Bimson ("Old Testament History and Sociology") describes the promises and pitfalls of reading biblical passages within their historical context. He uses several examples to show how the monuments and texts discovered by archaeologists can shed light on the Bible, and vice versa. In the essay, "Traditions, Intertextuality, and Canon," I explore the dynamic web of interconnections among biblical passages whereby the biblical collection acts as its own commentary and the whole of the canon becomes more than the sum of its passages and books. Since a text is also part of a wider ideology, Elmer Martens ("The History of Religion, Biblical Theology, and Exegesis") introduces us to the disciplines of the history of Israelite religion and Old Testament theology. Here we see how a passage contributes to the spirituality, theology, and worldview of the Old Testament. A text is also part of connected cultures, and Richard Hess ("Ancient Near Eastern Studies") helps us see how the Old Testament writers interacted creatively with surrounding peoples. He guides us to the many resources available on Canaan, Syria, Mesopotamia, and Egypt. Because the Bible is a product of a believing community and not merely authored by a few "heroic" individuals, Paul Hughes ("Compositional History: Source, Form, and Redaction Criticism") explores how we might make more sense of some biblical texts if we read them not simply as authored compositions but also as compositions edited over time. Finally, Jonathan Wilson ("Theology and the Old Testament") encourages us to see our contemporary situation and culture through the lens of the Old Testament by using a "this is that" model of biblical application, as suggested by Peter on the day of Pentecost (Acts 2:16).

As rich as these fields are, how can we be sure that after engaging in the hard work of textual and literary analysis, historical investigation, and theological interpretation, we will still remember to listen to the voice of God? This is not a question a book on interpretive tools and skills can answer but one that must be answered by every interpreter who uses these tools and skills before the living God who still speaks. I dedicate this book to my son Nathan and to all the child-theologians who keep us honest.

Abbreviations

ABD	*Anchor Bible Dictionary*. Edited by D. N. Freedman. 6 vols. New York, 1992
ANE	Ancient Near East(ern)
ANET	*Ancient Near Eastern Texts Relating to the Old Testament*. Edited by J. B. Pritchard. 3d ed. Princeton, 1969
ANEP	*The Ancient Near East in Pictures Relating to the Old Testament*. Edited by J. B. Pritchard. Princeton, 1954
ASOR	American Schools of Oriental Research
BAR	*Biblical Archaeology Review*
BASOR	*Bulletin of the American Schools of Oriental Research*
BDB	Brown, F., S. R. Driver, and C. A. Briggs. *A Hebrew and English Lexicon of the Old Testament*. Oxford, 1907
BHS	*Biblia Hebraica Stuttgartensia*. Edited by K. Elliger and W. Rudolph. Stuttgart, 1983
BZAW	Beihefte zur Zeitschrift für die alttestamentliche Wissenschaft
CBQ	*Catholic Biblical Quarterly*
CEV	Contemporary English Version
DOTT	*Documents from Old Testament Times*. Edited by D. W. Thomas. London, 1958
DSS	Dead Sea Scrolls
ET	English translation
FRLANT	Forschungen zur Religion und Literatur des Alten und Neuen Testaments
GBS	Guides to Biblical Scholarship
GKC	*Gesenius' Hebrew Grammar*. Edited by E. Kautzsch. Translated by A. E. Cowley. 2d ed. Oxford, 1910
HKAT	Handkommentar zum Alten Testament
HUB	*Hebrew University Bible*. M. H. Goshen-Gottstein and S. Talmon, general editors. Hebrew University Bible Project. Jerusalem, 1965–
IBR	Institute of Biblical Research
IEJ	*Israel Exploration Journal*
Int	*Interpretation*
JB	Jerusalem Bible
JBL	*Journal of Biblical Literature*

JETS	*Journal of the Evangelical Theological Society*
JSOT	*Journal for the Study of the Old Testament*
JSOTSup	Journal for the Study of the Old Testament: Supplement Series
JTS	*Journal of Theological Studies*
KJV	King James Version
LB	Living Bible
LXX	Septuagint
MT	Masoretic Text
NAB	New American Bible
NASB	New American Standard Bible
NCB	New Century Bible
NEB	New English Bible
NIBC	New International Biblical Commentary
NIDOTTE	*New International Dictionary of Old Testament Theology and Exegesis.* Edited by W. A. VanGemeren. 5 vols. Grand Rapids, 1997
NIV	New International Version
NJB	New Jerusalem Bible
NJPS	*Tanakh, the Holy Scriptures: The New JPS Translation according to the Traditional Hebrew Text*
NKJV	New King James Version
NLT	New Living Translation
NRSV	New Revised Standard Version
NT	New Testament
OT	Old Testament
OTL	Old Testament Library
PEQ	*Palestine Exploration Quarterly*
REB	Revised English Bible
RSV	Revised Standard Version
SBLDS	Society of Biblical Literature Dissertation Series
SBLSP	*Society of Biblical Literature Seminar Papers*
SWBA	Social World of Biblical Antiquity
TDOT	*Theological Dictionary of the Old Testament.* Edited by G. J. Botterweck and H. Ringgren. Translated by J. T. Willis, G. W. Bromiley, and D. E. Green. 8 vols. Grand Rapids, 1974–
TRu	*Theologische Rundschau*
TEV	Today's English Version (= Good News Bible)
VT	*Vetus Testamentum*
WBC	Word Biblical Commentary
WTJ	*Westminster Theological Journal*
ZAW	*Zeitschrift für die alttestamentliche Wissenschaft*
ZDPV	*Zeitschrift des deutschen Palästina-Vereins*

one

Interpreting the Old Testament

Principles and Steps

CRAIG C. BROYLES

The Nature of the Old Testament: Divine and Human

Divine Origins and Inspiration: Reading the Bible as Scripture

Before we study methods of interpreting the Bible, we must first consider briefly what the Bible is and how it works. The means we use to interpret an object depend on its nature and function. The most distinctive feature of the Bible is its claim to divine inspiration. Unlike other literature, its author is God. Much has been debated about the precise meaning of the claim that "all Scripture is God-breathed" (2 Tim. 3:16 NIV) and how the claim works out in the Bible itself, but even more important than our cognitive apprehension of this concept is our attitude. Exegesis of the Bible should be an adventure, filled with anticipation and holy fear, because in exegesis we hear the voice of the living God.

Our pursuit of the precise meaning and implications of the Bible's inspiration, we will discover, goes hand in hand with the exegetical process. If the exact meaning of "God-breathed" or "inspired" is simply a presupposition of our exegesis or derived from a theological system, our understanding of inspiration comes not from within but from without—in other words, the Bible becomes what we think it should mean. For example, if we respect the variety of forms in which God has packaged revelation, we recognize that a simplistic, prophetic model of inspiration (i.e., that "thus says the Lord" entails God's dictation to an individual prophet) does not work for the whole Old Testament.[1] Second Timothy 3:16 is clear on the Bible's ultimate cause, but it says nothing about the immediate causes or means that God used in the formation of Scripture.

Human Agency: Reading the Bible as Literature and History

Although divine in origin, the Bible is not a book "dropped from heaven," without human mediation. Nor is it a handbook of theological principles that are immediately accessible and applicable to all cultures at all times. It uses literary forms and imagery that are not immediately plain to modern readers (e.g., why does Yahweh call to the heavens and the earth when bringing an accusation against the people in Ps. 50:1–7 and Isa. 1:2–3?). Its many obscure references—from Abaddon to Zion—illustrate that the Bible is wrapped in history. The Bible makes the profound claim that God acts in history, but this entails a need for history lessons. Even the most uninitiated reader of the Bible soon becomes aware that God's means of revelation are human, including language, literature, history, and culture.

Much of biblical literature *refers* to historical people, places, and events. God has not packaged revelation in mere literature, whether through fictional stories or theological propositions (a systematic theology). God has revealed himself through both word (literature) and event (history). Revelation comes through the medium of historical events and a historical people and their culture. The benefits of this dual medium is that God grants us not mere ideas or mystical experiences but a historical basis for our faith. We can be sure that God can intervene in our own historical experience because we have historical precedents. The flip side of this form of revelation is that it is historically contingent. It is occasioned or elicited by particular historical circumstances (the Bible is *occasional* literature). To be sure, many cir-

---

1. Consider, e.g., Proverbs 24:30–34 and Joshua 10:13. Even within prophecy we should note that Amos and Hosea—although contemporaries—had remarkably different styles, that the Book of Habakkuk consists of a dialogue, and that Amos 5:4–6, which is introduced by "thus says Yahweh," strangely shifts from first-person speech to a third-person reference to God. See also Luke 1:1–4.

cumstances arise at God's initiative (the historic saving events of God), but many arise from Israel's doing (e.g., the history of Israel's kings) because Israel, or another ancient Near Eastern people, did something on its own. In other words, certain issues appear in the Bible by "historical accident." While the Bible has a universal message, it comes in a form that is contingent on circumstances and concepts of ancient times. We cannot limit "inspiration" to the original speech or the act of putting stylus to scroll; God supervises a process that includes authors and their personal experiences, audiences and their circumstances, historical events, cultural and social traditions, literary conventions (e.g., genres and figures of speech), and transmission history (including a book's adoption into canon).

The Nature of Interpretation: Interpreters and Processes

Table 1

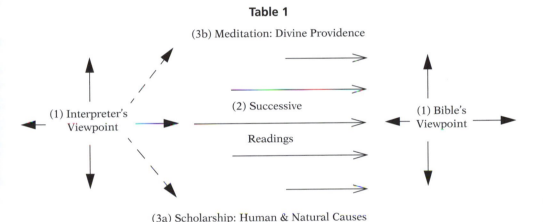

(3b) Meditation: Divine Providence

(1) Interpreter's Viewpoint

(2) Successive

Readings

(1) Bible's Viewpoint

(3a) Scholarship: Human & Natural Causes

The Interpreter's Viewpoint and Self-Examination

Table 1 illustrates some of the issues and processes involved in interpretation. To use Hans-Georg Gadamer's metaphor, the goal of interpretation is the "fusion of horizons" between text and interpreter (see the items numbered "1" in table 1). As Anthony Thiselton says, "The goal of biblical hermeneutics is to bring about an active and meaningful engagement between the interpreter and text, in such a way that the interpreter's own horizon is re-shaped and enlarged."[2] Interpretation

2. Anthony C. Thiselton, *The Two Horizons: New Testament Hermeneutics and Philosophical Description* (Grand Rapids: Eerdmans, 1980), xix; also, see esp. pp. 15–16, 439–45.

begins with the interpreter and the Bible, along with their respective "horizons" (depicted by the north-south-east-west grid), at some distance from each other.

The first subject for the interpretation of the Bible is thus not the Bible, but the interpreter. Before we consider the object of our study, we must consider our perspective or viewpoint. As phenomenology has made clear, whenever we observe phenomena, we never see the bare phenomena alone, objectively, in and of themselves. We see them through the eyeglasses of our language, culture, and personal experiences.

$$\longleftarrow \text{ sensory data}$$

observer/interpreter   object

$$\text{pre-understanding} \longrightarrow$$

Without being aware of it, we are not mere recipients of sensory data. To try to understand, we simultaneously attempt to integrate what we see with what we have learned. The arrows go in both directions: while the phenomena stimulate our senses, we likewise project on them our prior assumptions and experiences. We must therefore attempt to "bracket" our pre-understanding in order to come to terms with the phenomena in their own right. The telling question each must ask is, What are my vested interests and how might they bias and prejudice my reading of the Bible? What assumptions, presuppositions, and tendencies do I bring to the text? As humans, we must acknowledge our tendency to avoid the light the Bible casts upon us, especially its diagnosis of sin in the human condition.[3] We all bear cultural assumptions. In North America, for example, we tend to focus on techniques and technology when faced with problems, rather than on character. We all bear theological or denominational assumptions that act as eyeglasses. Passages that are an integral part of our theology are brought into focus, while the rest remains a blur. We all carry personal assumptions, which are the hardest to discern. We may, for example,

---

3. "According to Luther, the word of God always comes as *adversarius noster*, our adversary. It does not simply confirm and strengthen us in what we think we are and as what we wish to be taken for. It negates our nature, which has fallen prey to illusion; but this is the way the word of God affirms our being and makes it true. This is the way, the only way, in which the word draws us into concord and peace with God" (Gerhard Ebeling, *Introduction to Theological Theory of Language* [London: Collins, 1973], 17).

hold a belief tenaciously, not because we are exegetically and logically convinced, but simply because a trusted and beloved Bible teacher told us so. Self-examination is essential if we want to correct our inevitable astigmatism. A faith-affirming approach to Scripture means choosing to listen to it as God's medium of revelation, but it does not mean that we presume to know what its contents claim or what our theological conclusions should be.[4]

Successive Readings

As we begin our interpretation of the Bible and its viewpoint, we proceed through successive readings and approximations of its meaning, each time—theoretically at least—moving closer to fusing our horizons with those of the text (see item 2 in table 1). Through these successive readings and through trial and error, we alternate repeatedly through the processes of *analysis* and *synthesis*, and of *deduction* and *induction*. In the process of analysis we study the Bible by breaking it down into its constituent parts, thus uncovering its detail and depth. Through synthesis we study how those parts form a whole that is greater than their sum. If we engaged in mere synthesis, however, our interpretation would be too simplistic and flat.

In theory, our model of exegesis is primarily inductive, in which we go from the particulars of the text to inferring general principles. In practice, however, we must inevitably engage in deduction, in which we go from general principles, derived from our culture and theology, to their expression in the particulars of the text. The mere fact that the Bible comes in human words means we must have some pre-understanding of these codes. As soon as we read, "In the beginning God . . . ," we must project onto "God" our theological assumptions.

Scholarship. As noted in brief consideration of the nature of the Bible, it is "God-breathed" and thus divine, but it is also mediated through human agency. To appreciate the mystery of this "incarnation" of divine revelation we must, as part of our analysis, take deliberate steps to view it as both thoroughly divine and thoroughly human (see item 3 in table 1). Reading the Bible as Scripture means we submit to its authority; reading the Bible as literature and as history means we

---

4. We need to stop interrupting the Bible with our own questions and issues and to listen to it on its own terms. If we wish to be biblical people, we must be willing to surrender our preconceived notions, whether from our culture or from our church traditions. This inevitably involves us in a painful process. We must admit to ourselves that we may have been lazy, self-deceived, and intimidated by others. We must admit that others we have trusted in the past may not have an accurate or complete picture of the issues. We must work to distinguish what the Bible actually says from what we think it should say and what we think it "must" mean.

engage it "critically"—not with a faultfinding attitude, but with the exacting tools of scholarship. To understand what God says, we must study what God's human agents have said, according to the linguistic and literary conventions of their time. We must first acknowledge our "distance" from the Bible—to us today its language is foreign, its history remote, and its cultural assumptions sometimes strange. We need to employ the tools of the university—linguistics, literary criticism, history, archaeology, geography, anthropology, sociology, psychology, and philosophy—as they apply to biblical studies.[5]

If we, in fact, regard the Bible as "God-breathed," we should not shrink from asking any question or applying any exegetical tool, whether "critical" or not. Scripture, by virtue of its author, will prove itself when put to any legitimate test. If we assert the full divinity and humanity of Scripture, we must search both dimensions fully. An advantage of searching the human dimension is that it brings the Bible "closer to home." We see biblical writers and characters living amid life's complexities just as we do. Otherwise, if we imagine them as "saints," always in touch with God and never affected by the social conventions and pressures of their day, then we divest ourselves of models with whom we can identify.

Meditation and Faith. The exercise of scholarship is helpful so long as we also embrace the divine realities of Scripture and the world it describes. (The same holds, of course, for our interpretation of our own personal experiences, which are also affected by both divine and human, or natural, interventions.) The Bible's ultimate purpose follows from its unique claim. Because it is God-breathed, it is also God-revealing. Our primary goal in interpretation should follow from the Bible's reason for being.

5. In addition, it is often helpful to go one step further and deliberately distance ourselves from the text (a process called *distanciation*). To explore fully the Bible's human dimensions we may—temporarily—bracket its claims to divine inspiration and intervention (i.e., the "supernatural") and take a "reductionist" approach. We thus compel ourselves to uncover the human-oriented causes and effects that impinge on the Bible's formation. As we make ourselves "outsiders" to the Bible, we also remove ourselves—temporarily—from its authority. Suspicion is necessary for us to discern the possibility of self-deception. Otherwise we simply assume that the Bible's horizons, perspectives, and meanings are the same as ours. Moreover, we are then compelled to believe not simply because we ought; we grant our trust because of the Bible's inherent virtues and cogency. When we submit to its authority by reason and personal conviction, and not by mere decree, we take greater ownership of our own faith. The Bible is full of examples of believers who questioned God and their received traditions and who thus experienced breakthroughs in their understanding of God (e.g., Moses in the Torah, Habakkuk in the Prophets, Job and Psalm 73 in the Writings). While the Bible does enjoin obedience, it does not promote naive, docile, unquestioning acquiescence.

This realization poses a problem of how biblical exegesis is often taught in seminaries, universities, and Bible colleges. Whether one espouses the historical-critical method (often simplistically assigned to "liberals"), the historical-grammatical method (often simplistically assigned to "conservatives"), or the literary method (often simplistically assigned to "postmodernists"), the starting point is the text and factors such as genre, literary devices, traditions, and historical and social backgrounds. Thus, whether consciously or subconsciously, we begin with the human factors of the text. This is understandable, because the Bible is packaged as human communication, from authors and editors to various audiences. These are the features susceptible to the tools and skills of scholarly exegesis. But the effect of this starting point and the ensuing process is that we explain so much of the shaping of the text by human causes and influences that they may overshadow the spiritual and the divine. We then tend to relegate to God merely the aspects of the text that defy human probabilities. The theological deposit resulting from our exegesis is reduced to a "God of the gaps." In fact, the more "successful" we are at this form of exegesis, the more we explain the shaping of the Bible from historical, sociological, and literary factors, and the less we feel the need to invoke God.

Irrespective of the immediate agents of and influences upon the Bible's formation, its ultimate author and redactor is God. Before, during, and after our scholarly analysis of our passage, we must deliberately engage in prayerful meditation, whereby we access the text's primary author and speaker through the illumination of the Holy Spirit. We must recognize and acknowledge through deliberate, personal encounter that the transcendent God speaks to us. God who "dwells in unapproachable light, whom no one has ever seen or can see" (1 Tim. 6:16), to whom nothing can be compared (Isa. 40:18, 25)—no "likeness," image/symbol, metaphor, sign, or language—this God nonetheless "breathes" forth Scripture (2 Tim. 3:16) in words that liken him to human images, so we may gain a glimpse of him. Our exegesis of the Bible must always be imbued with this tension—otherwise we contradict its express nature and purpose. We should neither wish to devalue the Bible (a "liberal" tendency), nor to reduce the real God to the God "contained" in the Bible (a "conservative" tendency; cf. 1 Kings 8:27).

The leading question for the believing exegete should be, *What is at stake* in this passage? What difference does it make? By beginning with such questions, the interpreter focuses on the key existential issue. Our primary purpose and drive for reading the Bible should be existential, not literary, historical, or academic. Who is God, who are we, and what is the world? We should seek not mere information, but identity and direction. The Bible is not simply literature, history, or theology; it is our sustenance (Deut. 8:3). Second Timothy 3:16 does prescribe the Bible's use as "teaching," but such teaching is specifically "for training in righteousness" so we may be "equipped for every good work."

The Steps of Exegesis

Much can and should be said about methodology in biblical interpretation. Should we practice historical-critical or historical-grammatical exegesis? What of the more recent literary approaches and reader-response criticism? What about the questions raised by deconstruction and postmodernism regarding the agenda we bring to the Bible? But the essays in this volume focus on "how to." They presuppose particular philosophical and theological bases, but the intent is not to offer a method of interpretation as much as issues and questions helpful in bringing the various dimensions of biblical passages to light.

The following principles have guided the ordering of the exegetical steps below.

- Priority should be given to the spiritual dimension. Hence, once the passage and text have been established, meditation should be our first act.
- We proceed from the clear to the unclear.
- We move from text (what is said) to context (the factors that have a bearing on what is said).
- Among various contexts for reading, we proceed from those that are literary in nature (literary and generic contexts) to those that are cultural (historical and sociological, traditional, and extrabiblical contexts).
- We proceed from the "forest" to the "trees" (especially within literary analysis).

Two important caveats are necessary.

- We should not proceed through these exegetical steps in a linear fashion (i.e., attempting to finish a step before moving to the next) but in a spiral fashion (i.e., revisiting and revising earlier steps once discoveries have surfaced).
- There is inevitable overlap among these steps, especially among the six levels of context.[6] We should invest our energies,

6. For example, when we compare passages about divine retribution from Proverbs and Job, are we considering their canonical context or their traditional context (since both books stem from the wisdom tradition)?

not in splitting hairs between methodological boundaries, but in elucidating the passage(s) in question. The point of listing these six contexts is to insure that we try to appreciate the tapestry of biblical passages and all their colors, textures, and threads.

1. *Delimiting a passage*. Read the verses that you would like to focus on and those immediately surrounding them. Look for "markers" that set the passage/paragraph off as a "self-contained" unit.
2. *Translation and textual criticism*. Ascertain the "original" text and read it closely in Hebrew/Aramaic.
3. *Meditation*. In a prayerful manner read the passage aloud to yourself repeatedly and with imagination, emphasizing different words and roles in each reading.
4. *Literary analysis*. Do a "close reading" of the passage, with your attention focused on its "final form" and in relative isolation from its context. Unpack its meaning.
   4.1 *Theme*. Formulate a (preliminary) thematic statement of the passage.
   4.2 *Structure*. Trace the train of thought and plot development from verse to verse, also noting the emotive movement. Making an outline may be helpful.
   4.3 *Genre and social setting*. Identify the genre and setting of the passage, and note the genre's basic function and interpretive framework.
   4.4 *Point of view, characterization, style, mood, and selectivity*. Identify the point of view, the form of characterization, the literary style, and mood. Also consider the selectivity of material and plot development.
   4.5 *Grammar and word analysis*.
      4.5.1 *Grammar*. Be clear on the grammatical construction of sentences, noting connectives, main and subordinate clauses, subjects (divine, human), objects, verbs (declarative, imperative, and so on), and modifiers (adjectives and adverbs).
      4.5.2 *Figures of speech*. Note whether words are meant to be read literally or figuratively, and identify the figures of speech.
      4.5.3 *Word studies*. Using a concordance, do word studies to clarify the meaning of terms that are important and/or vague.

5. *Context.*
   5.1 *Literary and generic.* What light is shed by the immediate and broader context within the biblical book? Also, compare other passages of the same genre, noting similarities and areas of uniqueness.

   5.2 *Historical and sociological.* Using biblical and extrabiblical materials, describe the historical background of both the events recorded and the literary document itself. Also consider the sociological background, especially the social circles represented (e.g., priests, sages).

   5.3 *Traditional.* Study the traditions (e.g., exodus, Zion, Messiah) to which the passage alludes.

   5.4 *Intertextual/canonical* (literary connections). Does this passage echo and clarify earlier passages? Is it echoed and developed in later passages? What does this passage mean in the context of the biblical canon?

   5.5 *Biblical/theological* (conceptual connections). What are the theology, spirituality, and worldview reflected in the passage? How do they compare with other views in the Bible? How does the ancient writer's way of thinking differ from your own?

   5.6 *Extrabiblical and cultural* (ancient Near East). What parallels exist in other literatures, and what is the nature of their relationship (e.g., literary, conceptual, borrowing, polemical)? What light do these literatures shed on any of the items above?

6. *Compositional history.* What light does the reshaping of the passage shed on its possible reapplication in other contexts?
   6.1 *Oral transmission.* If the passage was composed and transmitted orally, how did this process shape its development?

   6.2 *Literary sources and redaction.* If the passage was composed from earlier written sources, what were their origins and functions? How did the redactor/editor shape his material?

7. *Theological implications and application.* While the preceding steps emphasize what the text *meant*, this step focuses on what it *means*. What general principles may be derived from this passage? Apply the passage to the modern context. Determine the points of contact and dissimilarity between the biblical and modern contexts. Seek to identify what is culturally relative and what is theologically binding.

8. *Secondary literature.*
   8.1. *Current interpretation.* Consult leading commentaries, reference works, and journal articles.
   8.2 *History of interpretation.* Deliberately consult older and ancient interpretations, Jewish and Christian.

An exegesis of Isaiah 41:21–29 will illustrate each step.

1. Delimiting a Passage

A "passage" can be anything from a verse to an entire Old Testament book, depending on the aim of one's sermon or exegetical paper. A short passage may illustrate the value of in-depth analysis, and a long passage may illustrate how the whole is more than the sum of its parts. Whether exploring an individual "tree" or a whole "forest," each range offers its respective challenges. The chief task of this exegetical step is to ensure that the verses chosen do not uncouple the train of thought. As a grammatical sentence is a "self-contained speech unit" and as a paragraph "deals with one point" (*Webster's Dictionary*), a biblical passage should present a self-contained point. The longer the passage, the more self-contained subpoints it will have.

The clues we use to delimit a passage derive from the same literary features we will explore in greater detail below. Opening and closing formulas may alert us to a passage's limits (e.g., *kōh ʾāmar* Yhwh in Amos 2:1, 4, 6; *nĕʾum-Yhwh* in 3:13, 15). Changes in genre (e.g., from narrative to law), subject/content, speaker/audience, or situational context may indicate a transition to a new passage. We should also observe grammatical changes in person (e.g., from second-person or direct address, "you," to third-person reference, "he") or tense (e.g., from present to past), and changes in tone/mood.

Isaiah 41:21–29 opens with the formula, "says the Lord." The following verses concern a challenge Yahweh offers, apparently to other "gods" (v. 23). This scenario unfolds in subsequent verses, until verse 29, in which Yahweh appears to offer a conclusion regarding the challenge. Verses 21–29 thus seem to have integrity as a unit. Isaiah 42:1 introduces a new topic: "Here is my servant." The verses preceding our passage (41:17–20) concern Yahweh's transforming the wilderness into a well-watered forest on behalf of the needy. Verse 20 appears to conclude it by showing how this act will result in a widespread revelation of God. Once we consult the commentaries, we will discover distinct changes in genre: our passage is a "trial speech against the nations," 41:17–20 is a "proclamation of salvation," and 42:1–4 is a "servant song."[7]

7. See, for example, Claus Westermann, *Isaiah 40–66* (Philadelphia: Westminster, 1969), 79, 82, 92.

2. Translation and Textual Criticism

Ideally, interpreters will translate their passage from the original Hebrew/Aramaic and assess each of the text-critical notations in *BHS*. But time often does not allow. Given the pressures that face all pastors, teachers, and students, they should at least endeavor to read their passage in the Hebrew Bible. (Minimally, they should read the passage in several translations, noting variations in translation and identifying the most accurate rendering.) We do not wish to undermine the confidence laypeople have in English translations. When Paul says, "All Scripture is God-breathed" (2 Tim. 3:16), his usual practice is to quote the Septuagint, a translation. The "inspired" quality of Scripture is thus not to be limited to supposed autographs but includes the Bible that lay readers hold in their hands. On the other hand, we must acknowledge that translation inevitably involves interpretation. There is no clear one-to-one correspondence between words in different languages, just as there is no one-to-one correspondence between words and concepts within any single language (see the discussion of the "word-concept fallacy" under "4.5.3. Word Studies"). The same Hebrew word may be translated by several English words, depending on the context and translators, and the same English word may be used to translate several Hebrew words. A translator's strategy may not match a reader's expectations for a translation. Just as adding a filter to a camera lens reduces the sharpness of the image, so a translation is a less precise representation of the original text. Reading the Bible in its original languages gives interpreters greater certainty of what a passage actually says. Moreover, we must acknowledge that inspired Scripture includes both its contents and its form, which is particularly manifest in the original Hebrew/Aramaic. In doing so, we come more in touch with the literary features of the text, such as Hebrew word play.

Reading the Bible from the original also guards against the presumption that we can immediately settle on what a passage or any of its words mean. It serves as a telling reminder that God's revelation is packaged in a language, culture, and history very foreign to our own. Our translation process, therefore, does not stop with a "translation" but continues through application of the passage to our contemporary context. Perhaps most significant, the awkwardness of reading a foreign language causes readers to slow down and to examine words and their relationships more closely. Often we gain insights we could have discovered from our English Bible, but our familiarity has blinded us to them. Although we must be cautious in assuming language indicates a particular mode of thinking (especially since J. Barr's *Semantics of Biblical Language* [Oxford: Oxford University Press, 1961]), we are more in touch with how biblical writers thought when we follow Hebrew words and sentences than English words and sentences.

> *Isaiah 41:21–29.* A close reading of the Hebrew text in *BHS* shows that the NRSV provides a reasonable translation. Regarding the textual difficulties, in verse 23 the Qere reading is *wĕnirĕʾeh* "so we may see," and the Kethib reading is *wĕnirāʾ* "so we may fear." (For more information on Kethib and Qere, see the discussion of Masoretic notes and accents in chapter 2.) The latter is probably the original reading. Instead of the MT's *yiqrāʾ bišmî,* "who calls on my name" (v. 25), we should probably read, "who is called by his name" (reading *yíqārēʾ* as implied by the LXX and *bišmô* with the DSS). Later, the "Cyrus Oracle" (discussed below under "5.1. Literary and Generic Context"), using very similar phrasing (*wāʾeqrāʾ lĕkā bišmekā* "I call you by your name," 45:4; cf. v. 3), is explicit that this figure is not a worshiper of Yahweh: "though you do not know me" (cf. also v. 5). Also in verse 25, instead of the MT's *wĕyābʾō* ("*and he come*s rulers like mortar"), we should probably emend it to *wayyābās* ("*and he tramples* rulers like mortar"). It is difficult to make sense of the MT in verse 27a: *riʾšôn lĕṣiyyôn hinnēh hinnām,* "First to Zion, behold, behold them." Instead of *hinnēh hinnām,* we should perhaps read, *higgadtî,* thus, "I first declared to Zion." In verse 29, the MT's *ʾāwen* is possible ("they are all *trouble*"), but reading *ʾayin* ("nothing, naught") is more appropriate to the parallel terms, *ʾepes* ("nothing") and *rûaḥ wātōhû* ("wind and emptiness").

3. Meditation

If we claim to believe that "all Scripture" may be characterized as "God-breathed" (2 Tim. 3:16), then—once we have established our text—our first recourse in interpretation should be to listen to the Bible as God's voice. We do not interpret a *text* that is merely literary or historical but a text that is characterized as present *speech*, and as speech we have access to the speaker. Because we regard the Bible as God's Word, our first act should be to surrender the initiative to God. The issue is not what we can get from the text, but what God wants us to hear. As "God-breathed" (*theopneustos*), the revelation of the Scriptures is inseparable from God's Spirit (*pneuma*). God's self-revelation must be "spiritually discerned" (1 Cor. 2:10–15). Knowledge of God has an unmistakably personal element: as humans know themselves by their inner spirit, so God is known only by God's Spirit (esp. 1 Cor. 2:10b–12). The very character of the "new covenant" is that it is communicated, not by mere literature, but by "letter" *and* "Spirit" (2 Cor. 3:6). The Scriptures are not to be an end in themselves but to lead us to encounter their author/speaker (John 5:39–40). We must be clear, however, that the Holy Spirit does not provide additional data in our interpretation of the Bible, so we might claim, "I know this is the correct interpretation because the Spirit told me so." The Spirit's role is in the illumination and personal apprehension of the Bible.

Meditation is not the property of Eastern mysticism—it is a biblical practice. Contrary to popular usage in today's culture, however, meditation is to be focused on a specific object, namely the Lord (Ps. 63:6), the Lord's works (77:12; 105:2; 143:5), or the Scriptures (Josh. 1:8; Ps. 1:2; 19:14; 119:15; etc.). It involves not only the mind but also the "mouth" (Josh. 1:8). The Hebrew verbs (*śyḥ* and especially *hgh*, which may be defined as "to mutter"[8]) point to an oral/audible act, as is consummately illustrated in "praising/meditating on" Yahweh (Ps. 35:28; 71:24). We must recall that silent reading is a relatively recent invention. Thus, meditation on the Bible involves reading aloud to oneself—repeatedly, or "day and night," as emphasized in the principal passages referring to meditation on Scripture (Josh. 1:8; Ps. 1:2). Paralleling these Hebrew verbs several times is *zkr*, "to remember" (Ps. 63:6; 77:3, 6, 11–12; 143:5). Meditation is thus associated with the act of "calling to mind." It does not necessarily provide readers with new information, but with a new quality of understanding by centering them in the Scriptures. Meditation is also an act of "searching" (*drš*, related to the noun *midrash*): Ezra is described as a person who "had set his heart to study (*drš*) the law of the Lord, and to do it, and to teach the statutes and ordinances in Israel" (Ezra 7:10; cf. 1 Chron. 28:8; Ps. 119:45, 94, 155).

Meditation is thus an act of *reading* aloud, wherein readers *center* themselves on the Scriptures and *search* them from every angle. Dramatic reading is especially appropriate because most of the Bible—stories, psalms, prophetic oracles, proverbs, and so on—was originally composed for oral performance. It is also helpful to emphasize different words in each reading (the verbs, the grammatical subjects and objects, adverbs and adjectives) and to role-play the various characters (Israel, the prophets, the wicked, God, and so on), so that we gain an appreciation of each perspective. At the same time meditation is also an act of *hearing*. We should endeavor to hear the Bible as though for the first time, and to hear it from the perspectives of various audiences: the original addressees, a later biblical audience (e.g., hearing the Pentateuch as one returning from Babylonian exile), a first-century Jewish/Gentile Christian audience, a postmodernist audience. Finally, meditation is also an act of *seeing*. The visual element in "hearing" the OT is particularly evident in prophetic visions (e.g., Isa. 1:1–2; 2:1; 6:1; 13:1). What was seen visually is then described verbally. We should thus hear

8. *TDOT* 3.321–22; W. L. Holladay, *A Concise Hebrew and Aramaic Lexicon of the Old Testament* (Grand Rapids: Eerdmans, 1971), 76.

the Bible with imagination, picturing in our minds the scenes portrayed before us. And each of these acts should be exercised in constant consultation with the speaker/author: "Open my eyes that I may see wonderful things in your teaching" (*torah*, Ps. 119:18, lit.).

At this interpretive stage we should not be overly concerned about being systematic or precise. We should go where we sense the passage and its author/speaker is leading us. To assume that all knowledge can be made objective and must be obtained by logical deduction (left brain) is reductionist and devalues intuitive ways of knowing (right brain). It is in the subsequent stages of interpretation that we confirm and unpack critically what we have learned in meditation, just as the Bible lays forth objective tests for prophecy (Deut. 13:1–5; 18:21–22).

The meditative and spiritual dimension of the interpretive process cannot be overemphasized. What sets the Bible apart from other literature and what should underlie our interpretation is that it is "God-breathed." Thus, while the bulk of the interpretive essays in this volume concern the critical use of the mind, we should not be misled that the intellect is the primary tool in interpretation. The engagement of the Spirit and the heart is vital. Meditation does not conclude here at step three—it should inform each step of exegesis, whereby we prayerfully and respectfully consult the author for each question we pose.

4. Literary Analysis

Reading the Bible as Scripture should not obscure that it comes packaged as literature.[9] Its verses cannot be lifted out as if from a "promise box," nor should they be read as part of a theological handbook. Both their *contents* and literary *form* are revelatory. God has packaged the contents of revelation in the form of literature, consisting of various genres. Broadly speaking, the genres found in the Bible are story or narrative (the Pentateuch and the historical books), law (parts

---

9. Martin Luther has said,

"I am persuaded that without knowledge of literature pure theology cannot at all endure, just as heretofore, when letters have declined and lain prostrate, theology too has wretchedly fallen and lain prostrate; nay, I see that there has never been a great revelation of the Word of God unless He has first prepared the way by the rise and prosperity of languages and letters, as though they were John the Baptists. . . . Certainly it is my desire that there shall be as many poets and rhetoricians as possible, because I see that by these studies, as by no other means, people are wonderfully fitted for the grasping of sacred truth and for handling it skillfully and happily. . . . Therefore I beg of you that at my request (if that has any weight) you will urge your young people to be diligent in the study of poetry and rhetoric." (Preserved Smith and Charles M. Jacobs, eds., *Luther's Correspondence* [Philadelphia: United Lutheran Publication House, 1918], 2. 176–77, cited in David J. A. Clines, "Story and Poem: The Old Testament as Literature and as Scripture," *Int* [1980]: 115.)

of the Pentateuch), and poetry (Psalms, Prophets, and wisdom literature). Each genre must be read according to its own set of ancient
rules. In other words, the Bible must be read *literarily* before it can be
read *literally*. If we think of Scripture as light (cf. Ps. 119:105), exegesis
acts like a prism revealing its colors. The following chart, although a
caricature, illustrates the importance of respecting the Bible's literary
forms.

Reading the Bible as a Theological Handbook	Reading the Bible as Canonical Literature
Content emphasized	Content and form emphasized
Emphasis on abstract concepts, ideas	Emphasis on concrete people and events, embodied ideas
Emphasis on universal principles, generalizations	Emphasis on specific examples, particulars (the typical)
Emphasis on ideals; what we should believe	Emphasis on ideals and realities (greater allowance for complexity, cross-purposes, ambiguity)
Text seen as prescriptive	Text seen as prescriptive and descriptive (thus it may be hard to discern if the behavior described is exemplary)
Text seen as transcultural	Text seen as culturally contingent
Logical order	Chronological order
Emphasis on nouns and adjectives (static), that is, on attributes	Emphasis on verbs (dynamic), that is, on acts
Emphasis on faith in principle	Emphasis on faith in practice
Emphasis on God as object of study	Emphasis on God as subject of action
God is defined/described	God is characterized and provides patterns of behavior (thus allowing for the freedom of God)
The interpreter is considered an objective observer	The interpreter is considered a personal participant (identifying with characters)
Cognitive (mind-focused) reading	Cognitive, intuitive, emotive, experiential, imaginative (mind and heart) reading

The text hits reader directly and theoretically	The text hits reader obliquely (can thus penetrate barriers) and practically
Text seen to have single meaning	Text seen to have different levels of meaning, open to multiple interpretations
Text presents homogenized point of view	Text presents canonized points of view

Reading the Bible as canonical literature reveals its depth and color. But perhaps more significant is what happens to the interpreters themselves: they cannot remain aloof but must personally engage with the literature. Canonical literature, however, does raise problems in interpretation; for example, discerning whether a character's actions are exemplary or simply one choice among many. This realization, however, does not cast us into a sea of relativism and subjective interpretations, because, since we are treating *canonical* literature, we must compare Scripture with Scripture (more on this point below).

To be clear on the object of our interpretation at this stage, we must distinguish a literary reading from an allegorical reading (seeking meaning *above* the text, as often practiced by laypeople) and a historical–critical reading (seeking meaning *beneath* the text, as often practiced by scholars).[10]

Historical Practitioners	Levels of Meaning	Examples
Medievalists	Anagogical/heavenly	Jerusalem = heavenly Jerusalem
	Spiritual (allegorical)	Jerusalem = Christian church
	Moral	Jerusalem = faithful soul
Reformers	Literary	Jerusalem = the city Synoptic Gospels
Historical-critical scholars	Redaction	Matthew's and Luke's redactions

continued

10. This chart is based on the insightful essay of Brevard S. Childs, "The Sensus Literalis of Scripture: An Ancient and Modern Problem," in *Beiträge zur alttestamentlichen Theologie, Festschrift* for W. Zimmerli, ed. H. Donner et al. (Göttingen: Vandenhoeck & Ruprecht, 1977), 80–93.

Historical Practitioners	Levels of Meaning	Examples
	Literary sources	Mark and Q
	Oral transmission	Jesus' sayings

The Medievalists often sought "spiritual" meanings from the Bible by positing allegorical equivalents to a text's referents (e.g., the city of Jerusalem typifies the Christian church). The Reformers, in their attempts to extricate the Bible from the authoritative, though speculative, interpretations of the church, sought to return to the literary level of the biblical text. But, as a pendulum swings in the opposite direction, the quest for the supposed "original core" soon displaced the text's literary meaning (e.g., the supposed actual sayings of Jesus took precedence over their final form and context in the Synoptic Gospels). Although we must not exclude outright the legitimacy of meanings "above" or "below" the text, attention must first be given to the literary meaning, for two reasons. First, it makes methodological sense to move from the clear to the unclear. Second, what the believing community has regarded as Scripture is the text in its canonized form ("the final form"), whether it be the "original" form or an edited form (e.g., whether the original sayings of Isaiah or Jesus or not).

4.1. Theme

Two definitions of *theme* are offered here. First, theme is "the abstract concept which is made concrete through its representation in person, action, and image in the work."[11] Second, theme is "a rationale of the content, structure, and development of the work."[12] The chief value of exploring a passage's theme is that it helps us to see the forest for the trees. Before we become immersed in details we should first get an impression of the whole; otherwise, the parts bear little relation to one another. They become mere segments of a photo, without any frame. Only with some grasp of the whole do we see the point of the parts. To change metaphors, a thematic statement serves as a kind of road map for the passage.

The best means for ascertaining a passage's theme are simply trial and error through successive readings and approximations (the "herme-

11. W. F. Thrall and A. Hibberd, *A Handbook to Literature* (New York: Odyssey, 1960), 486, cited in David J. A. Clines, *The Theme of the Pentateuch*, JSOTSup 10 (Sheffield: JSOT, 1978), 18.
12. Clines, *Theme of the Pentateuch*, 18.

neutical spiral"). Hints may surface particularly at the passage's beginning and end, at decisive breaks and turning points, in the development
of the main characters (especially a sudden realization), in surprises or
strange features, and in repetitions.

As noted above, the steps of exegesis must not be conceived as linear;
that is, one does not finish a step and then proceed to the next. Each
earlier step—especially the thematic statement—must be revised in
light of later findings. Its polished form should, in many respects, be
the prize of the exegetical process.

> *Isaiah 41:21–29.* Employing the hints above, we note that our passage be-
> gins with Yahweh's challenge to "gods" to present "proofs," and closes
> with his declaration, "They [other gods] are all a delusion." These proofs
> consist of interpreting "the former things" and predicting "the things to
> come" (v. 22). We detect a turning point when Yahweh shifts from imper-
> atives (vv. 21–23) to his own declaration of the gods' nonexistence (v. 24).
> This progression also reveals a striking development in the gods' charac-
> terization: the imperatives addressed to the "gods" allow for the possibil-
> ity that they are real, but their implicit silence and Yahweh's conclusion
> speak otherwise. The second half of the passage displays a similar turn-
> ing point. Yahweh presents his unique prediction (note "I" and "Who
> [else]?" in vv. 25–28), and then offers his own summation (v. 29). The rep-
> etition of these conclusions (vv. 24, 29) underscores the theme. We can,
> therefore, propose a provisional thematic statement: Because the gods,
> unlike Yahweh alone, cannot produce evidence of promises and fulfill-
> ments, they are nothing.

4.2. Structure

In light of the second definition of *theme* above, a passage's structure
consists of the same material as theme; it simply reflects a more detailed analysis. Interpreters must consider not only *what* is said (content) but also *how* it is said (form). To return to the notion of revelation,
it is not only a passage's conclusion that is revelatory but also its process, argument, or train of thought. Our structural analysis should consider the following:

- the overall theme (the whole)
- the constituent parts
- the transitions from each part to the next
- the relations of the parts to each other and how they contribute to
  the whole

When trying to discern a passage's structure, it is helpful to observe the same kinds of clues used to delimit a passage (see above). Delineating the structure in outline form is ideal, though it should not be pressed (as in a three-point alliterative sermon).

Isaiah 41:21–29. Our analysis of the passage's structure may begin with observing key grammatical shifts. There are imperatives (vv. 21–23) followed by a declaration (v. 24), and two "I" statements (vv. 25, 27) followed by two "who/no one" statements (vv. 26, 28) and by a declaration (v. 29). These observations confirm the passage's two main parts, as noted above: the first consisting of Yahweh's challenge to the gods to present proofs (vv. 21–24) and the second of Yahweh's own unique proofs (vv. 25–29). As for the transitions, we should note the striking absence of any answer to Yahweh's challenges after verse 23 and after his question of verse 26a. We are thus not "reading between the lines" to say there is an implicit interlude of silence after these verses. We may summarize our findings thus far in an outline:

21–23	Yahweh challenges the gods to make sense of the past and to predict the future
24	His preliminary conclusion: the gods are nothing
25–28	Yahweh's case: "I am first to declare that I have raised up a conqueror"
25, 27	"I have raised up a conqueror" and "I am first to tell Zion"
26, 28	No one else has declared it, and no one can explain it
29	Yahweh's repeated conclusion: the gods are nothing

4.3. Genre and Social Setting

We may define *genre* as a shared pattern of communication, usually shaped in a particular social context, that signals expectations of how a text/speech is to be understood and used.[13] Recognizing genres is an everyday but subconscious exercise. Whenever we read a newspaper we distinguish shared patterns of communication, such as journalistic reportage, editorials, advertisements, and cartoons. We take for granted their social functions of informing, persuading, advertising, and entertaining. A maxim of genre or "form criticism" is that recurring social situations give rise to recurring patterns of speech or genres. Because genres are usually tied to particular social functions, we should observe the various uses of language:[14]

13. See further C. C. Broyles, *The Conflict of Faith and Experience in the Psalms*, JSOTSup 52 (Sheffield: Sheffield Academic Press, 1989), 22–28.

14. This list is based on George B. Caird's helpful discussion in *The Language and Imagery of the Bible* (Philadelphia: Westminster; London: Duckworth, 1980), 7–36.

Referential Language
1. Informative: to talk about people, things, and ideas (e.g., news-paper journalism)
2. Cognitive: to think or talk about the above with oneself (e.g., newspaper editorials)
Commissive Language
3. Performative/causative: to do things and to get things done (e.g., legal pronouncements such as "I now pronounce you man and wife")
4. Expressive/evocative: to display or elicit attitudes and feelings (e.g., the laments "Why?" and "How long?" are not merely requests for information)
5. Cohesive: to provide a means of communal solidarity (e.g., "How do you do?" is not a request for psychological self-analysis)

Thus, for example, we must consider whether a statement is descriptive (no. 1), prescriptive (no. 3), or evaluative (no. 2). It may describe an actual condition, or it may prescribe an ideal or a solution to a problem. We should not assume that all prescriptive statements contain "should." To use a notable example, at face value "forty days more, and Nineveh shall be overthrown" (Jon. 3:4) sounds like a factual description informing the Ninevites what will take place (no. 1). We later learn that this oracle was God's prescribed punishment for the Ninevites' current behaviors (no. 3), and that it sought to elicit repentance (no. 4). Since the Ninevites later repented from these behaviors, the prescription was not executed.

The above definition of *genre* brings to light the components that all texts of the same genre share:

1. Literary motifs ("a shared pattern of communication")
2. Social setting (German: *Sitz im Leben*), speaker, and audience ("usually shaped in a particular social context")
3. Purpose/function ("signals certain expectations on how a text/speech is to be understood and used")

To identify genres we thus begin by noting the recurring, typical literary motifs that form shared patterns of communication. Because such motifs often appear within a literary structure, it is best to consider a passage's structure before attempting to identify its genre, although structure and genre often go hand in hand. This exercise naturally presupposes that the interpreter is familiar with OT literature. We compare Scripture with Scripture, with an eye not on content but on form and function. We then should ask, What social situation is presupposed in this genre? Who are the speaker and audience, and what are their relationships? Finally, to what use or function is this genre employed?

Once we recognize a passage's genre we are given the proper framework to interpret it. John Barton goes so far as to define "literary competence . . . principally as *the ability to recognize genre*."[15] Attention to genre keeps interpreters focused on the principal use or function of a passage. Interpreters are reminded not only to consider its contents but also why such content is present at all; for example, one might consider Psalms 105 and 106 contradictory accounts of the same historical period until one respects the distinct genres and functions of these historical recitals. With a clear idea of the overall function of a passage the exegete then can appreciate how the individual motifs contribute. Verses are understood, not just in isolation, but also in how they work together to form a whole. Another value of genre study is that by noting the typical features of passages, the distinctive features of each are brought into sharp focus.

To talk of a *genre* a "shared pattern of communication" must have been established in the society. But how do we, removed from Israelite society by some two to three thousand years, recognize the texts' generic signals? And given the importance of recognizing such signals, are we all therefore to be judged "incompetent readers"? At the very least, these questions must make us aware of the cautions and humility that should accompany our proposals. While archaeological discoveries, especially of the twentieth century, have provided many texts contemporary to the OT, our best source is still the OT. But we must also recognize that the OT forms a comparatively small sample of Israelite literary and speech forms used during the millennium of the OT's formation. The best we can do, whether scholar or lay reader, is to become thoroughly acquainted with biblical literature and to compare Scripture with Scripture (and to have good commentaries at hand). In any case, the primary goal of interpreters at this point should not be to arrive at a definitive generic label, but to consider features that make genre determination so important, namely (1) the passage's literary signals, (2) its key players and setting, and (3) its use of language (i.e., not merely its contents).

---

15. *Reading the Old Testament: Method in Biblical Study* (London: Darton, Longman and Todd, 1984), 16.

Isaiah 41:21–29. Several other passages in Isaiah 40–55 share a literary structure and motifs with our passage (41:1–5; 43:8–13; 44:6–8; 45:18–25). While we may have observed their similarities from our repeated readings of the Prophets, it may be more expedient here if we rely on the readings found mainly in commentaries. These passages represent the genre of "trial speech against the nations"[16] and share these literary motifs: imperatives summoning the nations and/or their gods (lacking in 44:6–8), questions asking who has foretold past and future events, and Yahweh's unique "I" claims, especially regarding his status as deity. The setting is an imagined one, namely a law court in which Yahweh is the prosecutor and the nations' gods the accused. The legal issue concerns who has foretold historical events and who thus is a legitimate deity. The function of this genre is to establish who is God by legal testimony and argument. The genre seeks to elicit and present evidence and to provoke the readers'/listeners' thinking (cognition, evaluation) about it, even to prompt them to judgment. It is possible Yahweh also plays the role of judge, but the assertions of 41:24 and 41:29 may serve as the summative arguments of the prosecution. If there is a "judge" in the scene, it is probably the audience.

4.4. Point of View, Characterization, Style, Mood, and Selectivity

Consideration of other literary features may shed light on the passage in question. Noting the *point of view* in Job, for example, is revealing. In the prologue and epilogue (1:1–2:13; 42:7–17) we are given a virtually universal perspective, with access to Job's inner thoughts (1:5) and heavenly conversations. But during the course of the dialogues (3:1–42:6), we become mere eavesdroppers. To understand the story we must recognize that while the readers are given the advantage of a universal perspective, the actual participant in the suffering, Job, is never told the full context of his suffering—not even after it is over.

Characterization, or information about a character's motives, attitudes, and moral nature, can be expressed at several levels:

1. Report of actions: what the character does, and what others do in relation to the character
2. Appearance, gestures, posture, or costume
3. One character's comments on another
4. Direct speech
5. Inward speech
6. Narrator's evaluation of the character's attitudes and intentions

Characters can be "static" or "dynamic" (i.e., undergo a radical change); they can be "flat" (i.e., built around a single quality without

16. See, for example, Westermann, *Isaiah 40–66*, 82 and 15–17.

individualizing detail) or "round" (with complex temperament and motivation). So, for example, Job in the prose prologue and epilogue is flat, but in the poetic speeches he is round.

Literary *style* "may be analyzed in terms of its *diction*, or choice of words; its sentence structure and syntax; the density and types of its figurative language; the patterns of its rhythm, component sound, and other formal features; and its rhetorical aims and devices."[17] Because biblical literature must be felt, not merely understood, we should also consider a passage's *mood* or emotional content. In addition, to grasp the weight of what is said we must consider the author's/editor's *selectivity*, and we must consider what is not said or what could have been said (which is called creating a "countertext").

> *Isaiah 41:21–29*. Yahweh is the speaker throughout, and the passage proceeds from his point of view. But it is important to note that he does not speak from privileged information but from what is publicly accessible and verifiable in a law court. He establishes his character, and the gods' lack thereof, strictly on the basis of verifiable predictions, fulfillments, and interpretations of historical events—in other words, through a deity's word and its historical effects. He characterizes himself as provocative and "in charge." The style of his speech, exhibited by his summonses and authoritative pronouncements, is confrontational and promotes this self-characterization. The gods, although given the opportunity to speak, are characterized as mute and worthless. In Yahweh's words, "[D]o good, or do harm, that we may be afraid and terrified" (v. 23), we also detect a tone of sarcasm. (We shall consider the passage's selectivity and what could have been said when we examine its extrabiblical context.)

4.5. Grammar and Word Analysis

4.5.1. GRAMMAR

Although sentence diagramming is not a stirring task, much light can be shed by observing the grammatical construction of sentences. By noting main and subordinate clauses we can discern the relative emphasis of the points made. Logical and temporal connectives (e.g., *kî*, "for") indicate how two clauses are related. We should also notice the grammatical subjects (divine and human), objects, verbs (declarative, imperative, and so on), and modifiers (adjectives and adverbs).

17. M. H. Abrams, *A Glossary of Literary Terms*, 4th ed. (New York: Holt, Rinehart and Winston, 1981), 190–91.

4.5.2. FIGURES OF SPEECH

Figures of speech are created by transferring words into new semantic fields. We are alerted to their presence by their strangeness. We recognize the metaphor in "the Lord is my shepherd" (Ps. 23:1) by the strangeness of perceiving God in a pastoral occupation. All speech figures are elliptical, meaning there is an inevitable gap to be filled by the interpreters, who must sort the relevant comparisons (e.g., the shepherd's care and protection) from irrelevant features (e.g., shepherds tend to perspire). The more common the figure of speech, the clearer the points of contact. Although literal speech is clearer, it is not better, because figurative speech adds richness, depth, and emotional impact. Because the Bible is rich in figures of speech, biblical interpreters should not assume that a passage is to be read literally unless such a reading is obvious. Passages must be read *literarily* (i.e., to determine the kind of speech employed) before they can be read *literally*.

The more common figures of speech are:

1. *Simile*: an explicit comparison (*x* is like *y*; "Now the appearance of the glory of the LORD was like a devouring fire on the top of the mountain in the sight of the people of Israel," Exod. 24:17)
2. *Metaphor*: an implicit comparison (*x = y*; "The LORD is my shepherd," Ps. 23:1)
3. *Synecdoche*: stating a part but referring to the whole (*x* fi *X*; "May the LORD cut off all flattering *lips* [i.e., wicked people]," Ps. 12:3) or vice versa (*X* fi *x*)
4. *Metonymy*: referring to something by naming an associated item ("The LORD has established his *throne* [i.e., royal rule] in the heavens, and his kingdom rules over all," Ps. 103:19)
5. *Personification*: attributing human qualities to what is not human (e.g., Lady Wisdom and Lady Folly in Proverbs 8–9)
6. *Anthropomorphism*: attributing human qualities to God (e.g., "the *arm* of the Lord," Isa. 51:9)
7. *Hyperbole*: overstatement ("every night I *flood* my bed with tears," Ps. 6:6)
8. *Irony*: saying one thing but intending the opposite, usually with sarcasm ("Come to Bethel—and transgress," Amos 4:4)

Isaiah 41:21–29. The imagined law-court setting is a metaphor for objective evidence (i.e., stripped of theological bias and political propaganda) and fair judgment. Theological language is characteristically figurative because God, who is ultimately incomparable (40:18, 25), can be known to humans only through images familiar to us from our experience. Especially evident in our passage are anthropomorphic figures: Yahweh is "the *King* of Jacob" (41:21), and he "looks" and "asks" (v. 28). He "aroused" (as though from sleep; *ʾwr* Hiphil, "stirred up" in NRSV) the "one from the north" (v. 25). Rather than merely saying "from the east," the phrase "from the rising of the sun" highlights this conqueror's dramatic and impressive arrival. Similes graphically portray the conqueror's aggression: "He shall trample on rulers *as* on mortar, *as* the potter treads clay" (v. 25). At the conclusion the "gods" are compared to "empty wind," showing that they lack substance. The sarcastic irony of "do good, or do harm, that we may be afraid" has already been noted. The identity of the "herald of good tidings" (*mĕbaśśēr*, v. 27) is not clear, but the parallelism suggests it is Yahweh's prophetic voice, which first announced the coming of the "one from the north" (probably the prophet of Isaiah 40–55). If so, the prophet is likened to the foot messengers who bring news, usually of military victory (cf. 1 Sam. 31:9; 2 Sam. 1:20; 4:10; 18:19, 20, 26, 31).

4.5.3. WORD STUDIES

We sometimes hear said to laypeople, "If you only knew the full weight of this Hebrew/Greek word. There really is no English equivalent." We must recall that the Bible is written in ordinary Hebrew and Greek. Its message is extraordinary, not the language itself. Its uniqueness lies not in its words but in its sentences. Although word studies are not *the* key to unlocking the meaning of the Bible, they can be very helpful. For example, we might do an exhaustive and exhausting study of *yšb* as it is used in contexts of "sitting." Lo and behold, we discover that the word matches the English verb "to sit." On the other hand, we might discover that, when collocated with God, the word portrays him as "sitting" enthroned as king (e.g., Isa. 40:22). This example also brings to light that if we want to study God as king and kingdom, we must include these passages in our study, even though the terms "king" and "kingdom" are absent.

This observation exposes a limitation of word studies. We need to be wary of the "word-concept fallacy," namely when we assume that words and concepts can be matched (cf. the issues of translation, discussed above). The lack of correspondence between words and concepts is best illustrated by *synonymy* (different words having the same meaning) and *polysemy* (one word having many meanings). Most concepts are covered by a variety of words, and most words cover a variety of concepts.

"The meaning of a word can be ascertained only by studying its use," and "the true meaning of a word is to be found by observing what a man does with it, not what he says about it."[18] A word's usage is best analyzed by noting the following features and categories.

1. Its syntactical (or syntagmatic) relationships, looking for common subjects, objects, kinds of action, and so on, especially if the word under study is a verb.
2. Its parallel (or paradigmatic) relationships. (Care must be taken, however, since the precise nature of the parallelism may not be clear. The parallelism may be antithetic, not synonymous.)
3. Its semantic field (i.e., a word's range of meaning and how it is distinguished from and overlaps with other words), noting synonyms and antonyms.
4. If the word is laden with religious/theological associations, it may be helpful to note its nontheological uses, which should elucidate its concrete meaning.[19] Nontheological uses may indicate that its religious/theological usage is metaphoric.
5. Rank the appearances of the word according to proximity: use of the word in the immediate context, in the same biblical book, by the same author, in the same historical period, in the same genre and social setting, in the same tradition or social circle, and in the same testament. Consider also the genres and situations in which the word appears.
6. Note the word's distribution among the various genres and blocks of biblical literature (e.g., legal and domestic contexts, the Prophets).
7. Check the versions, ancient and modern.

Isaiah 41:21–29. Doing exhaustive word studies of the passage's every word might shed some light, but it is simply too exhausting. The terms most in need of clarification are the parallel terms, "the former things" (*hāri šōnôt*) and "the things to come" (*habbāôt*, v. 22), and the near-synonym, "what is to come" (*hᵊōtîyôt*, v. 23). According to 42:9, "the former things" are simply Yahweh's former predictions that now "have come to pass." Its parallel expression is the "new things" that "I now declare" (42:9b), and these are probably to be equated with "the things to come" mentioned in our passage (cf. 48:3, 6). According to 43:18, among "the former things" is the "way in the sea," whereby Yahweh provided escape in the exodus from Egypt (vv. 16–17); the "new thing" he is "about to do"

18. Stephen Ullmann, *Semantics: An Introduction to the Science of Meaning* (Oxford: Blackwell, 1962), 67, 64.
19. For example, the concrete meaning of *ḥṭ᾽*, "to sin," is illustrated in Judges 20:16 ("and not miss"). Hence, "to sin" is "to miss (the mark)."

is to prepare "a way in the wilderness" for a second exodus. If the MT of 44:7 is correct, it similarly juxtaposes Yahweh's "establishing an ancient people" (*miššûmî 'am-ôlām*), presumably at the exodus liberation, with "the things to come." Because these expressions appear to be clarified adequately by the close context of Isaiah 40–48, we need look no further.[20]

5. Context

The issue of context is twofold: interpreters must both broaden and narrow their perspective on any given passage. First, and most obvious, we must broaden our horizons beyond mere words and verses. "The first and weightiest rule of speech is that context determines meaning."[21] Whenever words, or even sentences, are interpreted in isolation, more meanings become possible than are appropriate to the immediate context of the speech or writing. As we shall see, attention to various contexts will clarify many of the ambiguities inherent in an utterance taken in isolation.

Second, we must narrow our horizons from Christian theology and the New Testament to how a contemporary biblical audience would have understood a passage. The principle of "progressive revelation" means not only that God gradually unfolds his self-manifestation, but also that the process itself is revelatory, including each stage and its progression from previous stages. We must therefore "bracket" temporarily our knowledge of subsequent developments to appreciate the passage's original impact. We must endeavor to "forget" what the original writer and audience did not assume and to "remember" what they did. Readers of the eighth-century prophets, for example, must consider how much of the Old Testament had been "published" and circulated (and not merely composed) at that point. The OT itself admits that the Book of Deuteronomy, the covenant document par excellence, was only rediscovered in 622 B.C.E. (see esp. 2 Kings 22–23). We must therefore be careful not to assume that Isa-

---

20. We should also clarify the usage of *Zion* (41:27) in Isaiah 40–55. Elsewhere in the OT the word usually denotes Mount Zion, on which the temple resides, and by extension the city of Jerusalem and its inhabitants. But Isaiah 40–55 appears to be addressed to the exiles of Judah in Babylonia. Hence, in 49:14–22, Zion, here personified as a mother, feels "forsaken" and lies in "waste and desolate places" (cf. 51:3) without her "children," that is, her inhabitants. In 51:11, the inhabitants are identified as "the ransomed of the LORD," who "shall return . . . to Zion." Similarly, in 52:1–2, 7–10, Zion, though lying in "dust" and "ruins," will be restored. In these instances Zion is the abandoned city of Jerusalem and is personified as a mother. In 51:16, however, Zion is explicitly identified as "my people," that is, the people of Zion and not merely the abandoned city. In a prophetic section filled with lively imagery, we should not be surprised to see variations in the imagery surrounding Zion. In our passage it is not clear whether *Zion* refers merely to the abandoned city or includes the city's exiled inhabitants, although the latter seems to make more sense.

21. Caird, *Language and Imagery*, 49.

iah's or Micah's audiences had any grasp of a formal "covenant" contract with Yahweh. Given this realization, we are more prepared to study how these prophets endeavored to summon God's people back.

5.1. Literary and Generic Context

There are various ranges to a passage's literary context. First priority should be given to the most proximate range. The circles of context range from the verses immediately surrounding the passage, to the surrounding chapters and book, to works attributed to the same author, to the same block of the Hebrew Bible (Law, Prophets, Writings), to the same testament, and to the whole Bible itself (although these latter circles are formally part of the canonical context).

It is also helpful to compare a passage with others of the same genre. We have already considered our passage's genre, which we identified by noting other passages of the same genre and their *typical* features. We may now examine these other passages more closely, noting especially their *unique* features that contribute to an overall understanding of what is going on in this genre and social setting. Besides clarifying ambiguous points, this comparison should also reveal a passage's unique and perhaps key features.

Isaiah 41:21–29. The players and issues are difficult to determine from the immediate literary context. As noted above, the preceding and following passages concern very different subjects. The generic context is more revealing. Comparing our passage with other "trial speeches against the nations" (41:1–5; 43:8–13; 44:6–8; 45:18–25) sheds a great deal of light on the issues and parties involved. In our passage the pronoun "your" (v. 21) is strangely without antecedent. Two verses later we get clarification that the reference is to those who purport to be "gods." The preceding trial speech in 41:1–5 addresses "the peoples," thus elucidating that our passage concerns the nations and their gods. We also learn that the conquering by the "one from the north" (41:25) is specifically in Yahweh's "service" (41:2, lit. "with righteousness he calls him to his feet"). The third trial speech (43:8–13) uniquely introduces the "witnesses" of the law court. Opportunity is given first to the gods of the nations ("let them bring their witnesses to justify them," v. 9), and then Yahweh addresses his own: "You are my witnesses." The parallel expression, "my servant" (see, e.g., 41:8–9; 44:1–2, 21), and the later description of "my witnesses" as those who have had prior relationship with Yahweh as savior (see 43:12) identify these witnesses as the people of God in exile. So we here discover Israel's/Judah's role in these trial speeches against the nations. The fourth trial speech (44:6–8) has already clarified for us the meaning of "the former things" and "the things to come" (note also another reference to "my witnesses"). The fifth and final trial speech against the nations (45:18–25) comes after the pivotal "Cyrus Oracle" in 44:24–45:7. This time the "survivors of the nations" are addressed, and an "altar call" of sorts is offered ("Turn to me and be saved, all the ends of the earth!"), along with a confession ("Only in the LORD . . . are righteousness and strength"). Here we learn that Yahweh, as prosecutor, does not seek punitive damages against the nations, the accused party, but an acknowledgment that he alone has the right to be called God.

As part of the wider literary context of our passage, the Cyrus Oracle is particularly illustrative. Cyrus is named in this passage alone (44:28; 45:1). The description of his mode of operation in 45:1–3 is very similar to that of the "one from the north" in 41:25 and in 41:2–3, another trial speech. As already noted, both 41:25 and 45:3, 4 remark that Yahweh "calls him by name." We can now begin to make sense of why Yahweh's "arousing" a violent conqueror in 41:25 is "good tidings" (41:27). The Cyrus Oracle informs us that his conquering is "for the sake of my servant Jacob" (45:4), and in particular that both "Jerusalem" and its "temple" "shall be rebuilt" (44:28). In this oracle we also hear from Yahweh the same authoritative tone and exclusive claims (especially in 45:6) evident in our passage. It is possible that the reference to "the word of his servant" and "the prediction of his messengers" (44:26) points to the same declarations made by the "herald of good tidings" in 41:27.

We should also consider the use of the expression, the "herald of good tidings" (*měbaśśēr*, a masculine form, 41:27), elsewhere in Isaiah 40–55. In 40:9, the identity of the "herald of good tidings" (*měbaśśeret*, a feminine form) is ambiguous. Either the term is in apposition to "Zion" and "Jerusalem" (so NRSV main text), thus making this city a messenger to "the cities of Judah," or it is in construct with "Zion" and "Jerusalem" (so NRSV marginal note). The latter reading is corroborated in 52:7, in which the "herald of good tidings" (*měbaśśēr*, masculine) is sent "*to* Zion," as is the case in our passage: "I give to Jerusalem [= Zion] a herald of good tidings" (also a masculine form). Although in 52:7 the mention of the herald might simply be metaphoric, in our passage Yahweh refers to him as a historical figure—perhaps the actual prophet delivering this oracle.

5.2. Historical and Sociological Context

While the Bible is certainly literature, it also *refers* to historical people and events. It is literary, and thus works within the horizons of the stories and poems themselves, but it is also referential and thus tied to a stage of history. Considering the historical context to which a passage refers is essential to our beliefs about biblical revelation, namely that it consists of both word and event.[22]

---

22. When Moses asks, for example, "What other great nation has a god so near to it as the LORD our God is whenever we call to him?" (Deut. 4:7–8), he casts our eyes to the stage of history. Cf. Paul's argument in 1 Corinthians 15.

A passage may have two historical contexts. First is the historical context of the characters in the story or poem, that is, the history described in the text. Second is the historical context of the composition's author and audience, that is, the historical situation addressed by the text. So, for example, the Books of Samuel–Kings and Chronicles report the same history, but they address two different historical situations. The Books of Samuel–Kings conclude in the exilic period and address the issue of why Yahweh sent his people into exile. The Books of Chronicles conclude with Cyrus's decree allowing the Jews to return to their homeland and to restore the temple, and thus address the issue of restoring the people of God. As a result, the selectivity of each historian differs widely. Samuel–Kings focuses on human rebellion and divine judgment, and Chronicles focuses on human obedience, especially regarding worship at the temple, and divine blessing (i.e., historical patterns that foster restoration).

Our primary source for reconstructing these historical contexts is the OT itself, that is, comparing Scripture with Scripture. (Here there is overlap between a passage's historical and canonical contexts.) Most notably, the historical books (or the Former Prophets) and the Prophets (or the Latter Prophets) shed light on one another because they cover roughly the same historical periods. Another source for reconstructing the historical contexts lies in the ancient primary sources discovered by archaeologists (discussed further below under "5.6. Extrabiblical and Cultural Context").

Attention to the sociological context may also shed light. For example, among prophets, priests, wise sages, and the royal court, each group has its particular emphasis and point of view. Especially in passages in which historic (i.e., momentous) events are not in view, we must pay particular attention to the sociological context (e.g., most psalms and wisdom literature).

At this interpretive stage we consider what occasioned the passage. As noted above in the discussion of genre, recurring social situations give rise to recurring patterns of speech, or genres. Thus, studying a passage's situational context goes to the heart of its function and the all-important question of why it came to be in the first place. Given these circumstances, what is said in the passage? This analysis can be especially enlightening if we consider briefly what the text could have been (i.e., creating a "countertext"). For example, given that Yahweh could have given his people a big "I told you so" during the judgment of the Babylonian exile, Isaiah 40 surprises us all the more. Instead, Yahweh sends a "herald of good tidings" (v. 9, MT *mĕbaśśeret;* LXX *evan-*

gelizomenos, which is related to the antecedent of the NT's term, *gospel*) to proclaim his imminent advent to save: "Here is your God!"

In addition, these questions help us to see a level of interpretation often overlooked. On the surface many biblical stories focus on individuals, and so our eye is drawn to this level. Regrettably for many evangelicals, because our faith is very individual and personal, we limit our perspective to this level. But the ancients, without our preoccupation with individualism, did not so limit their understanding. For them an individual's identity drew heavily from "corporate solidarity." For example, the stories about David and Saul are not just about individuals, but also about tribes and the question of loyalty to whomever is the rightful king. In the story of Solomon we see the social tensions between tribes (a familial body) and the state (a political body), especially as he redraws the lines of his administrative districts and ignores old tribal boundaries (1 Kings 4:1–19).

> *Isaiah 41:21–29.* Irrespective of one's view of the authorship of the Book of Isaiah, it is generally agreed that most of chapters 1–39 is addressed primarily to a preexilic audience of the late eighth century, when the Assyrian empire was dominant, that is, during Isaiah's own lifetime. Chapters 40–55 are addressed to the Judahite exiles in the sixth century during the Babylonian period, and chapters 56–66 to the early postexilic community in the late sixth century, during the Persian period. In particular, chapters 40–55 reflect the period of Cyrus's emergence to power around 550 B.C.E., before he conquered Babylon.

5.3. Traditional Context (Traditional Connections)

We may define a *tradition* as a complex of beliefs associated with particular persons, events, places, institutions, symbols, or rituals. A sampling of OT traditions includes creation, ancestors, exodus, Sinai covenant and law, theophany, wilderness, conquest and Yahweh war, judges, Zion, divine kingship, Davidic kingship, day of Yahweh, wisdom, and apocalyptic. In addition, there are various traditions related to worship (i.e., the "cult"): the ark, tabernacle, temple, festivals, sacrifice, liturgies, and priests and Levites. This level of context is all the more important for the study of the Old Testament, during whose formation there was no consciousness of a body of written "scripture" as during the New Testament's formation. The Prophets, for example, generally do not appeal to written scripture as they do to these traditions (i.e., they tend not to cite each other or the Pentateuch). The question that is the focus of this interpretive stage is, From what sources does the author/speaker draw? Or, what antecedent tradition does the passage presuppose? Thus, we need to consider which traditions are echoed in a passage, what particular perspective of a tradition the passage reflects, and, finally, how it develops the tradition(s).

Because of the frequent association between a tradition and a key word or phrase, the mere mention of a key expression may signal a reference to a tradition. Thus, a word may signify more than its common denotation. This device acts as a kind of shorthand, giving biblical literature a sense of compactness and power. Thus, when Isaiah says, "Though your people Israel were like the sand of the sea, only a remnant of them will return" (10:22), he is using more than a simile. By alluding to the ancestral traditions he is threatening a reversal of the ancestral promise to multiply their descendants (Gen. 22:17; 32:12).

Isaiah 41:21–29. The genre of the "trial speech against the nations" is without parallel outside Isaiah 40–55. It may have been the prophet's own invention, one that uses the civil "lawsuit" (*rîb*, a term used in 41:21) as a metaphor (see, e.g., Exod. 23:2; Deut. 17:8; 19:17; 21:5; 25:1; 2 Sam. 15:2, 4). These trial speeches may also be indebted to the "psalms of Yahweh's kingship" (Psalms 47; 93; 96–99), a genre of psalm that addresses an international stage. The main characters are the same: Yahweh, the nations, their gods, and Israel, whose role is relatively minor when compared with corporate psalms of other genres. The primary conflict is between Yahweh and the nations with their gods. Israel simply plays the role of praising or testifying to Yahweh. In both the trial speeches and the psalms of Yahweh's kingship, Yahweh reveals his word and work internationally. Finally, the principal aim of both genres is the same, namely the acknowledgment of Yahweh.

5.4. Intertextual/Canonical Context (Literary Connections)

If a passage contains quotations, allusions, or echoes of other biblical passages, then it may be said to have an *intertextual context*. We need not hairsplit how quotations, allusions, and echoes are distinct. The point is that an apparent signal or flag must point distinctly to another passage. The passage thus means more than the sum of its words and sentences; elements of the echoed passage are "imported" into its meaning, because the author/speaker assumes the reader/listener is acquainted with another passage. In most cases the precise nature of the passages' relationship (e.g., whether complementary or polemical) is implicit and must therefore be inferred by the interpreter. In addition, it might also be helpful to consider if a passage is quoted, alluded to, or echoed in later passages, which should shed light on the earliest interpretations of our passage within the period of the Bible's formation. (For examples, see chapter 5, "Traditions, Intertextuality, and Canon.")

Strictly speaking, a passage's literary context extends as far as the "book" in which it is contained. Beyond this boundary we enter the *canonical context*. While we regard Scripture as "God-breathed," we also recognize that it is authored by humans and thus reflects their perspectives. If we liken God's revelation to a multifaceted diamond (cf. "the wisdom of God in its rich variety" revealed through the corporate body of "the church" in Eph. 3:10), then each author sees it from a particular perspective. For us to gain a sense of what the diamond looks like, we must consider as many perspectives as the Bible offers. When books were recognized as canonical, they were included "as is." By and large, they were not edited to produce "harmonized" or "homogenized" Scriptures told from a single perspective. Discrepancies or "rough edges" were not smoothed out. It does not follow that a synthesis is not possible; it simply means that God's perspective must be perceived through the variety of human perspectives ("for now we see in a mirror, dimly," 1 Cor. 13:12). Thus, to get the Bible's position on a matter, we cannot simply quote chapter and verse but must consider "the whole counsel [*boulēn*] of God" (Acts 20:27 my translation).

Before attempting to harmonize discrepancies, we should first respect the form in which God has committed revelation to us. The message of this medium (i.e., a canonical anthology) is that God's people may speak with a diversity of viewpoints. While, for certain issues, we may be able to achieve a synthesis, for many others we may simply achieve a mosaic or collage of viewpoints (there is thus a case for "biblical pluralism"—of course, within certain parameters).[23] (For examples, see chapter 5, "Traditions, Intertextuality, and Canon.")

Isaiah 41:21–29. Our passage does not appear to echo particular biblical texts, nor to be echoed in later texts. The reference to "the former things" (v. 22) in these trial speeches, however, presupposes Yahweh's predictions and fulfillments through the preexilic prophets (esp. 42:9). Although our passage mentions these "former things" in direct connection with the so-called gods, Yahweh's challenge naturally presupposes that he can meet the same test of presenting historical fulfillments of earlier predictions. (We could also treat the place our passage takes in the ca-

23. If we use an analogy of light (cf. Ps. 119:105), those looking at grass would say the light is green, those looking at the sky would say it is blue, and those looking at the soil would say it is brown. Each is correct from his or her perspective. If we attempted a synthesis, we might say that light is white (i.e., the combination of all visible colors). But if we pretended this was our summative description, it would be as limited a perspective as the others. To be accurate we must present both our synthesis (light is white) and our analysis of each of its discrete parts (as with a prism).

nonical development of monotheism, but this issue is probably more appropriate to the biblical/theological context.)

5.5. Biblical/Theological Context (Conceptual Connections)

While biblical literature naturally elicits imagination, it also purports to reveal the real God. As it is referential with respect to history, so it is referential when it comes to God. It dramatizes the persona of God, but it also reveals the person of God. Granted, we must admit God's accommodation to human understanding and language ("To whom then will you compare me?" Isa. 40:25). Nonetheless, while human language cannot grasp God, it can point to God.

The discipline of the *history of Israelite religion* has much to contribute to exegesis. While *biblical theology* tends to focus on normative faith (a *prescriptive* discipline), the history of Israelite religion tends to be more *descriptive*. It observes official religion, as promoted by kings and priests, and popular religion, and takes a more overtly "comparative religions" approach.

Biblical theology must be distinguished from *systematic theology*, which will be considered in step seven. As the name implies, the issues and categories emerge from the Bible itself. Because the discipline of biblical theology considers *traditions*, there is overlap with the traditional context above, but it also includes the issues that arise in the development of Israelite theology and religion (e.g., "salvation history," the election of the people of God, images/idolatry, monotheism, the land, social justice). In addition, it considers the relationships among various *streams of traditions* and how they complement one another—how they flow into a single "river." For example, in the traditions concerning the ancestors, the exodus, and the Sinai covenant, each has its distinctive perspective on God. The "God of the fathers" identifies himself with the family/clan; "Yahweh" presents himself as the social liberator; and in the covenant he presents himself as the overlord who guarantees himself to his vassal people in a contractual relationship. By viewing these perspectives together, we see a profound loyalty that responds to crises and a relationship that develops as the people develop into larger social units.

Among the many questions addressed by biblical theology, three deserve special mention. First, is our passage simply *describing* cultural practices or is it *prescribing* theological norms?[24] This is a complex

---

24. As part of this question we should also consider, Should the behavior of the human exemplars in our passage be considered normative or extraordinary? The point of a biography may be to show us something about God and what God can do, rather than to show us normative human behavior. For example, while Abraham and Daniel are upheld as models of faith, Abraham's willingness to sacrifice his son and Daniel's confidence while in the lions' den are presented as extraordinary behavior. Many a sermon has intimidated laypeople because it tries to institute heroic behavior as the norm.

question and one that may be aided by considering the extrabiblical context discussed below. To answer this question we should bear in mind whether the Bible has a uniform stance toward a particular issue or whether it shows variations, or whether a certain behavior is presented as inherently (im)moral or merely as culturally conditioned. Second, does the Bible reflect internal developments with respect to an issue? For example, in Exodus 21:2–11 no provision is made for the release of female Hebrew slaves in the seventh year, which is explicit for male slaves: "She shall not go out as the male slaves do" (21:7). In the later legislation of Deuteronomy 15:12–18, however, female Hebrew slaves are granted the same civil rights as the males. It becomes clear that we cannot take Exodus 21 as the last word on the subject of female civil rights. Because we observe such development within the biblical legislation, we then need to consider whether Deuteronomy 15 is the last word on this subject and the wider issue of slavery and human civil rights. In other words, is the last biblical passage on a subject (whether "last" chronologically or canonically is an open question) the normative biblical position, or are we meant to follow the "trajectory" established by internal biblical developments to its logical conclusion? This latter approach is simply an extension of "progressive revelation." So, for example, with respect to the wider issue of slavery the church has followed the trajectory established within the biblical canon. Although there are no explicit statements in the Bible condemning slavery, the biblical trajectory leads us to this conclusion. Third, how does the issue reflected in our passage rank among the Bible's priorities? Is it a major or minor issue? How much attention does it receive elsewhere?

Isaiah 41:21–29. Monotheism is so much a part of Judeo-Christian theology that we tend to assume it was normative from the time of Abraham. But closer examination of each historical stage of Israelite religion, within its own horizons, reveals interesting developments in progressive revelation. The primary conception of God in the ancestral period is as the personal "God of Abraham, Isaac, and Jacob" and of their clan (Exod. 3:6; see especially the Hebrew text of Gen. 31:53, and also vv. 29, 42). In the Mosaic period God is "the God of the Hebrews," whose name is "Yahweh" (Exod. 3:18, and so on). The emphasis here is on monolatry ("you shall have no other gods before me," Exod. 20:3), not on strict monotheism ("Who is like you, O LORD, among the gods?" Exod. 15:11). In the monarchical period Yahweh is the "God of Israel" and the divine king over the council of the "[sons of] the gods" (Ps. 29:1; 82:1–7; 89:5–8; 97:9; 1 Kings 22:19), and is thus sovereign. But in this section of the Book of Isaiah, addressed to the exiles (Isaiah 40–55), and especially in these trial speeches against the nations, we hear the OT's most explicit statements that Yahweh alone is God. It seems ironic that at Israel's lowest moment we hear most explicitly that the God of Israel is, in fact, the one true God. But it also makes sense that, during Israel's most desperate confrontation with Yahweh's apparent failure and with the apparent successes of other gods, Yahweh should assert that he alone is God. As Israel's/Judah's international horizons expand, so do their theological horizons.

5.6. Extrabiblical and Cultural Context (ANE Parallels)

As part of "word" and "event" revelation, God spoke to and through a particular people, who had a culture. Language does not consist of mere signs that point to unequivocal referents. Word meanings, and meanings of phrases and images, derive not from an objective dictionary but from cultural use. Revelation is packaged, in part, in a culture. If we claim the Bible is true in all that it affirms, then we must ask which statements are prescriptive of God's ways and which are merely descriptive of a culture's.

The histories of the ancestors, of the Hebrew people, and of the Israelite nation and its demise are inextricably influenced by ANE cultures and history. Thus, for us at great chronological and cultural distance from ancient Israel, we must use every resource available. Fortunately, we live at a landmark time for archaeological discoveries. Many believers are apprehensive of comparing the Bible with ANE literature, evidenced earlier in the twentieth century in the so-called Bible-Babel controversy. But our goal in these comparative studies is not to uncover the sources that biblical writers plundered for ideas, but to gain insight into the world to which God spoke. If we assume that God is a good communicator, he will not speak in a vacuum. Rather, God will first establish common ground with his people and lead them from there. Moreover, many OT passages respond to the issues of that ancient time and culture. To grasp the point of these passages we need to gain a sense of the culture's positions on the issues. By comparison and contrast with these ancient literatures we also gain an appreciation for the uniqueness of the OT revelation. If we eschew the ANE context, we unwittingly assume that the Bible speaks from the perspective we take for granted.

Here is a sampling of questions we need to ask in our comparative studies.

1. What parallels exist in other literatures?
2. How close are the parallels? Are they literary, traditional, or cultural?
3. What is their genetic relationship? Do they reflect direct dependence, a common source (diffusion), or independent origins?

4. If there is direct dependence on a common source, for what
purpose is the Bible echoing this source? Is there borrowing
(i.e., direct dependence of thought)? Or does the parallel serve
as a literary vehicle (e.g., a metaphor) or as a polemic?

Isaiah 41:21–29. First, we should observe that prophecy was not unique to
the people of Yahweh. *ANET,* for example, contains numerous ANE prophecies.[25] Second, the "Cyrus Cylinder,"[26] a historical text, bears some historical confirmations of and contrasting theological claims to our passage.
Cyrus, although a Persian king, claims that Marduk, the god of Babylon,
"scanned and looked (through) all the countries, searching for a righteous
ruler willing to lead him (i.e., Marduk) (in the annual procession). (Then)
he pronounced the name of Cyrus" (cf. Yahweh's claim: "I stirred up"
Cyrus and "he is called by his name" [Isa. 41:25]). The Cyrus Cylinder also
refers to the peoples "whom he (Marduk) has made him conquer" (cf.
41:25). It also confirms as fulfilled the promise of "good tidings" hinted in
our passage: "I returned to (these) sacred cities on the other side of the Ti-
gris, the sanctuaries of which have been ruins for a long time . . . . I (also)
gathered all their (former) inhabitants and returned (to them) their habi-
tations." Third, the Cyrus Cylinder and other ANE texts reflect a kind of
pluralism. As just noted, Cyrus's god is not Marduk, yet he credits his victory over Babylon to this Babylonian deity, admittedly for propagandistic
purposes. But for this propaganda to work there must have been a measure
of pluralism in the general ANE culture. Similarly, in Cyrus's edict found
in 2 Chronicles 36:22–23 and Ezra 1:1–4, he credits Yahweh with victory.[27]
Fourth, in the general culture of the ANE the status of a nation's god was
usually proven on the battlefield. Whichever nation prevailed over another,
that nation's god proved victorious over the loser. Our passage thus "shifts
the arena of decision from the battlefield to the law court."[28] Here the proof
of true deity lies in the ability to make proper sense of past events and to
forecast what is to come. The deity who shows that he has a measure of
control over history, by his explanatory and predictive word, is God, not
the one whose army has the upper hand at a given moment in history.

6. Compositional History

Tracing the compositional history of a passage is the most speculative
of the exegetical steps, requires the most expertise, and offers the least exegetical and theological payoff for the investment of time and energy. Nevertheless, the Bible itself demands some study of diachronic develop-

25. See *ANET* 441–52, 604–7, 623–26, 629–32.
26. Ibid., 315–16.
27. "In a text found at Ur," Cyrus claims "it is Sin, the Moon-god, who gives him victory. . . . His own god was Ahura-Mazda, creator of heaven and earth, and of man"
(*DOTT,* 94).
28. Westermann, *Isaiah 40–66,* 15.

ments, because they are an inherent part of progressive revelation. Not only do we see a chronological development of revelation among biblical books, as from Genesis through Ezra-Nehemiah, we can also see the same development within biblical passages. Signs that earlier sacred sources have been edited to apply to later situations surface most evidently in synoptic versions, for example, in Samuel–Kings and Chronicles. By comparing synoptic accounts we can discern the literary conventions considered acceptable to the ancient biblical writers, some of which might surprise modern readers. And while these literary conventions surface most clearly in parallel accounts, we have no reason to suppose that these practices were limited to this segment of biblical literature.

For example, a comparison of 2 Samuel 7:16 and 1 Chronicles 17:14 reveals that a biblical writer may edit speeches, even divine speech, to suit changed circumstances and to make a theological point. Instead of Yahweh saying, as in 2 Samuel "Your [i.e., David's] house and your kingdom shall be sure forever," in 1 Chronicles he says, "I will confirm him [i.e., Solomon] in my house and in my [i.e., Yahweh's] kingdom forever." Although the Chronicler "puts words in God's mouth," his interpretation has legitimacy because he simply replaces the immediate agent with the ultimate source, and it better suits his postexilic audience, which has no Davidic king, only a Persian king. Such a practice makes us uncomfortable only if we presume that the Chronicler is reporting historical events along the conventions of journalistic reportage. Rather, we must clearly read the Chronicler's work as an interpretive application of history to a later situation (a practice of any good sermon). Similarly, in a divine speech, 2 Chronicles 6:16 replaces the potentially vague "to walk before me" (1 Kings 8:25, when Yahweh's presence in the temple was center stage in Israelite religion) with the more specific "to walk in my law" (when the Torah moved center stage). In another example, a comparison of 2 Samuel 24:1 and 1 Chronicles 21:1 reveals a striking (and seemingly contradictory) reinterpretation of events based on intertextual interpretation. In light of the use of *incite* (*sût*, Hiphil) in Job 2:3, the Chronicler presents Satan as the one ultimately responsible for Yahweh's anger against David and for Israel's execution of a military census.[29] A final example reveals that a biblical writer may harmonize apparently discrepant texts. Exodus 12:8–9 ("they shall eat it [i.e., the Passover lamb] roasted over the fire [*şĕlî-ʾēš*] . . . Do not eat any of it raw or boiled in water [*bšl . . . bammāyim*], but roasted over the fire [*şĕlî-ʾēš*]") and Deuteronomy 16:7 ("You shall cook [*bšl*] it and eat it at the place that the LORD your God will choose") appear to be in contradiction, so 2 Chronicles 35:13 at-

---

29. See further Williamson, *1 and 2 Chronicles*, 142–44.

tempts to reconcile them ("They roasted [*bsˇl*] the passover lamb with fire [*ba⁻ʾeˉsˇ*] according to the ordinance; and they boiled [*bsˇl*] the holy offerings in pots"). Other examples of ancient, biblical literary conventions are noted below, especially in the treatment of 1 Chronicles 13–16.

6.1. Oral Transmission (Genre and Tradition Transmission)

In considering the period of the OT's formation, it would be anachronistic to think that it circulated as written literature. (Gideon didn't have a "pocket Pentateuch.") Stories and poems were passed from one generation to the next within the family (e.g., Deut. 6:7, 20–25) and within the worship services at the temple (see the discussion of 1 Chronicles 16 below).[30] This is understandably the most speculative task of exegesis, because we have no direct access to what was said apart from what was written. Our chief means for tracing the oral transmission of passages begins with the passage's genre and its social setting (*Sitz im Leben*, which is part of *form criticism*). In other words, if the genre is suited for oral performance in a particular setting, then we are in a position to conjecture its oral transmission and development (what is sometimes called "tradition history" or the "history of the transmission of tradition"). Because our deductions derive primarily from inferences regarding the basic genre and its setting, they usually shed light only on the genre and its traditions, not on particulars within a passage.

While some proverbs of the wisdom tradition were written (Prov. 22:20–21; 25:1), these short, pithy sayings were primarily suited for oral transmission (22:17–18; 26:7, 9), especially from parent to child (1:8, 10; 2:1; and so on). This observation helps us to understand why the *Book* of Proverbs shows little evident thematic arrangement and why there are duplications and slight variations of common phrases. Similarly, writing was not the preferred means of broadcasting prophetic oracles (Jer. 36:5–6, 32; Isa. 8:16–18). The prophets should be conceived more as preachers than as writers. Thus, prophetic books reflect characteristics similar to Proverbs. Interpreters should thus be cautious about making too strong a point from an oracle's immediate literary context, because the juxtaposition of oracles may not have been intentional, only conve-

---

30. "As in the case of all the literature of Israel, we must think of the Psalms as primarily not written literature at all. We must put away all thoughts of paper and ink and look on the Psalms as having their source in the life of the people. They played a part there before they took literary form at all. The most important fact in this connection is that the singing of Psalms was originally a part of worship" (H. Gunkel, "The Religion of the Psalms," in *What Remains of the Old Testament* [London: George Allen and Unwin, 1928], 70–71).

nient.[31] The exodus story was transmitted and published primarily not through written Torah, but through the celebration of Passover, which is presented as both a domestic (Exod. 12:1–13:16) and a national meal (Exod. 34:18; Lev. 23:4–14; Num. 28:16–25; Deut. 16:1–8).

Ironically, this method of biblical "criticism" can be used to support a "conservative" view of the Bible's authenticity. One of the problems with the ancestral narratives of Genesis 12–50 is the difficulty of finding confirmation of their historicity in archaeological finds. Because there are no people or events mentioned in Genesis 12–50 that can be correlated with archaeological texts and monuments, and vice versa, some scholars have argued that they are mere stories. But if we consider how these stories must have been transmitted, namely through family storytelling, we should not be surprised to see that political history fails to appear on the scene. In addition, identifying this means of transmission within the family provides a model for our own religious education in the home.

6.2. Literary Sources and Redaction

Is our passage an authored or an edited work?[32] (For our purposes, "redaction" may simply be considered "editing," and the "redactor" as

31. At a meeting of the Book of Jeremiah section of the Society of Biblical Literature, there was considerable discussion among members of the panel and audience about the rationale guiding the arrangement of oracles in the book. William Holladay, who has written arguably the most detailed commentary on the book (*Jeremiah*, 2 vols., Hermeneia [Philadelphia: Fortress, 1986–89]), spoke from the audience. I recall his relating a "dream" that in heaven he spoke with Baruch, Jeremiah's scribe, who said, "I put this oracle here simply because there was just enough room left for it on the scroll I was working with."

32. This is a legitimate question to raise.

The Bible has functioned as authoritative Scripture for believers not because it was written by extraordinary people of God; it commands our obedience because we believe it is inspired or, more literally, "God-breathed" by Yahweh himself (2 Tim. 3:16). Many of the "books" in the OT are anonymous (e.g., Josh., Judg., Ruth, 1–2 Sam., 1–2 Kgs., 1–2 Chron., Esther, and Job), yet they are no less authoritative than those associated with real historical figures. Many of the references within the Bible to other parts of the Bible are simply that; they are references to where one may find a passage, not claims to historical authorship. . . . The names of biblical books, which we take for granted, were anachronistic to biblical times, as were chapter and verse numbers. So texts were often identified by prominent historical figures. The Pentateuch or Torah was associated with Moses, Proverbs with Solomon, and the Psalms with David. (Note also Mark 1:2–3, which says, "It is written in Isaiah the prophet," and then proceeds to quote Malachi first and then Isaiah.) (C. C. Broyles, *Psalms* NIBC [Peabody, Mass.: Hendrickson, 1999], 27)

The entire Pentateuch, as we know it, was not formally called "the book of Moses" until the exilic or early postexilic literature (2 Chron. 25:4; 35:12; Ezra 6:18; Neh. 13:1). (Ibid., 31)

The designation, "(the book of) the law of Moses," in Josh. 8:31–32; 23:6; 1 Kgs. 2:3; 2 Kgs. 14:6; 23:25 refers only to the book of Deuteronomy. The appearance of this phrase is traceable to the editing of Joshua and 1–2 Kings (i.e., the "Deuteronomistic History") that was instigated by the re-discovery of Deuteronomy during Josiah's reform in 622 B.C. (Ibid., 40 n. 27)

the "editor.") This question has *historical* value because it helps us formulate what claims are appropriate to biblical compositions, especially
regarding literary conventions and the issue of authorship. It has *literary*
value because a composition might make more sense if regarded as an
edited work than as an authored work. In other words, the question not
only may help us elucidate the diachronic formation of compositions but
also help make sense of them in their final form.[33] It also has *pastoral*
value, for we may gain insight into how biblical writers applied sacred
texts and traditions to their contemporary situations, thus providing a
model for how present-day sermons might apply the ancient Scriptures.

We cannot talk about "evidence of editing" or "criteria for determining sources" because we must acknowledge our limited understanding
of ancient literary conventions. We should therefore consider the following list as possible "clues" that *may* point to edited sources.

1. Duplications (e.g., Psalms 14 and 53 were probably first transmitted independently in the so-called Yahwistic and Elohistic
   collections of the Psalter)
2. Discontinuous narrative or train of thought (e.g., Isa. 7:1 appears to be drawn from 2 Kings 16:5 and inserted into "Isaiah's
   memoirs," 6:1–8:18)
3. Changes in vocabulary (e.g., different divine names), style, or
   point of view—changes that are not traceable to changes in
   subject matter (e.g., the style of the narrative found in Isa. 36:1–
   39:8 is much closer to the style found in 1–2 Kings than that
   found in Isaiah 1–35, and virtually the entire passage is paralleled verbatim in 2 Kings 18:13; 18:17–20:19)
4. Anachronisms (e.g., Gen. 36:31, which is a later explanatory
   comment)

The search for literary sources and redaction is, in fact, an extension
of our literary and contextual analysis. If we had found that our passage does not seem to be from a single author, then we should consider
the possibility that we are reading an edited work. The following incongruities may point to earlier sources.

33. It is difficult to make sense of Psalm 108 as an authored composition. Why does
this lament psalm uniquely *begin* with a vow of praise, and what does a battle with neighboring "Edom" (vv. 9–10) have to do with God's cosmic and international self-revelation
(v. 5)? But once we recognize that it forms a creative composite of earlier psalms (vv. 1–
5 are drawn from 57:7–11, and vv. 6–13 from 60:5–12) and once we recognize their intertextuality with Isaiah 34:1–11; 63:1–6, we can begin to make sense of this composite (see
further Broyles, *Psalms*, 411).

- Difficulties in determining a coherent theme and structure
- Dissonant points of view or characterizations, or varying literary styles, including grammar and word choice
- Awkward fit of a passage with the literary context
- Audiences reflecting different historical periods, or traditions reflecting different social circles
- Incongruous theological perspectives

The probability increases if we discern "strands" of passages that can be separated into more or less continuous narratives.[34] The probability increases if the reconstructed strands match developments found in other OT literature.[35]

We might regard these clues as "discrepancies," "rough edges," or "seams." They might also be considered "flaws" if they served no rhetorical value or if they were part of an authored composition (the possibility of poor composition notwithstanding). But if the work were an edited composition, these "rough edges," in fact, reflect the editor's respect for his sacred sources, because he has left them untouched and restricted his "authorship" to the arrangement of the source material and to transitions and parenthetical comments. (In this respect, the tools that traditionally have been called "source" and "redaction criticism" can support the Bible's integrity and authenticity.[36])

34. Thus, not only do Genesis 1:1–2:4a and 2:4b–25 contain the incongruities noted above but they also cohere with the so-called P and J strands, which some scholars claim formed originally independent and somewhat continuous narratives. But even here we must admit to the possibility that some "duplications" may reflect, not an editor's splicing together of originally separate accounts, but an author's extension of parallelism, where repetitions or "seconding" may be to add emphasis, specificity, or a different perspective (e.g., in the Psalms "God" sometimes appears in the first line and "the LORD" or "Yahweh" adds specificity in the parallel line: 47:5; 56:10; 58:6; 68:26).

35. Thus, the legislation found in JE generally matches that reflected in 1–2 Samuel, the laws in D match those reflected in 1–2 Kings, and the laws in P match those reflected in 1–2 Chronicles. Exemplary cases concern the issues of multiple altars or a single, central altar and distinctions between priests and Levites. Yet here we must also consider the OT's own admission that the Book of Deuteronomy was lost, but, once found, it profoundly influenced the interpretation of the Israelite and Judahite monarchies, as reflected in 1–2 Kings.

36. Whether or not interpreters agree with the *conclusion* that a literary work, such as the Pentateuch, is an edited composition, we must acknowledge the *observations* of scholars, irrespective of their presuppositions. They have helped us see the diversity of theological perspectives and emphases within biblical compositions—whether from one author or several may be irrelevant. They have, in fact, helped us read the Bible more closely. In the twentieth century both the so-called conservatives and liberals agreed on a premise that has proven ill-founded, namely the claim of single authorship for certain biblical books and passages. Hence, assertions that they were edited would make them "forgeries" and thus fallacious. Both sides have needed to surrender their modern presuppositions about what is "proper" in good literature and to respect the literary conventions acceptable in ancient times.

A final caveat: we must be extremely cautious that we not apply modern expectations about literary conventions to ancient texts. For example, we might consider the apparent contradiction between Proverbs 26:4 and 26:5 as indicative of separate sources. But if we show respect to the ancient author/editor, and we assume that he did not fall asleep between verses, we should admit that the tension between these proverbs is intentional. We should be aware that such literary tensions may be part and parcel of ancient Hebrew literary style. Before we propose that certain features would have been inappropriate to a biblical writer, we must first become thoroughly familiar with ancient literary conventions. Speculating on a passage's compositional history must come toward the end of the exegetical process, lest we presume that an infelicity (as detected by our modern expectations of literature) indicates multiple authorship, without having given full consideration to the passage's literary and rhetorical function according to ancient Near Eastern conventions.

1 Chronicles 13–16. Rather than Isaiah 41:21–29, we shall use 1 Chronicles 13–16, the account of David bringing the ark into Jerusalem, as our exemplary passage, because it has a clearly discernible compositional history. A comparison with its parallels results in the following observations.[37]

1 Chronicles	2 Samuel	Psalms
13:1–4 Priests and Levites distinguished	none	
13:5–14	6:1–11	
14:1–17	5:11–25	
15:1–24 Priests and Levites distinguished; Levites to carry the ark "as Moses had commanded according to the word of the LORD" (v. 15)	none	
15:25–16:3	6:12b–19a 6:12a, 13 are omitted	

37. Especially helpful here is a synopsis, such as *A Synoptic Harmony of Samuel, Kings, and Chronicles*, ed. James D. Newsome Jr. (Grand Rapids: Baker, 1986). See further the very informative commentary by H. G. M. Williamson, *1 and 2 Chronicles*, NCB (Grand Rapids: Eerdmans, 1982).

16:4–7 Levitical assignments	none	
16:8–22		105:1–15
16:23–33		96:1–13
16:34–36		106:1, 47–48
16:37–42 Priests and Levites distinguished	none	
16:43	6:19b–20a 6:20b–23 is omitted	

First, we should note that the Chronicler *reorders the sequence of events* as narrated in 2 Samuel. Whereas, in the latter, David defeats the Philistines and then, after two attempts, brings the ark into Jerusalem, in the former his first attempt to bring the ark precedes his defeat of the Philistines. During these military engagements with the Philistines, David twice "inquired of the Lord" (2 Sam. 5:19, 23 // 1 Chron. 14:10, 14). In 1 Samuel he apparently does so by means of the ephod (23:1–12; 30:7–8), which was associated with the Urim and Thummim (Exod. 28:28–30; Lev. 8:7–8; Num. 27:21). None of these implements is mentioned in Chronicles (it is possible the Chronicler was mindful that the ephod had at times been associated with idolatry, in Judg. 8:27; 17:5; Hos. 3:4), so we are left with the impression David consulted Yahweh by means of the ark (cf. Exod. 25:22; Num. 7:89).

Second, the Chronicler *omits material from his source that would detract from his thematic interests and the purpose of his work.* He omits 2 Samuel 6:12a because it implies that David is motivated to make a second attempt at retrieving the ark because he envies the blessing that had fallen on Obed-edom. Instead, the insertion in 1 Chronicles 15:1–24 implies that David is motivated by his discovery of the Mosaic legislation prescribing the Levites to carry the ark. The Chronicler omits virtually all of 2 Samuel 6:13, in which "an ox and a fatling" are sacrificed at every "six paces," because none of this has a precedent in pentateuchal or priestly legislation. Instead, he specifies that "the Levites . . . were carrying the ark" (1 Chron. 15:26, 27) and "they sacrificed seven bulls and seven rams," animals frequently named for sacrifice in pentateuchal and priestly legislation (note especially the number "seven" in Ezek. 45:23; 2 Chron. 29:21; cf. Num. 23:4). These omissions and additions support the purpose of 1–2 Chronicles to instruct the postexilic generation on how to restore the temple worship prescribed by the priestly legislation. The Chronicler also omits the conflict between David and Michal, Saul's daughter, and implicitly the conflict between Judah and the northern tribes (2 Sam. 6:20b–23). Because the northern kingdom worshiped at illegitimate sanctuaries, this material does not fall within the Chronicler's thematic interests.

Third, the Chronicler *uses source material that postdates the story he is narrating*, and he *edits it accordingly*. He includes a psalm, which is paralleled in three psalms of the Psalter. Several variations among them make clear that the Chronicler edits these later psalms to remove anachronistic references to a temple structure.[38] He replaces "his sanctuary" (Ps. 96:6) with "his place" (1 Chron. 16:27), and "into his courts" (Ps. 96:8) with "before him" (1 Chron. 16:29). Instead of "beauty" in Psalm 96:6, 1 Chronicles 16:27 reads "joy" (*ḥedĕwāh*), a term found elsewhere only in postexilic passages (Neh. 8:10 and Ezra 6:16, which is in Aramaic). The Chronicler, however, retains the anachronistic petition, "gather . . . us from among the nations" (1 Chron. 16:35 = Ps. 106:47), because it suits the setting of his audience in the postexilic period. ("Deliver us" may have been added by the Chronicler to suit David's victories over neighboring nations in 1 Chronicles 18.) We should also note that, in addition to 1–2 Samuel and the Psalms, the Chronicler draws on a source that emphasizes the respective responsibilities of priests and Levites (1 Chron. 13:1–4; 15:1–24, 26–27; 16:4–7, 37–42).[39]

It thus appears that the Chronicler endeavors to instruct the postexilic community by means of a key historical figure, who acts as a model for the kind of obedience that should brings God's blessing. He uses the momentous event of David's bringing the ark into Jerusalem to illustrate later liturgical practices. In view of this overarching purpose, this biblical

---

38. Although it is not impossible that later psalmists had edited a psalm originally from the Davidic, pre-temple period, this theory makes less sense. Besides the petition "gather us . . . from among the nations" (Ps. 106:47), other features in Psalm 106 have affinity to the (post-) exilic period (see Broyles, *Psalms*, 406–7). While there are obvious reasons why the Chronicler would make the changes noted above, there are no obvious reasons why later psalmists should change the text transmitted in 1 Chronicles. The expressions "his place" (1 Chron. 16:27) and "before him" (1 Chron. 16:29), are well attested in the extant psalms (24:3; 26:8; 132:5; and 18:6; 96:6; 100:2).

We should note what we might call the criterion of "affinity"; that is, if a passage's style and word choice, theological and sociological perspective, traditions, and so on show strong affinity to a particular historical period, then it is likely that it was either composed or edited in that period. While this criterion may not prove the passage's origins, it should at least cause us to reevaluate our assumptions about the passage's ostensible authorship and origins.

39. We do not have the space to speculate whether this was the so-called P source.

writer-editor considered it legitimate to subsume historical accuracy to thematic concerns.[40]

7. Theological Implications and Application

To this point we have emphasized what the biblical passage *meant* to its biblical audiences. Now we focus our attention on what it *means* to us. In this final stage of inferring theological implications and applying the Bible to our situation, we become readers/interpreters, not only of the Bible, but also of our own contemporary circumstances and needs. Our theological emphases should first be driven by the literary theme of the passage. The main points of the passage should guide the points we wish to make to our audience. We also need to note where these points rank within the Bible's priorities, as we determined in our analysis of the biblical-theological context. In this way we align ourselves not only with the Bible's content but also with its priorities.

In the process of deriving theological implications we can ask the following questions.

- What is said explicitly about theology, spirituality, and worldviews?
- What is assumed? For example, a prayer may make few explicit theological claims, but the very act of saying it implies divine condescension and compassion.
- What general principles may be derived from this specific case? The Bible is much more relevant than it initially appears. Although a passage may focus on an issue that does not concern us, it may employ general principles or lines of argument that may be applied to a variety of situations.[41]
- How does the passage match my modern-day expectations and those of my audience? What surprises does it offer? These questions may bring to light what our audience most needs to hear from the Bible. How do our historical, social, traditional, and cultural contexts match with those reflected in our passage? If in our

---

40. The issue is thus not one of historical truth and falsehood but one of genre and purpose. If 1–2 Chronicles was not intended as a strict historical chronicle, as we might understand it, it cannot be faulted for historical imprecision.

41. For example, Jesus went beyond the immediate issues of the OT Scriptures to the principles underlying them. In Matthew, Jesus twice appeals to Hosea 6:6, which in its immediate context concerns ritual sacrifice. At first glance, this has little to do with dining with "tax collectors and sinners" (Matt. 9:10–13) and with plucking grain on the Sabbath (12:1–8). But underlying each of these cases is the principle of God's priorities and values within God's revealed Torah.

biblical-theological analysis we discerned a biblical "trajectory," where does that trajectory lead us in our current situation?
• Do I genuinely believe what I have read? We must distinguish between what we should believe (orthodoxy) and what we actually believe (existential faith). The Bible is about beliefs, not mere doctrines or theological dogma.[42] A further question that helps bring an honest response to the surface is, How do I feel about this passage?

This final stage is often the most controversial. Our own readers/listeners may be in full agreement with us on what our passage meant, but they may disagree when we come to what it means. It is therefore critical that we do all our homework prior to this stage. It is a tactful strategy for our audience, because the less of a leap we take to our (post-) modern context, the clearer the Bible's application becomes. It is a shrewd strategy with respect to the interpreter's own biases and prejudices, because the more sharply we can bracket our interests from what the Bible meant, the more likely we are to present a truer reflection of its claims. Take, for example, the problem of distinguishing what is culturally relative and what is theologically binding in the Bible. If we have taken care to note that the Bible is simply describing a cultural practice, or that it shows a variety of perspectives within the canon, then we and our audience are more prepared to show flexibility. Similarly, if the Bible does take a consistent position and prescribes a theological norm, then we and our audience are more prepared to submit to the Bible's mandate.

Isaiah 41:21–29. From our exegetical analysis of this passage we can make the following points, which can be applied to the church today.

• Which god is indeed God is not to be determined by whose religion (including secular humanism) holds the military, political, or cultural advantage. It is determined by the God who can make sense of history, promise something for the future, and make good on that word.
• Impartial, "legal" criteria can be established to determine a religion's truth claims. Biblical faith is, at least to some extent, verifiable, which also means that it must admit to being falsifiable. These inferences support the need for "apologetic" arguments for a faith to be credible.
• A measure of pluralism exists both in the culture of the Babylonian exile and that of today. This "trial speech against the nations" tactfully

42. For example, "If I really believed Isaiah 40, why do I view Monday mornings the way I do?"

admits to the possibility of other gods. But after their failure to produce evidence, this passage declares a verdict, without apology.
- God's power is not limited to God's people and their institutions.
- God can use politicians! They can do God's will unwittingly.
- While this passage does argue for monotheism, it is a functional monotheism, not a theoretical one derived from metaphysics or ontology (tools frequently used in systematic theology). A "god" is a god if he or she can say something and make good on his or her word.

8. Secondary Literature

It is important, especially for the interpreters themselves, that they take an initial run through the exegetical steps before turning to what others have said. Just as the process of composition, and not merely its conclusions, is part of biblical revelation (e.g., progressive revelation), it is also vital that interpreters engage in the process of exegesis and not merely assemble exegetical conclusions. Those who have engaged in Bible study—whether formal or informal, academic or not—know there is as much joy in the process of discovery as in a notable conclusion.

Ignoring the research and reflections of others, whether believers or not, will shortchange a sermon or exegetical paper. Secondary literature can help us avoid superficiality and our own idiosyncrasies. If we seek depth and breadth of insight, then we must continue in this task of listening, which is what exegesis is all about. (Without good listening there should be no preaching or writing.) As we must respect the variety of perspectives within the Bible itself (see above, §5.4), we must also listen to the church's insights that have continued beyond the canonical period (again see Eph. 3:10). To escape the issues and agenda of our postmodern culture and Christian subculture, we must read works beyond our own times. It is best to sample the major periods of church history (e.g., the patristic, medieval, Reformation, and Enlightenment periods) and of Jewish interpretation (e.g., Pseudepigrapha, Qumran, Targums, Mishnah, Talmud, Midrash, medieval commentators).

We should not limit our reading to authors of our own theological persuasion or even to "believing" authors. As noted above, God has mediated his self-revelation through human language, agents, circumstances, and culture. These features of Scripture are susceptible to human investigation through the tools of the university (e.g., linguistics, literary criticism, history, and sociology). To ignore the insights even of secularists is to ignore this dimension of God's revelation. Similar to the way that we regard science as a valid means of studying creation, literary and historical study are also valid means of investigating the Bible, especially its contextual features.

We must be mindful that we should use secondary literature simply as a resource for shedding light on our primary literature, the Bible. We do not submit to its authority as we do the Bible's, so we must evaluate its claims critically. We must be especially cautious not to be driven by the issues and agenda of secondary literature. It is best to be as clear as we can on the passage itself before we adopt the views of later commentators; otherwise we will not escape being tossed by the waves of scholarly opinion (cf. Eph 4:14; and, especially, Prov. 18:17). [43]

43. For further information, see John Barton, *Reading the Old Testament: Method in Biblical Study* (London: Darton, Longman and Todd, 1984); John H. Hayes and Carl R. Holladay, *Biblical Exegesis: A Beginner's Handbook* (Atlanta: John Knox, 1982); William W. Klein, Craig L. Blomberg, and Robert L. Hubbard Jr., *Introduction to Biblical Interpretation* (Dallas: Word, 1993); and Willem A. VanGemeren, ed., "Guide to Old Testament Theology and Exegesis," *NIDOTTE* 1.1–218.

two

Language and Text of the Old Testament

David W. Baker

Constant exposure to Scripture in one's native tongue can easily lull the reader into thinking that it originally appeared in that language. After all, Genesis 1:3 does record that God said, "Let there be light," so those are the exact words which God must have used, in English and with cadences very reminiscent of the Authorized Version! It comes as a surprise that Swedish or Cantonese friends are equally convinced that God spoke in the same words with which they grew up. While we never will be sure in which language these first recorded words were spoken, we do know that they were recorded in Hebrew, that other Old Testament portions were recorded in Aramaic (two words in Gen. 31:47; Dan. 2:4–7:28; Ezra 4:8–6:18; 7:12–26; Jer. 10:11), and that the words of Jesus, while probably spoken in Aramaic, have reached us in Greek.

In this chapter we will explore some of the implications of these languages being the means of revelation, the necessity of determining as accurately as possible what the original text actually said, and the translation of that text into contemporary languages.

Hebrew and Aramaic

Hebrew and Aramaic are members of the Semitic language family. In addition to a number of languages no longer spoken, this family includes several languages that are used today, including Arabic, Aramaic (in a few villages in Syria and south India), the Hebrew of Israel, and some of the languages spoken in Ethiopia.[1] Hebrew and Aramaic

---

1. See John Huehnergard, "Languages (Introductory Survey)," *ABD*, 4.155–70, and articles on individual languages, 4.170–229; Robert Hetzron, ed., *The Semitic Languages* (London and New York: Routledge, 1997).

are linguistic "cousins," sharing the same ancestry in a way similar to the relationship of Spanish to French, through their predecessor, Latin. In addition to a large percentage of shared vocabulary, the two also share morphological (word form) and syntactical (word order) features. Since the majority of the OT is in Hebrew, Hebrew will be the focus here.

The core component of Hebrew words is a root that usually consists of three letters, although two- and four-letter roots also exist. Roots indicate the basic semantic field of the word, showing what part of the universe it describes. Changes in morphology or word form, by adding elements before, after, and/or among the root letters, identify the word according to its part of speech and syntactical function. This is somewhat similar to English words such as *cook*, whose meaning is ambiguous in that specific form. Adding a definite or indefinite article (*the* or *a*) before it indicates a noun, and *s* following one of these forms shows that there are more than one. An added suffix *-ie* changes it to a different, though related, noun. If the base form is preceded by the preposition *to* or supplemented by the suffixes *-ed* or *-ing*, various verbal forms are recognizable. Thus, by knowing just one of the words in this semantic group, one is able to tell fairly clearly what is being talked about even if that form had never been encountered.

A Hebrew example is the root *zbḥ*, which concerns the semantic field of ritual or sacrificial slaughter.[2] As *zābaḥ* it is a verb meaning "he has sacrificed," while *yizbaḥ* indicates that the verbal action is not yet completed. A *zōbēaḥ* describes one who regularly performs the sacrifice, which itself is called a *zebaḥ* and is sacrificed on a *mizbēaḥ* ("altar").

The linguistic feature of a modifiable root can have great advantages for the language learner. When one word from the root is learned, the semantic field of the associated root words becomes easier to postulate.[3] Vocabulary acquisition can be eased when this feature is exploited. It is important not to make this a hard-and-fast rule, however, since for various reasons, some words that appear to share the same root have no apparent semantic connection.[4]

---

2. BDB 256–59; David J. A. Clines, ed., *The Dictionary of Classical Hebrew*, vol. 3 (Sheffield: Sheffield Academic Press, 1996), 76–80; vol. 5 (forthcoming), under מִזְבֵּחַ.

3. George M. Landes lists the vocabulary in his book *A Student's Vocabulary of Biblical Hebrew* (New York: Scribner's, 1961) according to these roots, as does BDB in its organization of entries.

4. A warning against the "root fallacy" is found in James Barr, *The Semantics of Biblical Language* (Oxford: Oxford University Press, 1961); see especially 100. See also Grant Osborne, *The Hermeneutical Spiral: A Comprehensive Introduction to Biblical Interpretation* (Downers Grove, Ill.: InterVarsity, 1991), 66–71.

In Hebrew, grammatical forms regularly follow set patterns and thus allow understanding to be transportable from one root to another. That is, the structure of the form *zābaḥ*, with this vowel combination between the three root letters, regularly indicates a single male having completed the action of the root. The form, will, as a rule, be similar no matter which root is used, so one would expect to be able to translate any similar form as "he has done *X*."[5] Fortunately for Hebrew learners, there is comparative regularity in the patterns, with very few "irregular" forms. This is a stark contrast with English. This feature allows the learner to master a limited number of grammatical forms, applying them repeatedly to different roots, rather than needing to learn each form for each root separately.[6]

Language and Worldview

Claims have been made about the ability to derive insight into the mind of a group, into the very worldview under which the group functions, by analyzing its language. Through language people express their worldview, and they are constrained, it is argued, by this language. This argument led to proposing a significant distinction between the Hebrew and Greek minds based on differences in linguistic structure and usage.[7] This proposal was soundly refuted by James Barr more than thirty years ago, even though the hypothesis is still evident today in many pulpits and classrooms.[8] This refutation is an important counter to claims that Hebrew-speaking people see everything as living, since there is no neuter gender, "it," in Hebrew.[9] This understand-

5. For discussion of these and numerous other morphological and syntactic features, see the standard grammars: GKC; Paul Joüon, *A Grammar of Biblical Hebrew*, trans. T. Muraoka (Rome: Pontifical Biblical Institute, 1993); Bruce K. Waltke and M. O'Connor, *An Introduction to Biblical Hebrew Syntax* (Winona Lake, Ind.: Eisenbrauns, 1990).

6. For comments on language teaching and learning, see David W. Baker, "Studying the Original Texts: Effective Learning and Teaching of Biblical Hebrew," in *Make the Old Testament Live: From Curriculum to Classroom*, ed. Richard S. Hess and Gordon J. Wenham (Grand Rapids and Cambridge, England: Eerdmans, 1998), 161–72.

7. For example, Thorlief Boman, *Hebrew Thought Compared with Greek* (Philadelphia: Westminster, 1960), and Gerhard Kittel, ed., *Theological Dictionary of the New Testament* (Grand Rapids: Eerdmans, 1964–76).

8. Barr, *Semantics of Biblical Language*; idem, *Biblical Words for Time* (London: SCM; Naperville, Ill.: A. R. Allenson, 1962). See also Moises Silva, *Biblical Words and Their Meaning: An Introduction to Lexical Semantics*, 2d ed. (Grand Rapids: Zondervan, 1994), 18–23; D. A. Carson, *Exegetical Fallacies*, 2d ed. (Grand Rapids: Baker; Carlisle, Pa.: Paternoster, 1996), 44–45. A useful introduction to a more positive use of linguistics is Peter Cotterell and Max Turner, *Linguistics and Biblical Interpretation* (Downers Grove, Ill.: InterVarsity; London: SPCK, 1989).

9. Norman L. Geisler and William A. Nix, *A General Introduction to the Bible* (Chicago: Moody Press, 1968), 219.

ing would border on pantheism, which is far from the Israelite concept of reality. The claim that Hebrew is oriented on the verb rather than noun[10] could be supported by its paucity of adjectives.[11] Rather than seeing this as evidence that the Hebrews lived in a bland world, it must be noted that they used another formulation, the *genitive construct*, to fulfill the same adjectival function, so they are not deprived of descriptive capability.[12] No language should be considered inferior, since each is sufficient to express what is necessary and what is desired by its speakers.

While the claim that language, on its own, is a completely adequate window into a person's worldview is fallacious, language does indicate what is important to a society. One aspect of this is the breadth of vocabulary dealing with the issues central to a people's life and culture. The ubiquitous examples of Eskimo words for snow or Arabic words for camels and their accoutrements—words that are more numerous than among peoples for whom these items play a lesser role—will need to be verified elsewhere. It is clear that the Hebrews gave much thought to unacceptable activity, since they used numerous words to speak of sin and transgression, yielding nuances of meaning that are muted in English.[13] This raises the interesting question as to what seems important to contemporary North American English speakers, with their numerous words for intoxication.

Establishing the Text

Before one can determine what a text means, it is necessary to identify what it says. That this needs stating is due to the process of textual transmission, which lies behind the biblical text, as it does behind every written document. In this day of photocopying and electronic transmission of texts, errors in transmission are rare and surprising.

10. Barr, *Semantics of Biblical Language*, 14 n. 2.
11. The lack is noted by, for example, G. Bergsträsser, *Introduction to the Semitic Languages*, trans. Peter T. Daniels (Winona Lake, Ind.: Eisenbrauns, 1983), 8; and Waltke and O'Connor, *Introduction to Biblical Hebrew Syntax*, 255, though they do not support this claim based upon it.
12. Waltke and O'Connor, *Introduction to Biblical Hebrew Syntax*, 255; GKC §128; J. Weingreen, *A Practical Grammar for Classical Hebrew*, 2d ed. (Oxford: Clarendon, 1959), 136.
13. For example, ʿāwōn 'iniquity', ʾāšām 'offense, guilt', ḥăṭāʾāh 'sin', ʿawlāh 'unrighteousness', hēpek or ʾiqqĕšût 'perversion', pešaʿ 'rebellion, transgression', raʿ 'evil', rešaʿ 'wickedness', mirmāh 'deceit', kāzāb or šeqer 'falsehood'. A detailed study of the development of the listed English glosses would most likely indicate that a number of them were proposed, not to express nuanced differences in English connotation, but rather to provide discrete matches for each Hebrew term.

We need to be reminded, however, that the biblical documents were hand-copied, and this is a different story. Most of us have written a document by hand and passed it to a typist for transcription. The result is often different from the original, due mainly to, from personal experience, the illegibility of the original handwriting. There can be errors in different stages of the transmission process.

The problem increases geometrically when the time gap between original composition, on the one hand, and the existing witnesses to it, on the other, becomes longer. This is most certainly the case with the biblical text. For example, there is a long gap between the original composition of the Pentateuch, or its elements, and the earliest witness we have to the pentateuchal text, which is the LXX. Various dates have been proposed for the original composition, which would lead to a transmission history measured in centuries (envisioning a postexilic pentateuchal composition)[14] or even a millennium (envisioning Mosaic composition in the early to mid–second millennium B.C.E.).[15] The nature and steps of textual transmission of the Old Testament are both convoluted and debated, and are not of direct concern to our topic.[16] Whatever the process of transmission, much can happen to a text during such transmission, giving need for the discipline of text criticism, whose task is "pre-hermeneutical"[17]—determining, as far as possible, what the "original text" actually said.

Textual Transmission

A brief history of textual transmission will provide some context for discussion. No original documents of the Old Testament are known to us today. After leaving the hand of the author/editor, they were preserved and copied for future generations. Care was taken, but in the days prior to the printing press, copying was done by hand. Changes inevitably arose from either the copyist's error or intentional updating of the text. Even an authoritative, canonical text would have slowly

14. For example, Richard Elliott Friedman, *Who Wrote the Bible?* (Englewood Cliffs, N.J.: Prentice Hall, 1987), who posits Ezra as the one who brought the Pentateuch to its final form.

15. For example, Duane Garrett, *Rethinking Genesis: The Sources and Authorship of the First Book of the Pentateuch* (Grand Rapids: Baker, 1991).

16. See F. E. Deist, *Witnesses to the Old Testament: Introducing Old Testament Textual Criticism*, The Literature of the Old Testament 5 (Pretoria, South Africa: N. G. Boekhandel, 1988); Emmanuel Tov, *Textual Criticism of the Hebrew Bible* (Minneapolis: Fortress; Assen: Van Gorcum, 1992); Ernst Würthwein, *The Text of the Old Testament: An Introduction to the "Biblia Hebraica,"* 2d ed. (Grand Rapids: Eerdmans, 1995).

17. A term that I first came across in lecture material of Walter Wessel.

drifted from the original over time, no matter how careful those entrusted with it were.[18]

At various times, Israelites were exiled to Assyria (722 B.C.E.; 2 Kings 17:7–40) and Babylonia (597 B.C.E.; 2 Kings 24:10–16, or 586 B.C.E.; 2 Kings 24:20b–25:21), fled to Egypt (c. 581 B.C.E.; 2 Kings 25:26), or intermarried with non-Israelite exiles and were thus denied contact with orthodox Yahwists due to their syncretistic religion (2 Kings 17:24–41; cf. Ezra 4:2). Each disenfranchised group wanted its sacred writings, and thus took copies with them. Each of these copies independently developed its own idiosyncratic departures from the original text, following the process of hand-copying mentioned above. There thus developed several slightly different witnesses to the original text.

While the Israelites were in Babylonian exile, Aramaic replaced Hebrew as the daily language of many Israelites. When returned exiles heard Ezra read the law in Hebrew after the rebuilding of the wall of Jerusalem, it needed translation into Aramaic for them to understand (Neh. 8:8). This is the first record of the need for translation. This led later to full-blown Aramaic translations (or paraphrases) called the Targums, dating from approximately the first through fourth centuries C.E.[19] In Egypt, Hellenization during the last pre-Christian centuries led to the translation of the Hebrew Scriptures into Greek in what is called the Septuagint, abbreviated LXX. This translation started in the third century B.C.E. for the Pentateuch, and it also provides an important witness to textual transmission history.[20]

The Qumran community on the northwest shore of the Dead Sea preserved archives of biblical and extrabiblical material collected during their occupation of the site between c. 150 B.C.E. and C.E. 70.[21] They had

18. The topic of canonization is theologically very significant, but is beyond the scope of this study. For entry into the topic, see Sid Z. Leiman, *The Canonization of Hebrew Scripture: The Talmudic and Midrashic Evidence* (Hamden, Conn.: Archon, 1976); Roger Beckwith, *The Old Testament Canon of the New Testament Church and Its Background in Early Judaism* (Grand Rapids: Eerdmans; London: SPCK, 1985); F. F. Bruce, *The Canon of Scripture* (Downers Grove, Ill.: InterVarsity, 1988); Lee M. McDonald, *The Formation of the Christian Biblical Canon* (Nashville: Abingdon, 1988); John W. Miller, *The Origins of the Bible: Rethinking Canon History* (New York: Paulist, 1994).

19. Philip S. Alexander, "Targum, Targumim," *ABD* 6.320–31.

20. See E. Tov, *The Text-Critical Use of the Septuagint in Biblical Research* (Jerusalem: Simor, 1981); Melvin K. H. Peters, "Septuagint," *ABD* 4.1093–104.

21. See John J. Collins, "Dead Sea Scrolls," *ABD* 2.85–101; Lawrence Schiffman, *Reclaiming the Dead Sea Scrolls* (New York: Doubleday, 1994); James C. VanderKam, *The Dead Sea Scrolls Today* (Grand Rapids: Eerdmans, 1994); Florentino Garcia Martinez and Julio Trebolle Barrera, *The People of the Dead Sea Scrolls: Their Writings, Beliefs, and Practices* (Leiden: Brill, 1995). For the scrolls themselves, see the series Discoveries in the Judaean Desert (Oxford: Clarendon), and, for English translations, Geza Vermes, *The Dead Sea Scrolls in English*, 4th ed. (New York and London: Penguin, 1995); Florentino Garcia Martinez, *The Dead Sea Scrolls Translated: The Qumran Texts in English*, 2d ed. (Grand Rapids: Eerdmans, 1996).

Hebrew texts reflecting several different transmission traditions, including those behind the LXX and Targums. These are very important for text criticism in that they predate the next available Hebrew texts by a millennium, and the earliest major LXX texts available by half a millennium.

Early in the Christian era, Jewish religious leaders attempted to establish a common text, rather than having several similar but divergent versions. The variety of versions in use at the time caused the same problem it does in a contemporary church, in which parishioners might have four or five different translations among them. This "official" text became known as the Masoretic Text (MT).[22] It is this text that lies behind today's standard critical editions of the Hebrew Bible.[23] As is clear from the abbreviated narrative above, even the best example of the MT is far removed in time from the original text.

Textual Criticism

In order to work with and evaluate the evidence available from these and other early versions and translations, experts in Old Testament text criticism must possess an arsenal of languages, since relevant resources are written in Hebrew, Greek, Syriac, Aramaic, Latin, Sahidic, Coptic, Ethiopic, Arabic, and Armenian.[24] This should not lead those lacking this competence to despair, however, since all students of Scripture can find text-critical assistance at whatever level of expertise. Basic but important information is available in almost all editions of English translations, in footnotes noting the important differences among English, Hebrew, and Greek. Of more concern for readers of this volume is how to do text criticism using the Hebrew competence achieved in a year of Hebrew study at the seminary level.[25]

There are two critical editions of the Hebrew Old Testament currently on the market. Only the *Biblia Hebraica Stuttgartensia*[26] is com-

22. E. J. Revell, "Masoretic Text," *ABD* 4.597–99.

23. The MT is dated relatively late, coming from the early tenth century C.E. (the Aleppo Codex, underlying *HUB*; see n. 27 below) and approximately a century later (Codex Leningradensis, which underlies *BHS*; see n. 26).

24. Based on a list organized "in roughly the order of their significance for textual criticism" from Würthwein, *Text of the Old Testament*, 114.

25. Text-critical method is explained in numerous sources. Useful introductions are P. Kyle McCarter Jr., *Textual Criticism: Recovering the Text of the Hebrew Bible*, Guides to Biblical Scholarship, Old Testament Series (Philadelphia: Fortress, 1986), and Ellis R. Brotzman, *Old Testament Textual Criticism: A Practical Introduction* (Grand Rapids: Baker, 1994). A more technical study is Tov's *Textual Criticism*.

26. K. Elliger and W. Rudolph, eds., *Biblia Hebraica Stuttgartensia* (Stuttgart: Deutsche Bibelstiftung, 1977). Henceforth *BHS*. This is a new edition of Rudolph Kittel, *Biblia Hebraica* (Stuttgart: Württembergische Bibelanstalt, 1937). A further revision is under way.

plete, while the *Hebrew University Bible*[27] edition is only in its infancy, with two volumes completed.[28] Each of these editions starts with a good, early example of the MT as the basis for its analysis.[29] The MT is printed as the basic text, and significant variations between it and other texts and versions are recorded in footnotes. This is a different methodology than that adopted for the critical Greek New Testament editions,[30] in which an eclectic text is made by analyzing the various texts and editions and choosing what is determined to be the best reading for each word. The textual footnotes then record and evaluate the other options not chosen by the editors. The difference results in, on the part of the Old Testament, a Hebrew text that is almost identical to an early manuscript that one can actually study today, while the Greek text is different from any presently existing Greek text. The Greek text is thus a carefully weighed approximation of what the original text would have been, while the *BHS* necessitates regular visits to the textual apparatus at the bottom of the page in order for the reader to reconstruct an original text.

HUB has four sets of apparatus at the bottom of the page. The first provides readings from the *"primary* versions" (MT, LXX, Targum, Syriac, Vulgate) retroverted, or back-translated, into the original Hebrew.[31] The second includes readings from the Judean desert witnesses (the Dead Sea Scrolls) and Jewish rabbinic literature;[32] the third, evidence from medieval, or "Masoretic" manuscripts;[33] and the fourth, less important variants.[34] There is much important information here, and it will prove a valuable resource for biblical scholars. But since it is so far from completion, *HUB* will not be discussed further. The meth-

27. M. H. Goshen-Gottstein and S. Talmon, general editors, *The Hebrew University Bible*, Hebrew University Bible Project (Jerusalem: Magnes Press, 1965–). Henceforth *HUB*.

28. M. H. Goshen-Gottstein, *The Hebrew University Bible: The Book of Isaiah* (Jerusalem: Magnes, 1995); C. Rabin, S. Talmon, and E. Tov, *The Hebrew University Bible: The Book of Jeremiah* (Jerusalem: Magnes, 1997).

29. *BHS* uses the Leningrad Codex B19[A], identified by P. Kahle (*The Cairo Geniza*, 2d ed. [Oxford: Blackwell, 1959]) as "the oldest dated manuscript of the complete Hebrew Bible" (cited in *BHS*, xi), dating from 1008–9 C.E. *HUB* uses the Aleppo Codex, which its editors claim to be "the oldest extant codex of the entire Bible" (Rabin, Salmon, and Tov, *Book of Jeremiah*, xii). Though incomplete, it is earlier, dating from the start of the tenth century C.E (ibid., xxxv).

30. B. Aland et al., eds., *The Greek New Testament*, 4th rev. ed. (Stuttgart: Deutsche Bibelgesellschaft, 1994).

31. See Rabin, Salmon, and Tov, *Book of Jeremiah*, xv–xxviii.

32. Ibid., xxviii–xxxii.

33. Ibid., xxxii–xxxiii.

34. Ibid., xxxiii–xxxvi.

odology of text criticism laid out below is applicable to *HUB* as well as to *BHS*.

Text-Critical Apparatus

BHS has three sets of marginal notes that aid in textual study. The most important of these is the text-critical apparatus compiled by the editor of each of the biblical books and placed as the second apparatus at the bottom of each page. There, the different readings from other witnesses are presented. Sometimes, but not always, there is a Hebrew retroversion, but often it is either left in the original (LXX, Vulgate) or transliterated (Syriac).

If a word has a textual note pertaining to it, a following superscript, lowercase letter directs the reader to the relevant apparatus. If a phrase or clause receives comment, the letter appears before and after the relevant word string. The apparatus itself orders the comments by chapter (Cp, for Latin *caput*) and verse. For example Cp 15,1[b] would refer to the second ("b") textual note for verse one of chapter 15.

The textual notes themselves are not transparent, since they rely heavily on abbreviations to preserve space. These abbreviations are explained in detail in a chapter early in *BHS* entitled "Sigla et compendia apparatum" (Apparatus signs and abbreviations).[35] This title indicates another reason why the textual apparatus is opaque to most readers. While the introduction to the volume is presented in German, English, French, Spanish, and Latin, in order not to favor anyone, Latin is the language of choice for comments in the apparatus, placing everyone at an equal disadvantage. Students thus need to plow through the Latin before they can dig into the evidence presented.

There are two important resources to help the student over these twin hurdles of abbreviation and language: William R. Scott, *A Simplified Guide to BHS*,[36] and Reinhard Wonneberger, *Understanding BHS*.[37] The former is much more user-friendly, especially for a novice. It has a brief chapter explaining the operation of the textual apparatus (18–22), a very abbreviated list of signs and symbols (86–87)—truncated from the *BHS* chapter mentioned earlier—and a translation of Latin terms and abbreviations (61–86).[38] Wonneberger has a much more de-

---

35. *BHS* xliv–l.

36. Subtitled *Critical Apparatus, Masora, Accents, Unusual Letters, and Other Markings*, 3d ed. (North Richland Hills, Tex.: BIBAL, 1995). This volume also contains "An English Key to the Latin Words and Abbreviations and the Symbols of *Biblia Hebraica Stuttgartensia*" by H. P. Rüger.

37. Subtitled *A Manual for the Users of "Biblia Hebraica Stuttgartensia,"* trans. Dwight R. Daniels, 2d ed., Subsidia Biblica 8 (Rome: Pontifical Biblical Institute, 1990).

38. Also found in Brotzman, *Old Testament Textual Criticism*, 171–92.

tailed explanation of how the various *BHS* reference systems work, along with helpful examples, but its layout makes it less accessible as a reference work.

For an example of the kind of information available in this text-critical apparatus, and a demonstration on how to use it, consider the text of Genesis 4:8. It reads, in part:

8 וַיֹּאמֶר קַיִן אֶל־הֶבֶל אָחִיו* וַיְהִי בִּהְיוֹתָם בַּשָּׂדֶה וַיָּקָם קַיִן

A literal translation ("Then Cain said to his brother Abel, [ ] When they were in the field, Cain arose . . .") shows that there is difficulty with the text. Something is missing from the middle of the cited passage. This is reflected in the textual apparatus, to which the reader is referred by the superscript letter [a]. The apparatus reads: 8[a] mlt Mss Edd hic interv; frt ins c 𝔰 𝔊𝔰𝔳 נֵלְכָה הַשָּׂדֶה cf 𝔗𝔍𝔍𝔦 (surely a strong encouragement to consult Scott or Wonneberger!). It indicates that we are not the first to appreciate the problem with the text, but that "many medieval manuscripts and editions of the Hebrew Bible have a gap here; perhaps the Hebrew clause נֵלְכָה הַשָּׂדֶה should be inserted as it is with the Samaritan, Septuagint, Syriac, and Vulgate; compare with *Targum Pseudo-Jonathan* and other Palestinian Targum fragments." All of this information was found by consulting Scott and the *BHS* introduction. The length of the note, and the number of important witnesses to the variant text, is a strong indicator that the suggested interpolation has validity.[39]

The above example illustrates why textual criticism is both a science and an art. The "science" side of the equation involves collecting the different readings of the textual witnesses, and amassing the raw data for analysis. This is the sum of the various manuscripts noted above. Some of this evidence is in languages other than the Hebrew (or Aramaic) in which the text was originally written. In our case, variants were found in Greek, Syriac, and Latin, as well as the Aramaic Targums. This step also involves a retroversion of these languages into what was probably the Hebrew (or Aramaic) original.

The "art" side of the equation concerns the interpretation of this gathered data. Not all evidence is of equal importance, so each point must be evaluated. While there are some "rules" to assist in this interpretation, they are not hard-and-fast. Each case must be studied on its own merits.

39. See n. 24 above and the list in Stuart, *Old Testament Exegesis*, 2d ed. (Philadelphia: Westminster, 1984), 91–92, where witnesses to the text are ranked by relative importance.

The various witnesses do not have equal weight, as indicated above. The MT and LXX are by far the most important, although there are differences in validity even within these two witnesses. Some portions of each are better preserved than other portions. There is also debate over which should have priority in a particular case. This evaluative step is not simply accomplished by comparing the number of witnesses holding one reading with the number holding another. If only one rendering of a superior text were copied for each generation, while numerous copies of an inferior text were made, the numerical superiority would not reflect greater textual integrity. A maxim of textual criticism is that witnesses must be weighed, not simply counted.

Several rules aid in the evaluation process. Two of these regard the more difficult and shorter readings. It is held that an obscure reading would more likely have been made plain than a plain reading made difficult. This act of making plain would have been done by adding explanatory words rather than removing words already in place. The related rules are: (1) the shorter text is more likely to be original (known by the Latin phrase *lectio brevior*), and (2) the more obscure text is more likely to be original (Latin *lectio difficilior*). For example, the LXX adds sixteen words to the end of Genesis 1:9, "so the waters under the heavens were gathered into their pools and the dry land appeared." These make explicit what was implied in the Hebrew phrase "and it was so," which is most likely the original reading, without the addition. Genesis 7:6 shows the opposite phenomenon, in which the Hebrew explains the rare word *flood* (*mabûl*) by adding the common *water*, which the LXX does not have.

The art of biblical criticism makes itself felt in the application of these "rules" to actual situations. Our example of Genesis 4:8 above shows that logic stands *against* the rule of the shorter reading. The MT is shorter than the other witnesses mentioned, but the clear lack of an essential phrase leads to the preferred reading being the longer one, as reflected in the other witnesses.[40]

Masoretic Notes and Accents

Two other sources of textual information are available in *BHS*. The Masoretes were scribes of the mid–first millennium C.E. They preserved and transmitted the Hebrew text. During the course of textual transmission they supplemented the originally consonantal text with

40. See also the problem of the shorter, and reordered, LXX of Jeremiah in, for example, Sven Soderlund, *The Greek Text of Jeremiah: A Revised Hypothesis*, JSOTSup 47 (Sheffield : JSOT Press, 1985); Jack R. Lundbom, "Jeremiah, Book of; B. MT and LXX," *ABD* 3.707–9.

vowels and accents, and added notes on matters of text and exegesis. The material is a Masoretic commentary, providing their understanding of how the text should be interpreted.⁴¹ Many of the notes involve points of grammar rather than text (e.g., the note that the verb "they were shipwrecked" in 1 Kings 22:49 NJB should end with the regular *mater lectionis* ‎ו rather than the unusual ‎ה). These grammatical points are more relevant to translation and interpretation, the step after establishing the text itself, but use of the Masoretic information will be introduced here.

Notes. The most visible Masoretic notes are those located on the outside margins of *BHS*. These notes are called the Masora Parva. They are indicated by a small, superscript circle in the text, above the word to which the note refers. If the note refers to a phrase or clause, there are similar circles between each of the words of the relevant segment. Each marginal note, if there are more than one for a line of text, is separated from its neighbor in the margin by a dot. In Genesis 4:8, *BHS* has a circle between the last two words of the example discussed above, so the note concerns the clause "Cain arose." In the margin there is the single letter ‎ל with a tiny dot above it. This is a note of frequency, the most common of the Masoretic notations. The note indicates that the clause occurs only one time in the OT.

Hebrew scribes, *sōfrîm* 'counters', were so named because among their tasks was enumeration (*sfr*). Since they were dealing with Scripture, the very Word of God, each letter was sacred and none could be lost. Counting served as a partial control over the accuracy of the text.⁴² The Masoretic notations, like the textual apparatus, use abbreviations heavily, although this time the abbreviated language is Aramaic, so most readers again will need some help in using them.⁴³

The first Masoretic notation on Genesis 4:7 concerns the first word of the verse, ‎הֲלוֹא. The note indicates that this specific *plene* form (with

41. For an introduction to the Masoretes and their work, see Page H. Kelley et al., *The Masorah of the "Biblia Hebraica Stuttgartensia": Introduction and Annotated Glossary* (Grand Rapids and Cambridge, England: Eerdmans, 1998), 13–30.

42. An example of this enumerative practice is found in the colophon or endnote to the Pentateuch (*BHS* 353). Translated, it reads: "Sum of the verses of the book [Deuteronomy]—nine hundred fifty-five (5 + 50 + 900). . . . Sum of the verses of the Torah—five thousand eight hundred and forty-five (5[,000] + 800 + 40 + 5. . . . Sum of the letters of the Torah—four hundred thousand nine hundred and forty-five." Some of these final notes include notice of the midpoint in the enumerated portion, so one could tell whether a missing letter or word was from the first or last half.

43. *BHS* l–lv provides a Latin key to the abbreviations. This is translated into English in Scott, *Simplified Guide*, chap. 6, with a handy key to the Hebrew letter-number equivalents on the back cover. A much fuller translation with explanation and examples is provided in Kelley et al., *Masorah*, chap. 5.

the vowel letter ו) occurs twelve times in the Pentateuch. The marginal notation has a small, superscript number 6, which refers to the first set of notes at the bottom of the *BHS* page. There we find a code, "Mm 27," referring to another set of Masoretic notes called the Masora Magna, which is published in a separate volume.[44] This resource lists all of the references to the verses in which this form occurs.[45] Sometimes these Masoretic notes appear to have academic rather than practical value, but this is not always the case. An important application of the list of parallel uses is to counter some text critics who are wont to emend the text willy-nilly, even if there is no textual support for the emendation based on the appearance of what seems to be an anomalous or odd form.[46] The Masoretic notes can furnish evidence that a peculiar form is not in fact unique. This provides a useful brake to overabundant conjectural emendation.

Accents. Almost every individual Hebrew word has at least one Masoretic accent.[47] They have served at least two functions in the history of interpretation. One concerns the cantillation or singing of the Hebrew text in the Jewish community, but this is not relevant to us.[48] The Masoretes used accents not only to show where the stress fell on each word,[49] but also the relationship between one word and the next. Each accent is either *conjunctive*, joining the word on which it falls in some way with the next word, or *disjunctive*, separating the word from the next.[50]

44. Gérard E. Weil, *Massorah Gedolah iuxta Codicem Leningradensem B19 a* (Rome: Pontifical Biblical Institute, 1971).

45. Genesis 4:7; 31:15; 34:23; 37:13; 40:8; 42:22; 44:5, 15; Exodus 33:16; Numbers 14:3; 22:30; Deuteronomy 32:6; Weil, *Massorah Gedolah*, 4.

46. Kittel's *Biblia Hebraica* (see above, n. 26) did this often. See also what are at times seemingly arbitrary, and undocumented, emendations in the NEB.

47. Walter Wickes, *Two Treatises on the Accentuation of the Old Testament*, ed. A. Dotan (1881, 1887; New York: Ktav, 1970).

48. See Scott, *Simplified Guide*, 35–36; Suzanne Haïk-Vantoura, *The Music of the Bible Revealed: The Deciphering of a Millenary Notation* (Berkeley, Calif.: BIBAL; San Francisco: King David's Harp, 1991).

49. This use of accents has phonetic implications. Beginning, and even intermediate, students are often unable to determine whether a *qamets* is regular (pronounced /ā/) or a *qamets khatuf* (pronounced /o/). If the syllable in which the sign occurs is accented, the former possibility is almost certain. In an unaccented syllable, there is a possibility of the latter option, but that is less regular.

50. Lists and descriptions of the accents are included in Scott, *Simplified Guide*, 27–35. Note that there is a slightly different accentuation system used in three books, Job, Psalms, and Proverbs (ibid., 32–35), than in the remainder (ibid., 27–32). Cf. GKC §15; Wickes, *Two Treatises*; and Yeivin, *Introduction*, 157–274. See Lars Lode, "A Discourse Perspective on the Significance of the Masoretic Accents," in *Biblical Hebrew and Discourse Linguistics*, ed. Robert D. Bergen (Dallas: Summer Institute of Linguistics, 1994), 155–72, for a detailed explanation of the accents' function.

These accents are scribal interpretations that can provide some syntactical help for the reader. For example, in Genesis 4:8, the clause "And Cain said to Abel, his brother," is separated from what follows by an *ʾathnaḥ*, one of the two major disjunctive accents in a verse. This indicates that the scribes saw the following clause as separate from the preceding clause; thus, the second clause does not contain the direct object, which in this case would have been the quotation. There is no statement as to what Cain actually said to Abel. Accents can be especially helpful when two nouns occur side by side, when the reader is unsure whether or not they are in a construct relationship. By definition, nouns in construct are closely bound together. This is frequently indicated by the Masoretic *maqqef*,[51] but where this is lacking, a disjunctive accent indicates that the scribes did not view the two nouns in construct. A conjunctive accent could indicate that the nouns are a construct. A simple example is Genesis 1:2, in which the words תֹהוּ וָבֹהוּ 'formless void' are joined by a conjunctive accent, while the following וְחֹשֶׁךְ 'and darkness' is separated by a disjunctive accent. This would indicate that "the earth" is characterized by the first two of these words, while the third word, instead of joining them and making a list of three, starts a new clause.

Vowels and other notes. The Masoretes also added the vowel signs to the original, consonantal text. This became necessary when Hebrew was no longer the native language of Bible readers, and the traditional pronunciation was being lost.[52] Their vowel signs generally reflected the received pronunciation, but at times a new interpretation is evident in the text. The most common example is the reluctance to pronounce the Tetragrammaton, the four-letter personal name of God. Since the consonantal text itself was canonically fixed and could not be altered, where the name יהוה 'Yahweh' was written in the original text, the scribes indicated through vocalization how they preferred the form to be pronounced. Thus the two forms יְהוָה and יֱהוִה are to be read as אֲדֹנָי 'Lord' and אֱלֹהִים 'God', respectively. This is one example of rereading that is to be done routinely whenever encountered in the MT. There are several of these cases throughout the Old Testament text.[53]

---

51. The "small horizontal stroke between the upper part of two words [resembling the English hyphen] which so connects them that in respect of tone and pointing they are regarded as one, and therefore have one accent" (GKC §16a, p. 63).

52. The challenge of vowel-less writing can be illustrated in English. If one were meeting someone to buy a car, a note saying "frd-nrk" would clearly indicate what car was desired (a Ford) but not where the meeting was to take place (Newark, New York, Norwalk [based on pronunciation], since the English vowels are "a, e, i, o, u, and sometimes y and w").

53. See Scott, *Simplified Guide*, 13–14, for others.

Other, more occasional rereadings are also indicated by the Masoretes through altered vocalization. This is known as the *qᵉrê/kᵉtîv* (קרי כתיב) since it concerns what is read (*qᵉrê*)[54] in contrast to what is written (*kᵉtîv*).[55] These occasional rereadings are indicated by using the proposed vocalization in the text body. The proposed change in consonants is written as superscript in the *BHS* Masora Parva, marked with a subscript ק (for קרי). An example of this is the last word in Isaiah 13:16. There the scribes seem to think that the last written verb ("they will be raped") is too indelicate, so they substitute a euphemism ("they will be lain with").[56] Correction of a misread letter is found in Genesis 14:2, 8. The Hebrew text is written *ṣĕbyōyîm*, but is to be read as *ṣĕbôyim* based on its spelling in Deuteronomy 29:22 (cf. Hos. 11:8).

Sample Exercises

A. First Samuel 13:1 is a textually corrupt verse, as indicated not only by the numerous textual variants in *BHS*, but also by the disagreement among English versions. The MT reads:

בֶּן־שָׁנָהᵇ שָׁאוּל וּמָלְכוֹ ᵈוּשְׁתֵּי שָׁנִים ᶜמָלַךְ עַל־יִשְׂרָאֵל׃ᵃ

Literally it can be translated: "A year old (was) Saul when he reigned and a pair of years he reigned over Israel." There seems to be some difficulty in this literal translation (translation itself is discussed in the next section), unless the reason the boy David was unable to wear King Saul's armor (1 Sam. 17:38–39) was really because it was too small for him! Various versions and early translations have tried to solve the problem. The reader, before continuing, is urged to decipher the notes using the aids mentioned above.

The first text-critical footnote reference, at the beginning of the verse, indicates that "verse one is absent in some manuscripts of the Septuagint versions of Origen and Lucian." This could be interpreted in at least two ways. First, the verse originally could have been a scribal gloss that later crept into the body of the text itself, although not into the Hebrew text from which Origen and Lucian were working. This still does not address the problem inherent in the verse itself—why the scribe would leave out the necessary numbers. On the other hand, due to the obvious problems, the portion could have been deleted. In other

54. The Aramaic passive participial form from the root *qrᵓ* 'something which is read'.
55. The Aramaic passive participial form from the root *ktb* 'something which is written'.
56. See Yeivin, *Introduction*, 56–58, for additional examples.

words, if you leave out the verse, the problem goes away.[57] While this is true, this is generally not an acceptable way to handle Scripture (even if much of the church does this in practical terms with most of the Old Testament!). It is more honest to grapple with a problem rather than ignoring it.

The second footnote shows how others addressed the issue. It says that "some Septuagint Lucianic versions read '30'; Syriac reads '21.'" In other words, rather than being only one year old (MT), Saul is at least twenty or thirty years old when this episode takes place.[58] This fits much better into the historical context. In order to determine which, if any, of the options is best requires historical investigation that goes beyond the parameters of this chapter. Our two "rules" are not very helpful in making the decision here.

The third footnote points out a second difficulty with the verse, since the context indicates that Saul must have reigned more than the two years allocated to him in the MT. Interestingly enough, the note reads that the two words bounded by the superscript letters are "lacking in Syriac." The problem is removed in Syriac and thus ignored as it was in the first footnote. Here there is no other textual evidence given in *BHS*, indicating that the major manuscripts support the MT and its claim for the two-year reign. Most modern translations see a missing number here, many adding "forty" based on Acts 13:21. Some translations decide to reflect the MT accurately by indicating a blank—"Saul was . . . years old when he began to reign; and he reigned . . . and two years over Israel" (RSV; NJB; similarly NJPS, although it takes his reign as two years).

This exercise should serve several functions. First, it shows that some texts are obviously corrupt in the MT and that other critics have noticed the difficulties before now. Second, based on the marginal notes of the standard critical Hebrew text, there are tools available to determine what others have proposed. Third, text criticism needs to be supplemented by other exegetical steps, in our case the study of historical context. Finally, there is place for hypothetical reconstruction that goes beyond the text-critical evidence, although this must be used with caution and a note must appear when the interpretation goes beyond the available evidence. This last step can be especially evident in translation, to which task we turn below.

57. JB follows this path, omitting this verse, although noting the difficulty in a footnote.

58. Or even forty; see Ralph W. Klein, *1 Samuel*, WBC 10 (Waco, Tex.: Word, 1983), 122.

B. Amos 9:12 is theologically important from a text-critical point of view. It reads in the MT:

לְמַעַן יִירְשׁוּ אֶת־שְׁאֵרִית אֱדוֹם וְכָל־הַגּוֹיִם אֲשֶׁר־נִקְרָא שְׁמִי עֲלֵיהֶם

The text is clear and makes good contextual sense as, "in order that they [i.e., ruined Israel] might possess Edom's remnant and all of the nations over whom my name is proclaimed." *BHS* has no textual notes for this verse, so there is no pressing problem from the Old Testament itself.

Things become exegetically interesting, however, when the passage is quoted in Acts 15:17 as:

[17]ὅπως ἂν ἐκζητήσωσιν οἱ κατάλοιποι τῶν ἀνθρώπων τὸν κύριον καὶ πάντα τὰ ἔθνη ἐφ᾽ οὓς ἐπικέκληται τὸ ὄνομά μου ἐπ᾽ αὐτούς.[59]

This is translated, "in order that the remainder of humanity may seek the Lord, and all of the people over whom my name is called." The latter is based on the LXX rather than the MT.

The differences between the two readings can be understood on text-critical grounds, after the Greek has been retroverted to Hebrew. The MT *yrš* 'possess' has been read as *drš* 'seek', a misreading of letters that are similar in the square script, adopted between the return from exile (538 B.C.E.) and the Hellenistic period.[60] The misreading could not have taken place earlier, since the previous Hebrew forms of the letters were quite different. Another rereading involves the unvocalized form *'dm*, which the MT reads as "Edom" and the LXX reads as *ādām* 'humanity'. The third difference is taking what was the direct object of the verb in the MT ("the remnant of Edom") and seeing it as the verbal subject in the LXX/NT. The combination of these creates a striking difference between the two renditions. Since the NT use is so theologically significant, the interpretation of the differences is important, but that moves to hermeneutics, a step beyond our pre-hermeneutical study.[61]

59. Kurt Aland et al., *The Greek New Testament* (Stuttgart: Deutsche Bibelgesellschaft, 1983).

60. Angel Sáenz-Badillos, *A History of the Hebrew Language*, trans. J. Elwolde (Cambridge and New York: Cambridge University Press, 1993), 113.

61. For a brief study that claims no great theological distance between the two readings, see David M. King, "The Use of Amos 9:11–12 in Acts 15:16–18," *Ashland Theological Journal* 21 (1989): 8–13.

Translation

Text criticism involves the transmission of the text vertically, through time. Its goal is to move back as far as possible in that stream of transmission to reconstruct, as accurately as possible, what the original reading was at the source. Translation, on the other hand, concerns the flow of the text horizontally through space, to peoples of different cultures and languages. The study of past translations is also a part of text criticism, as seen with the Aramaic and Greek translations above, since they are witnesses to the vertical transmission of the text. Students today also need to be involved in the translation process, since most contemporary readers and hearers of the Old Testament are not able to do so in the original Hebrew and Aramaic. Once the text-critical task has been performed to the best of our ability, the resulting text needs to be made available to our congregations and classes, as well as for our own study and understanding.

"The measure of the adequacy of a translation . . . is the comparison between what the original source intended to write or say and what the receptor in the second language actually understands, together with the style and effectiveness of the language that is used."[62] The message and its meaning must be transmitted to the new audience with as little distortion as possible. Ideally, the impact on the new hearers/readers should parallel that on the original audience. While there is great benefit in using existing translations, there are also decided advantages in doing one's own translation. It requires careful attention to each word and nuance of the text, not allowing the reader to skip thorny or difficult issues. Our own translation makes the text our own, informing subsequent interpretation and allowing reasoned rebuttal to alternative interpretations. All do not have either the time or expertise to do a polished translation, but it is not desirable to leave the entire enterprise in the hands of a few experts. The latter are needed, and they work constantly on presenting Scripture to each new generation, but all readers need some critical ability to evaluate the fruit of these translators' labors. The pastor and teacher can work alongside these experts—using their own work to evaluate and appreciate what is provided—while also providing their own insights and joining in the community of learning.

There are two different philosophies of translation, with each translation falling along a spectrum between these two poles.[63] The *literal,*

62. Donald N. Larson and William A. Smalley, *Becoming Bilingual: A Guide to Language Learning* (South Pasadena, Calif.: William Carey Library, 1972), 391.
63. *Translation* differs from a *paraphrase*, which sets out to make a text clearer by completely rewording it.

formal equivalence, or "word-for-word" approach, seeks to parallel the original wording and form of the source language as much as possible in the target language. This goal is pursued even if the product might not be understood by the target audience. The most extreme literal translation is an interlinear translation, which provides an English rendering immediately below or above each word of the Hebrew text.[64] This is so literal, even following the Hebrew word order that goes from right to left on the page, that it is of no practical use to an English reader who has no Hebrew competence, and a person who knows Hebrew does not really need it.[65] There is no attempt to close the time and culture gap between then and now.

One problem area is the translation of idioms, expressions whose meaning is different from the sum of the meanings of the constituent words. An American idiom is "the check bounced." Each word can be looked up in a dictionary, but the sum of the individual meanings does not equal the meaning of the clause itself. This type of usage is the most difficult for non-native speakers to grasp. This is true for any language, not just English. A Hebrew idiom that is translated literally into English appears in 1 Samuel 24:3. In his pursuit of David, Saul goes into a cave to "cover his feet" (KJV, MLB, NJB). From this translation we know exactly what the Hebrew said, which is the goal of a literal translation, but we have no idea what Saul did.

The second approach to translation is called *dynamic* or *functional equivalence,* or "meaning-for-meaning." It seeks to produce "the closest natural equivalent of the original text,"[66] resulting in the same response from the present audience that it produced in the original audience. This type of translation seeks to bridge the gap between the original text and today's readers.

The difference between the two approaches can be illustrated by looking at 1 Samuel 20:30, in which Saul expressees his extreme anger at Jonathan by using a phrase deriding Jonathan's mother. This is rendered fairly literally by calling him a "son of the perverse rebellious woman" (KJV, NASB, NIV, NRSV, NJPS). While this is literally what is said, it does not carry the visceral insult from Hebrew into English. The TEV tries to convey the outrage by having Saul

64. For example, John R. Kohlenberger III, *The NIV Interlinear Hebrew-English Old Testament,* 4 vols. (Grand Rapids: Zondervan, 1979).

65. There are examples of even greater exercises in futility, such as when the KJV translators were not sure what a Hebrew word (*parbar;* 1 Chron. 26:18) meant. They simply transliterated the term from Hebrew into English, more or less saying to the reader, "Since we couldn't figure this out, maybe you can."

66. Jan de Waard and Eugene A. Nida, *From One Language to Another: Functional Equivalence in Bible Translating* (Nashville: Thomas Nelson, 1986), 41.

call Jonathan a "bastard," but this insult to him and his parentage is not the equivalent to the Hebrew, which is better rendered more functionally as "son of a rebellious slut" (NJB) or even "you son of a bitch" (LB).[67] The shock value of the latter, which seems totally inappropriate and an expression that should not be used in polite—or indeed, any—company, is exactly the response the insult would have elicited from its first hearers, and is therefore completely appropriate, and in fact necessary, in a dynamic equivalence translation.

Returning to the idiom in 1 Samuel 24:3, the dynamic-translation approach wants readers to understand what the clause means in everyday terms. This is accomplished in the Living Bible by stating that Saul went in the cave "to go to the bathroom." This is in fact what the Hebrew idiom meant, so the translation would be appropriate as meaning-for-meaning. There was, however, a reason why the Hebrew, rather than starkly stating the bodily function, used an idiom in the first place. This involves another aspect of language that is relevant to translation, namely the use of euphemisms. Numerous cultures, including that of the ancient Hebrews as well as our own, share an aversion to speaking bluntly of bodily functions or death and cloak them in more discreet forms. Since the original and target languages both share this view of this bodily function, it would be even more appropriate to render the Hebrew euphemism by an equivalent English euphemism, which numerous versions do by saying that Saul went in "to relieve himself" (NASB, RSV, TEV, NEB, CEV, NLT). This rendering preserves not only the meaning but also the delicacy of the text.

A danger in functional equivalency is importing too much into the target language, supplying more meaning than the original provided.[68] An example is adding specificity lacking in the original. Many English translations did this in Isaiah 7:14 when they rendered the Hebrew word ʿalmah, meaning "a female . . . who has not yet borne a child,"[69] as "virgin." The lack of sexual experience that is an integral part of the meaning of the English term *virgin* is not part of the specific meaning of the Hebrew term. That is, an ʿalmah may (Isa. 54:4) or may not have had sexual relations, since that is not the distinguishing semantic fea-

67. The vulgarity, though not necessarily the tone, is somewhat muted by the New Living Translation's "you stupid son of a whore." The blunt derogation of mother and son comes through here, but there is also an added slur on Jonathan's intelligence that is not explicit in the original.

68. See the previous note for an example.

69. John Walton, *NIDOTTE* 3.415–19, here 418. The LXX renders the word as *parthenos*, which also indicates sexual maturity but not sexual experience or its lack (ibid.).

ture for the word, while a virgin by definition cannot have had sexual relations.[70]

These are some of the issues that can be overlooked if one simply consults an already existing translation. The options mentioned also indicate why a Bible student might want to use both translation procedures in the course of sermon or lesson preparation. It is important to be able to read the words that the original audience read, so a literal translation has its place. One needs, using the words of Thiselton, to "pay attention to the historical particularities and historical conditionedness of the text."[71] It is not enough to stop there, however, for one should continue to translate for understanding, bridging the gap from the past to the present. According to Thiselton, "The modern reader is also conditioned by his own place in history and tradition."[72] This conditioning and pre-understanding must also be addressed.

Even if one is unable to produce a translation, English is blessed with multitude of translations that can help in this step of interpretation. In studying the text it is helpful to consult resources from across the spectrum of translations, from the more literal, such as the KJV or NASB, to the more dynamic, such as the TEV or NLT. Such research would include translations representing the middle of the spectrum, for example, NRSV, NIV, and NJB. In this, as in many aspects of life, there cannot be too much help.

70. For a useful bibliography on the interpretation of this verse, see ibid., 419. For an introduction to the process of analyzing the semantic components that make up the meaning of a word, see Eugene A. Nida, *Componential Analysis of Meaning: An Introduction to Semantic Structures* (The Hague and Paris: Mouton, 1975).

71. These features form the historical horizon of the original reader (Anthony C. Thiselton, *The Two Horizons: New Testament Hermeneutics and Philosophical Description with Special Reference to Heidegger, Bultmann, Gadamer, and Wittgenstein* [Grand Rapids: Eerdmans, 1980], 15).

72. Ibid. This is the second horizon, that of the current reader.

three

Reading the Old Testament as Literature

V. Philips Long

Is the Bible Literature?

It seems a simple question, but finding an answer to it is not always easy. Most today are quick to recognize that the Bible is in some sense literary; it does, after all, consist of words on paper. But is it literature in a narrower sense? Leland Ryken describes the Bible as "the story of all things, embodied in a collection of all major literary genres." As a diverse, yet unified, anthology, the Bible evinces a "truthfulness to human experience" that "preserves the complexities and polarities of life to an unusual degree." Its style is at once simple and yet majestic.[1] Observations such as these affirm that the Bible can rightly be called literature, as do the titles to such works as Robert Alter's *The World of Biblical Literature*[2] or John B. Gabel, Charles B. Wheeler, and Anthony D. York's *The Bible as Literature: An Introduction*.[3]

---

1. L. Ryken, "Bible as Literature," in *Foundations for Biblical Interpretation*, ed. D. S. Dockery et al. (Nashville: Broadman & Holman, 1994), 55–72.
2. New York: Basic Books, 1991.
3. New York and Oxford: Oxford University Press, 1996.

Some prefer to define literature as a "social category": "Literary texts are defined as those that are used by the society in such a way that *the text is not taken as specifically relevant to the immediate context of its origin.*"[4] Such a definition tends toward what David Robertson decribes as *pure* (i.e., imaginative, nonutilitarian) literature as opposed to *applied* (i.e., utilitarian) literature.[5] To be sure, the Bible, like much great literature, involves "an interpretive presentation of experience in an artistic form,"[6] and it is marked by "artful verbal expression and compelling ideas."[7] But it is not merely art for art's sake. As Robertson has noted, much of the Bible "was originally written as applied literature: as history, liturgy, laws, preaching, and the like."[8]

Provided that we define *literature* to include the utilitarian sense, then the Old Testament is correctly called literature. This means that if interpreters wish to do the OT justice, they must include literary considerations in their exegetical practice. The OT *requires* a literary approach. But what does this mean?

What It Means to Read the Bible as Literature

Lack of clarity on what a "literary approach" should look like may in part be accounted for by the youthfulness of the field.[9] As Berlin explains, "Because the field is young, growing rapidly, and still rather undisciplined, its rules and procedures have yet to be spelled out. The situation in literary studies of the Bible is somewhat like that portrayed

4. So John Ellis, *The Theory of Literary Criticism: A Logical Analysis* (Berkeley: University of California Press, 1974), 44 (emphasis in original); quoted by M. Z. Brettler, *The Creation of History in Ancient Israel* (London and New York: Routledge, 1995), 16.

5. *The Old Testament and the Literary Critic* (Philadelphia: Fortress, 1977), 3. For fuller discussion of these issues, see V. P. Long, *The Art of Biblical History*, Foundations of Contemporary Interpretation 5 (Grand Rapids: Zondervan, 1994), 152–53.

6. L. Ryken, *The Literature of the Bible* (Grand Rapids: Zondervan, 1974), 13.

7. A. Berlin, "On the Bible as Literature," *Prooftexts* 2 (1982): 324.

8. *Old Testament and the Literary Critic*, 3. Cf. Gabel, Wheeler, and York, *Bible as Literature*, 4: "We are using the term 'literature' in its broadest sense. There is a narrower sense of the term that encompasses only what is known as belles lettres: poetry, short stories, novels, plays, essays. Although the Bible does contain this kind of material, it also contains genealogies, laws, letters, royal decrees, instructions for building, prayers, proverbial wisdom, prophetic messages, historical narratives, tribal lists, archival data, ritual regulations, and other kinds of material more difficult to classify."

9. Biblical scholarship has taken a literary turn since the 1970s, though, in view of such earlier works as Richard G. Moulton's *The Literary Study of the Bible* (London: Isbister, 1896) and of even earlier interpretive practices, it would be more accurate to speak of a literary *return*. This is not to deny, of course, that significant advances have been made in recent years in understanding the workings (that is, the *poetics*) of the narratives and poems of the OT—and of the many subgenres within these broad categories.

in the Book of Judges: each person does what seems right in his or her eyes."[10] So-called literary approaches to biblical exegesis range from formalist to structuralist to deconstructionist, and so on. Some of these are quite irreconcilable with one another.[11] Deconstructionist criticism, for example, recently in vogue in some quarters, would have us believe that words and language are so unstable that all attempts at communication ultimately begin to unravel, or deconstruct. In "The Status of Biblical Narrative," Stephen Prickett offers the following wry comment on the excesses of deconstructionist literary criticism:

> Literary criticism has perhaps been plunged into the greatest crisis of them all, radically problematised to the point where some of its most respected prophets have proclaimed the ultimate meaninglessness and futility of words themselves. That they have done so by means of words at often inordinate length is only a minor irony. Those of us with a more typological cast of mind can, in our less charitable moments, perhaps take a certain malicious pleasure over one eminent scholar who had authoritatively pronounced that there was essentially no difference in status between literature and a laundry-list, and who was subsequently run over and killed by a laundry-van outside the gates of his own university.[12]

Whatever may be granted about a certain indeterminacy (or polyvalence) of meaning in literary texts, the notion of indeterminacy should not be carried to extremes, especially not in *applied* literature. As Robert Morgan has noted: "A thousand interpretations of Lear may be enriching, even two of the *Highway Code* disastrous. A single agreed interpretation of legal statutes is necessary for the life of society."[13]

While few trends in contemporary literary study are as counterintuitive as deconstructionism, there are sufficient pitfalls in many literary approaches to commend caution. Given the trend toward destabilization of meaning, a first caution would be to safeguard a commonsense approach to the ability of language to convey meaning. Recent work in text linguistics (pragmatics, discourse analysis, speech-act theory, and so on) stresses the recognition that communicative acts in texts correspond in many respects to communicative acts in real life. A second

10. A. Berlin, "Literary Exegesis of Biblical Narrative: Between Poetics and Hermeneutics," in J. P. Rosenblatt and J. C. Sitterson Jr., eds., *"Not In Heaven": Coherence and Complexity in Biblical Narrative* (Bloomington: Indiana University Press, 1991), 120.

11. For a recent, helpful survey of the rise and current status of modern literary study of the Bible, see T. Longman III, "Literary Approaches and Interpretation," *NIDOTTE* 1.103–24.

12. S. Prickett, "The Status of Biblical Narrative," *Pacifica* 2 (1989): 26–46, at 28.

13. R. Morgan and J. Barton, *Biblical Interpretation* (Oxford: Oxford University Press, 1988), 12.

caution is made necessary by one of the strengths of literary approaches in general, namely, that they are, as Gale Yee remarks, text-centered: "One encounters the *text* firsthand and not simply the formative historical situations *behind the text*."[14] This very text-centeredness can run the risk of "severing the text from its author and history," thus becoming "an ahistorical inquiry that regards the text primarily as an aesthetic object unto itself rather than a social practice intimately bound to a particular history."[15] The second caution, then, is to avoid the ahistorical turn that reduces the biblical texts to something they were never intended to be, that is, *pure* literature, as discussed above. After all, "The biblical texts were not written [merely] to be objects of aesthetic beauty or contemplation, but as persuasive forces that during their own time formed opinion, made judgments, and exerted change. Moreover, in all its historical, cultural, and literary constraints, the Bible continues to be a powerful standard for present-day social, as well as religious, attitudes and behavior."[16]

Our discussion of the potential dangers of adopting a literary approach to biblical interpretation could be extended, but that would deter us from the real point of this chapter. Many of the problems associated with literary approaches stem from the entirely unwarranted reductions of the Bible to art for art's sake and of meaning to absolute indeterminacy. So long as such missteps are avoided, and so long as the literary approach does not lead to neglect of the Bible's two other impulses—historical and theological[17]—then much can be gained from reading the Bible as literature. Indeed, it is fair to say that unless one gives the Bible an appropriate literary reading, one may misperceive its historical and theological import. This brings us back to the primary question in this section: "What does it mean to read the Bible as literature?"

First, it should mean taking an appropriately eclectic approach. The best literary approach to the Bible, given the Bible's unique character, may not fall under any of the current "*isms*." As Longman points out, "The cutting edge of the field . . . is not only varied in its approach to the study of the Bible, it is eclectic. That is, it utilizes not one but a variety of approaches at the same time."[18] Second, and this is the most fundamental

14. G. A. Yee, *Judges and Method: New Approaches in Biblical Studies* (Minneapolis: Fortress, 1995), 11.

15. Ibid.

16. Ibid., 11–12.

17. As Longman ("Literary Approaches and Interpretation," 113) maintains, "It is not only possible, it is necessary to integrate literary analysis with the study of history and the text's ideology (theology)."

18. Ibid., 110.

point, to read the Bible as literature should mean to use all available means to read it on its own terms and to discover its message(s). That is, the goal of a literary approach to the biblical text is to hear the text as clearly as possible, to discern correctly the text's *truth claims* (irrespective of the issue of *truth value*). We shall return to the issue of truth claims and truth value below, but for now an analogy may suffice to elucidate the concepts. A child visiting her grandfather back in the "old country" may have little trouble assuming the truth value of what her loving forebear says, and yet have great trouble (due to linguistic, cultural, generational, and various other factors) in discerning what truth claims he may be making. In other words, she is quite ready to *believe* him but has great difficulty *understanding* him. On the other hand, this same child may have little difficulty understanding a truth claim uttered by a stranger on the street outside her school ("Your mother sent me to take you home"), but she is wise not to assume the truth value of this statement.

The goal of a literary approach to biblical interpretation is to discover the truth claims of the text, to hear what it is trying to say—to hear its propositions, descriptions, exhortations, and all its other "speech-acts" as they were intended to be heard.[19] Put most simply, the goal of a literary approach is to make the interpreter a good (competent) listener to the text. It is not always easy to discover truth claims, whether one is dealing with a "foreign" grandfather (separated by time, culture, language, and so on) or with a "foreign" book like the Bible (similarly separated from the modern reader),[20] but unless the effort is made, true understanding will never occur. In discovering truth claims, literary interpretation must take priority. Thus, the tendency of "some biblical specialists" to view the "turn to literary theory as little more than optional icing on the cake" is, as A. C. Thiselton has observed, gravely mistaken.[21] Rather, literary interpretation is the initial ingredient of the recipe, although at some point(s) in the process it must be mixed with historical and theological considerations, if anything edible is to emerge from the oven.[22]

19. For an insightful discussion of the Bible's varied literary speech-acts, see K. J. Vanhoozer, "The Semantics of Biblical Literature: Truth and Scripture's Diverse Literary Forms," in *Hermeneutics, Authority, and Canon*, ed. D. A. Carson and J. D. Woodbridge (Grand Rapids: Zondervan, 1986), 49–104.

20. On the Bible as a foreign book, see Long, *Art of Biblical History*, 30–38.

21. A. C. Thiselton, *New Horizons in Hermeneutics: The Theory and Practice of Transforming Biblical Reading* (Grand Rapids: Zondervan; London: Marshall Pickering, 1992), 471.

22. On the symbiotic relationship that exists between, for instance, historical and literary study, see M. A. Powell, *What Is Narrative Criticism?* (Minneapolis: Fortress, 1990), 29.

What does it take to become a good listener to texts? In two words, it takes *competence* and *cooperation*.

Competence: Linguistic and Literary

By *competence* I have two types in mind. The first, and most obvious, is *linguistic competence*. If the granddaughter and her "old country" grandfather do not speak the same language, they may communicate a little, if face-to-face, through gestures and expressions, but imagine how little they will accomplish over the telephone! A parent serving as interpreter will help a great deal, but the ideal situation would be for one or the other to develop a high degree of linguistic competence in the other's language. In the case of a foreign book like the Bible, gestures and facial expressions are, of course, out of the question. The reader without Hebrew (or Aramaic), for instance, if faced with the Old Testament in its original language(s), would get about as much from the encounter as the aforementioned individuals on the telephone. Scholars who have translated the OT into English have helped English readers a great deal, of course, but a vital need remains for those who will seek as much linguistic competence in the original languages of the Bible as possible.[23]

In addition to *linguistic* competence, the best interpreters will need to make every effort to develop *literary* competence. "To be literarily competent," as Longman explains, "does not mean knowing the literature exhaustively, but being aware of the major conventions, or literary devices, genres, and so forth."[24] The granddaughter may learn the language of her grandfather, but unless she also gains some competence in the protocols of telephone conversations (and anyone who has traveled outside his or her own culture will know how these can vary), then much misunderstanding could still result. In the same way, students of the OT may learn much Hebrew and yet seriously misunderstand the biblical texts if they do not learn as much as possible about the idioms, the literary conventions, the rhetorical devices, and so on at work in the foreign literature that is the Bible.

Some may balk at the challenge of developing an ancient literary competence, insisting that it is impossible—after all, how can we ever really put ourselves in someone else's shoes (or sandals)? But those with such hesitations need to hear Meir Sternberg's remonstrance:

23. For practical wisdom on cultivating hard-earned language skills, see P. M. Doriani, "A Pastor's Advice on Maintaining Original Language Skills [Hebrew and Greek]," *Presbyterion* 19 (1993): 103–15.
24. "Literary Approaches and Interpretation," 124.

From the premise that we cannot become people of the past, it does not follow that we cannot approximate to this state by imagination and training—just as we learn the rules of any other cultural game—still less that we must not or do not make the effort. Indeed the antihistorical argument never goes all the way, usually balking as early as the hurdle of language.[25]

Just as one cannot hope to get far with the Hebrew Bible without first learning something of the conventions of the Hebrew language (or depending on the translations of those who have), one cannot hope to get far without learning something of Hebrew literature (or depending on the commentaries of those who have). Competence, both linguistic and literary, is required of those who would read the Bible as literature. This is not just a matter of literary "appreciation" but, as Robert Alter insists, "a discipline of understanding: the literary vehicle is so much the necessary medium through which the Hebrew writers realized their meanings that we will grasp the meanings at best imperfectly if we ignore their fine articulations as literature."[26]

In addition to linguistic and literary competence, right reading requires something else as well—a cooperative attitude that, whether willing to *believe* a particular text or not, at least tries to *understand* it on its own terms.

Cooperation: Taking the Bible on Its Own Terms

The cooperative interpreter tries to read the text as the "implied reader" would. M. A. Powell, citing J. D. Kingsbury, explains:

[T]he implied reader [is] the "imaginary person in whom the intention of the text is to be thought of as always reaching its fulfillment." To read in this way, it is necessary to know everything that the text assumes the reader knows and to "forget" everything that the text does not assume the reader knows. The critic should ask the questions that the text assumes its reader will ask but should not be distracted by questions that the implied reader would not ask. The implied reader, furthermore, is not necessarily to be thought of as a first-time reader. In some instances the narrative text apparently assumes the reader will come to an understanding only after multiple readings.[27]

25. *The Poetics of Biblical Narrative: Ideological Literature and the Drama of Reading* (Bloomington: Indiana University Press, 1985), 10.

26. "Introduction to the Old Testament," in *The Literary Guide to the Bible*, ed. R. Alter and F. Kermode (Cambridge: Harvard University Press, Belknap Press, 1987), 21.

27. *What Is Narrative Criticism?* 20.

In the same vein, the cooperative interpreter will assume, at least as a *reading strategy*, the fundamental philosophical or metaphysical convictions of the "implied reader." For instance, as Sternberg has argued, in biblical narrative the narrating persona is always privileged in being privy to information that has not necessarily been empirically obtained—the narrator sometimes knows what has transpired behind closed doors, or in the mind of a character, or even in the mind of God.[28] Some modern interpreters automatically regard an "omniscient narrator" as a mark of fiction, but Sternberg contends that this privilege (omniscience) is not to be explained according to the "quasi-inspirational model" of modern fiction, but in the "inspirational" model at home in the Bible.[29] His essential point is that

> personal opinion about fact or faith is one thing, and interpretive strategy another. Interpreters must either invent their own biblical text or grant the storyteller all the storytelling authority (divine and otherwise) he enjoys in cultural context. Across all doctrinal boundaries, inspiration simply figures as an institutional rule for writing and reading; and it is no more liable to questioning than the Bible's rules of grammar (or the reality of *Hamlet*'s ghost). To make sense of the Bible in terms of its own conventions, one need not believe in either, but one must postulate both.[30]

The cooperative reader, then, will not infer from "omniscient narration" that the biblical narrator *intended* to write fiction. Nor would the cooperative reader infer from narratives involving miracles or direct divine intervention that the biblical narrators did not *intend* to write history. Some modern interpreters may refuse to allow a place for either divine inspiration or divine intervention in "their world," but this then is no longer a question of what truth claims the text is making but of what truth value interpreters are willing to invest in those claims. The task of literary interpretation is, in the first instance, to discover the biblical texts' truth claims, not to rule on their truth value. The former requires competence and cooperation, the latter is a matter of faith, however one rules.

A Basic Plan for Reading the Bible as Literature

Books on how to read and interpret the Bible abound, and many treat the specifically literary aspect of biblical interpretation. So the direction that a section on the "basic steps" in literary interpretation

28. See Sternberg, *Poetics of Biblical Narrative*, 73ff.
29. Ibid., 76ff.
30. Ibid., 81.

might take is by no means a foregone conclusion. In the next major section, we look at some of the specific competencies that will facilitate sound literary interpretation of biblical texts. Since our focus in the present volume is on the Old Testament, the emphases and examples in our discussion will relate mostly to the "larger testament." But much of what we shall learn about OT narrative, for example, will find ready analogues in and applications to New Testament narratives. Our immediate concern, however, is to lay out a simple, basic strategy for doing literary interpretation of biblical texts.

The four-stage strategy presented represents a loose adaptation of guidelines that Leland Ryken commends in his book *Words of Delight: A Literary Introduction to the Bible*.[31] Ryken introduces his guidelines in a discussion of how to explicate biblical poetry, but I have discovered, having worked with the guidelines for several years, that they offer a useful approach not just to explication but, with some modification, to interpretation as well, and not just to poetry but to any literary text. In the process of literary interpretation, then, the interpreter will need to gain understanding in each of the following areas: (1) genre and setting; (2) topic and theme; (3) structure and unity; (4) literary texture and artistry.[32] While explication of a text might logically follow the above order, the process of interpretation will necessarily involve moving back and forth among the various elements, insights gained in one area prompting refinement of earlier judgments in another.

In what follows, I describe each element in the process and then briefly exemplify it, using the story of the rise of Saul in 1 Samuel 9–11. Aspects of the four elements and of the chosen example will be developed more fully in the next major section.

Genre and Setting

"Genre may well be the literary concept most important to the interpretive task."[33] But what is *genre*? John Barton describes a genre as "any recognizable and distinguishable type of writing or speech—whether 'literary' in the complementary sense of that word or merely utilitarian, like a business letter—which operates within certain conventions that are in principle (not necessarily in practice) stateable."[34] At a high level

31. Grand Rapids: Baker, 1987.

32. As my previous comments imply, this scheme represents a modification of Ryken's approach to explication. It is not necessary, for our purposes, to highlight the differences, but they can be easily discovered by consulting Ryken's work, esp. 207–11.

33. Longman, "Literary Approaches and Interpretation," 114.

34. *Reading the Old Testament: Method in Biblical Study* (London: Darton, Longman, and Todd, 1984), 16.

of generality, the OT can be divided into sections of narrative and poetry.[35] But far more specific descriptions of genres are also possible. For instance, 1 and 2 Samuel tell a remarkable *story*. Do they also recount *history?* More specifically, do they constitute a *royal apology* in defense of the Davidic monarchy? To take another example: we may recognize an OT text as *poetry*, but then we should ask more specific questions about its genre. Is it a *psalm?* a *lament* psalm? an individual or communal lament psalm? a *God-lament* psalm? As complex as genre considerations can become, they are indispensable in literary interpretation, for genre recognition plays a vital role in enabling readers "to interpret meaning and to recognize what kinds of truth claims are being made in and by a text."[36] Genre has to do with *what a text is*. As a simple illustration of how decisions about genre enter everyday communication, one might think of the way in which the daily mail is sorted at the desk or kitchen table. Third-class advertisements and solicitations in one stack, bills in another, business letters in another, personal letters, letters from the tax office (!), and so forth. In order to make the stacks, genre decisions are made, almost without thinking, and often on the basis of conventional signals. But once the genre of a piece of mail is determined, certain expectations arise regarding what kind of information it will contain (or whether it will even get opened).

Closely related to genre is the issue of *setting*. Certain genres operate generally within certain settings. Personal letters function within personal relationships, business letters are used for transacting business, and so forth. In OT interpretation, the issue of setting can be approached from several angles. The most important issue with respect to the *literary* task of interpretation is, of course, the *literary* setting: what is the literary context in which a text is found? What comes before it? after it? What part does it play within the larger story or poem, and so on? But other settings must be considered in the interpretive process. With much OT narrative, for instance, one must give thought to the historical setting of the events described, and also to the historical setting(s) in which the narrative was written and passed down. Definite answers to these latter questions are often not easy (sometimes impossible) to discover, but the issues at least need to be raised.

As regards our test case (i.e., the story of the rise of Saul in 1 Samuel), its genre is mostly narrative, Hebrew narrative, and, more specifically (although some will contest this), historiographical narrative. Its literary setting is in the middle of 1 Samuel, which begins with Samuel

35. Cf. D. J. A. Clines, "Story and Poem: The Old Testament as Literature and Scripture," *Int* 34 (1980): 115–27.
36. Vanhoozer, "Semantics of Biblical Literature," 80.

and ends with David. The historical setting it describes falls between the dusk of the period of the judges and the dawn of kingship. The setting of the text's composition is, of course, much debated, ranging from near the time of the events described to the postexilic period. The compositional history of the Saul narratives and of the Books of Samuel can be deferred, as far as the central task of literary interpretation is concerned; in fact, the results of the literary interpretation may at some stage play a part in coming to understand the compositional setting.

Topic and Theme

Borrowing from Ryken's discussion of the "intellectual core" of a text, we may distinguish *topic*—what a text is about—from *theme*—what the text asserts or implies about the topic.[37] The topic can sometimes be expressed in one word, whereas theme generally requires at least a verb as well as a noun. In the sample text before us, the topic could be expressed as *kingship*, or *the beginning of kingship in Israel*. The theme might be something like; *a king who will not submit to God will not succeed in Israel*. It is easy to see how such a theme, underlying the account of Saul's rise to power, could lay the foundation for the subsequent defense of David's right, as a "man after God's own heart" (1 Sam. 13:14), to replace Saul. These initial attempts to state topic and theme are of course dependent on prior knowledge of the texts, and they should remain tentative and open to refinement or correction as literary interpretation proceeds. When approaching a text for the first time, a reader may have no idea of topic or theme, but some ideas will begin to surface as the reading progresses. Even in instances in which one feels confident about topic and theme, one should expect that each new reading may bring new understanding and prompt revision. Moreover, while it is a healthy exercise to push oneself to discern the "big idea" in a text, it would be unwise to assume that a text can have only one topic and theme.

Structure and Unity

The central questions in this part of the process are whether the text hangs together (*unity*) and how (*structure*). It is generally a good idea to outline the passage and, especially with narrative texts, to explore how the passage fits within the larger literary context. Some texts, especially poetical texts, may exhibit specialized structures that should

---

37. *Words of Delight*, 208. Cf. D. J. A. Clines's distinction between *plot* and *theme* in *The Theme of the Pentateuch*, JSOTSup 10 (Sheffield: JSOT, 1978), 17–18: plot involves "a narrative of events, the emphasis falling on causality," whereas theme involves a "conceptualization of its plot" that "tends to focus its significance and state its implications."

be considered in outlining, but even narrative texts can be expected to exhibit a beginning, middle, and end. Longer stretches of narrative are generally comprised of episodes, each with its own beginning, middle, and end, but the larger narrative itself will also show this tripartite progression. The more technical skills one acquires, in areas such as text linguistics for example, the more precisely one may be able to trace the discourse of a text. But even without such skills, literary sensitivity and common sense can often yield a serviceable outline. Since outlining is a descriptive and, to some extent, subjective exercise, there is unlikely to be only one correct outline for a given text. There are, however, better and worse outlines, and good outlines of a given text should show at least some resemblance.

If the *structure* of a text can be convincingly presented in an outline, although it would not be quite right to say that the *unity* of the text is proven, the burden of proof would at least shift to those who would assert the opposite. Modern literary interpretation generally begins with the assumption that a text is unified and that its parts will hang together, whereas older-style literary criticism (such as source criticism) generally began with the assumption that a text is not unified and that tensions and inconsistencies in the text often allow earlier source material to be discerned and divided. Neither of these assumptions is patently correct, and both should be open to correction in the light of the evidence. Nevertheless, the literary interpreter is best advised to assume the unity of the text as a working principle and to make every legitimate effort to make sense of the text as it stands. Such an approach forestalls overhasty judgments about disunity that would truncate serious exegetical engagement with the text and preclude the discovery of genuine resolutions to perceived difficulties.

Returning to our test case, the chapters recounting the rise of Saul (1 Samuel 8–12, especially 9–11) have been described as the *locus classicus* of source criticism in 1 Samuel. Here, more than anywhere else, vying traditions have been juxtaposed in an attempted combination that is at best only partially successful—so Wellhausen's traditional view, which continues to dominate many commentaries. Tonal and logical inconsistencies among the episodes are believed to stand in the way of a coherent reading of all the texts in their present sequence. As regards tone, some passages are deemed promonarchical (i.e., 9:1–10:16 and 11:1–11) and others antimonarchical (chap. 8; 10:17–27; chap. 12). As regards logic, Saul appears to be elevated to the throne in too many different ways—he is anointed (9:1–10:16), he is selected by lot (10:17–27), and he gains popular support by delivering Jabesh-Gilead from Ammonite oppression (11:1–11). To make matters worse, there appears to be some textual dislocation or distortion, as Samuel's command in 10:8 that Saul should repair to Gilgal and wait seven days for Samuel's arrival is not mentioned again until chapter 13 (after many intervening episodes), at which time Samuel is late and Saul fails to wait for the appointed time (13:8).

In short, the traditional critical approach has concluded that the rise of Saul is a disunified and not particularly coherent stretch of text. A literary approach of the more modern variety, however, will not simply accept the validity of this conclusion and will reread the texts in the light of newer understandings of the poetics (or workings) of Hebrew narrative, in the hope of perhaps discovering a more coherent text than has generally been assumed. We review some of these newer understandings below, with regard to both narrative and poetical texts in the OT, but for now we need only note that such a literary reading, combining literary competence and a cooperative attitude, does indeed discover the rise of Saul to comprise a coherent narrative. There is neither space nor necessity in this essay for a full summary of what is covered extensively elsewhere,[38] but we shall return to this issue from time to time in illustrating points in the next major section.

Texture and Artistry

In his description of how to explicate biblical poetry, Ryken treats "poetic texture" and "artistry" separately. For our purposes, they can be combined. The central point is that while the three categories above concern the text as a whole, the exploration of *texture* and *artistry* focuses on the details of the text. Ryken employs an architectural metaphor to explain what is involved in this exploration.[39] Modifying Ryken's description slightly, we might say that the *structure* of a text can be compared to the framing timbers that hold up a wall; *texture* is the plaster (or "drywall"); and *artistry* is the paint or wallpaper. The texture of a poem, or of a narrative, includes "words (including their connotations and overtones)," and may also include "images, metaphors, similes, apostrophes, personifications, hyperboles, and any other figures of speech."[40] Imagery and figures of speech naturally occur in higher concentration in poetical texts, but they may also occur in nar-

38. See, for example, V. P. Long, *The Reign and Rejection of King Saul: A Case for Literary and Theological Coherence*, SBLDS 118 (Atlanta: Scholars, 1989); idem, "How Did Saul Become King? Literary Reading and Historical Reconstruction," in *Faith, Tradition, and History*, ed. A. R. Millard, J. K. Hoffmeier, and D. W. Baker (Winona Lake, Ind.: Eisenbrauns, 1994), 271–84.

39. *Words of Delight*, 210.

40. Ibid.

ratives. The division between narrative and poetry in the OT is not absolute but simply a matter of degree. The "artistry" of a text is closely tied not only to texture but to earlier categories as well. In exploring artistry, the interpreter focuses on what gives "color" to the poem or narrative. Focus on artistry asks, for instance, what makes the poem beautiful or powerful? What makes the narrative convincing or compelling? Even in asking such questions, we are reminded that biblical interpretation is as much an art as a science.

In our example of the Saul narratives, much could be said about texture and artistry: the economy of the narratives; the dramatic mode of presentation, whereby the narrator presents the words and actions of the characters with but sparse *explicit* evaluative commentary; the narrator's use of contrastive speech and actions to build his characterizations; the use of key words and wordplays, of irony, and so forth. The subtleties of OT narrative and poetry are such that they easily escape the untrained eye, but this is where efforts expended to improve one's ancient literary competence begin to pay rich dividends. To be sure, it is possible to get the basic point of most biblical texts with a fairly rudimentary set of interpretive skills, just as it is possible to gauge the basic shape of a wall from the framing timbers alone, but the serious student of the Bible will hardly be content to "live there." Indeed, sometimes extremely important issues turn on seemingly small details in the texts. We consider an example as we move into the next section.

Specific Competencies

So far we have seen that the Bible is literature, broadly conceived to include utilitarian literature, and as such demands a literary approach. Further, we have seen that a proper literary approach to the Bible requires both a cooperative attitude and certain competencies, not least linguistic and literary competencies. In this section we expand on these competencies. In the discussion just completed of a basic plan for literary interpretation, we noted four concerns to which a proper literary interpretation must do justice—genre and setting, topic and theme, structure and unity, texture and artistry. Whatever our initial judgments regarding the first three concerns, the refining of these judgments only begins when we get down to the "close reading" involved in the exploration of texture and artistry. We begin our discussion of specific competencies, then, with a focus on words.

Linguistic Competence

Text and translations. The present volume is aimed especially at theology students and pastors, in other words at those who have (or have had!) Hebrew, and perhaps even a bit of Aramaic. Rare is the pastor or student, however, who does not have frequent recourse to a translation of the OT into his or her mother tongue. And so a brief word on translations is in order. What is the best English translation? The homespun adage that the best translation is the one you will read should not be gainsaid. But more also needs to be said. When asked what is the best translation, the proper response is another question: "Best for what purpose?" One translation may be particularly good in *lexical* accuracy (choosing the best English word in a given context from the full range of meaning of the Hebrew word), but another may sacrifice a degree of lexical accuracy in order to gain *rhetorical* accuracy. Compare for instance the following two translations of Amos 8:2.

> He [the Lord] said, "Amos, what do you see?" And I said, "A basket of summer fruit." Then the LORD said to me, "The end has come upon my people Israel; I will never again pass them by." (NRSV)

> "What do you see, Amos?" he asked. "A basket of ripe fruit," I answered. Then the Lord said to me, "The time is ripe for my people Israel; I will spare them no longer." (NIV)

The first rendering is *lexically* more accurate than the second, but not immediately comprehensible without further research. The second is less precise in its rendering of a couple of Hebrew words, but it is comprehensible and *rhetorically* more accurate than the first. Neither translation is categorically "more accurate" than the other. The key difference between the two is over how the Hebrew words *qāyiṣ* and *qêṣ* are translated. The most accurate rendering of the first is "summer" and of the second is "end," as in the NRSV, but there is also a wordplay in the Hebrew, for the two words sound very much alike. To capture this latter feature, which is central to the logic of the exchange between the Lord and Amos, the NIV simply uses "ripe" for both words—though neither *qāyiṣ* nor *qêṣ* actually means "ripe." This and many other examples demonstrate that, as the saying goes, "You always lose something in the translation." Effective translation involves, as Bruce Metzger notes, "the art of making the right sacrifice."[41] This suggests that when attempting serious study without the benefit of the original languages, one should at least consult several translations that emphasize different kinds of accuracy.

41. "Problems Confronting Translators of the Bible," in *The Making of the New Revised Standard Version of the Bible,* ed. B. M. Metzger, R. C. Denton, and W. Harrelson (Grand Rapids: Eerdmans, 1991), 47.

The following graphic illustrates the impossibility of achieving a completely accurate translation. The placement of the various translations on the chart is approximate and is only intended to illustrate the principle that translations stand in differing relationships to the three points of the triangle.

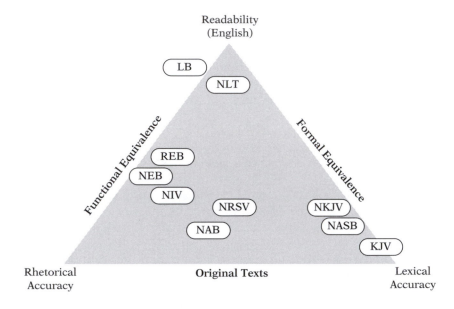

While on the topic of translations, we should also note that the rendering of a particular passage is only as good as the translator's understanding of that passage. Sometimes an apparently insignificant difference can take on great import. This can be illustrated from our example dealing with the rise of Saul. At the time of Saul's anointing by Samuel, Samuel predicts three signs that will confirm Saul's election (1 Sam. 10:1–6). The third sign is to take place at Gibeah of God, "where there is a Philistine outpost" (10:5 NIV). After describing the signs, Samuel issues Saul a two-part charge in 10:7–8. Many English translations render verse 7 along lines similar to the following: "Once these signs are fulfilled, do whatever your hand finds to do, for God is with you" (so NIV). Such a rendering, by using the word "whatever," suggests that Saul, in response to the signs, is to begin to act in a kingly fashion, doing *whatever* seems right, *whenever* an opportunity shall arise. The Hebrew text, however, does not read "do *whatever* your hand finds to do" but, rather, "do *what* your hand finds to do" (*'ăśēh lĕkā 'ăšer timṣā' yādekā*). "Do what . . . " suggests that Samuel has something specific in mind that Saul should do as soon as the signs are fulfilled. The seemingly slight variation in the translation is, in fact, quite significant for the overall interpretation of Saul's anointing and its aftermath, and indeed for a proper understanding of how the texts recounting Saul's rise hang together. We return to this matter in the next section.

Lexical, grammatical, syntactical, and discourse analysis. Lexical analysis concerns itself with the meaning of words. *Grammatical analysis* concerns how words are inflected to add nuance to their meaning—how, for instance, a verb may be conjugated to show the person, gender, and number of its subject. *Syntactical analysis* concerns how words work together in phrases and clauses to create meaningful expressions. And *discourse analysis*, or text linguistics, focuses on how larger units (sentences, paragraphs, and beyond) work together to create meaningful discourses. It is probably fair to say that most students feel more comfortable with lexical and perhaps grammatical analysis and less comfortable with syntactical and discourse analysis. Even students of the Bible without specialized training often have some idea of how to use a concordance or an English-accessible theological dictionary to do a word study. Students with theological training are familiar with original-language dictionaries, concordances, and grammars that facilitate more precise word studies. Syntactical study generally proves more challenging for students and pastors without more advanced training, in part due to a relative sparsity of good, intermediate-level discussions of Hebrew syntax. And discourse anaysis is still a relatively young, though rapidly maturing, field.

Faced with the challenge of doing responsible study of the OT in its original language(s), many pastors simply give up. This situation elicits a few observations. First, it is certainly the case that different individuals are more or less gifted in different areas, and this variety is something to be celebrated. Nevertheless, all who have opportunity to study the original languages of Scripture stand to gain something, even if only the ability to read and understand higher-level, language-based commentaries. Second, because of the direct applicability of linguistic competence in the study of Scripture, those who have once studied Hebrew or Greek tend to develop a guilt complex about what they inevitably forget. Everytime they open the Bible, a little voice inside their head says, "I wonder what this says in the Hebrew? or the Greek?" It is easy to see how these daily reminders can lead eventually to a sense of failure and defeatism. This need not happen. Instead, remember that forgetting is a natural result of being human; if we stop and think about it, we have forgotten much of what we learned in our theological studies—we are just not forced to face our losses on a daily basis as we are with the biblical languages, if we are studying the Bible regularly.

Third, linguistic competence in a foreign language, ancient or modern, is not gained in just a year or two. During one's theological training, one may make a good start, just as one makes a good start in mastering Bible content or in developing theological understanding and convictions or in learning to work with people, but these latter tasks continue to be the pursuits of a lifetime. So should the learning of the original languages of Scripture.

To illustrate how important grammatical, syntactical, and higher-level linguistic competence can be for understanding the message of a text, we return to the issue of Saul's first charge in 1 Samuel 10:7. Earlier we noted that Samuel's charge should read, "Do what [not *whatever*] your hand finds to do." How do we know this? The imperative *do* in Hebrew is singular (and, of course, second person), addressed to Saul. It is immediately followed by a preposition (*lĕ*) to which a second-person, singular suffix is attached. A wooden rendering of the injunction would read, "Do for yourself what your hand finds to do." But what is the significance of "for yourself"? Awareness of Hebrew grammar and syntax can sharpen our understanding at this point. The particular feature before us is discussed in *Gesenius' Hebrew Grammar*, in a section dealing with the way in which (pro)nouns can be subordinated to verbs by means of prepositions.[42] Our feature would come under the heading of a *dativus commodi*, which, according to Gesenius,

> is used . . . in the form of a pronoun with ל, as an apparently pleonastic *dativus ethicus*, with many verbs, in order to give emphasis to the significance of the occurrence in question *for* a particular subject. In this construction the person of the pronoun must always agree with that of the verbal form. By far the most frequent use of this ל is with the pronoun of the second person after imperatives, . . .[43]

T. Muraoka has challenged the aptness of using the term *dativus ethicus* to designate the usage described above, suggesting instead the designation "centripetal Lamedh."[44] He writes:

> In the light of these examples and also, of course, on the basis of a fresh examination of relevant biblical data, it now appears to me that this idiomatic preposition can be best described as centripetal. Basically it serves to convey the impression on the part of the speaker or author that the sub-

42. GKC §119.
43. Ibid., §119s.
44. See T. Muraoka, "The So-Called *dativus ethicus* in Hebrew," *JTS* 29 (1978): 495–98; cf. also P. Joüon, *A Grammar of Biblical Hebrew*, translated and revised by T. Muraoka, 2 vols., Subsidia Biblica 14 (Rome: Editrice Pontifico Istituto Biblico, 1991), 2.133d.

ject establishes his own identity, recovering or finding his own place by de-terminedly dissociating himself from his familiar surrounding.[45]

Whatever precise terminology we choose, it is clear that the idio-matic feature described above suits very nicely in 1 Samuel 10:7. Sam-uel's charge to Saul to "do (for yourself) what your hand finds to do" suggests that in taking action Saul will begin to "establish his own iden-tity" (Muraoka)—that is, as God's chosen leader. As noted earlier, Sam-uel seems to have something specific in mind—"do what [not *whatever*] your hand finds to do"—just as in the closest biblical parallel to this us-age, in Judges 9:33, Abimelech is exhorted by Zebul, governor of Shechem, to take specific action against the rebellious Gaal: "In the morning at sunrise, advance against the city. When Gaal and his men come out against you, do to him what[46] your hand finds to do."

As I have argued elsewhere, the context of 1 Samuel 10:7 indicates what specific action Samuel has in mind for Saul. Samuel's explicit mention of the "Philistine outpost" in verse 5 is not necessary for pur-poses of orientation—Saul would have been well familiar with the area and its features (as commentators have noted). Rather, Samuel's re-mark seems designed as a hint to Saul of what his hand should do (i.e., attack the outpost), once the three signs are fulfilled. Such an attack would be in keeping with the rationale for Saul's elevation, namely to "deliver my people from the hand of the Philistines" (1 Sam. 9:16 NIV), and it would begin to demonstrate that Saul had been designated by the Lord, which then could have led to Saul's *confirmation* by the peo-ple.[47] Saul's failure to do so in chapter 10 is significant, although the re-strained narrator does not offer explicit commentary, preferring rather to employ a narrative technique called *gapping*. In gapping, the narra-tor provides enough information to create gaps, or to raise questions, in the reader's mind, but delays filling the gaps until later in the narra-tive.[48] Such a device operates above the syntactical level—on the dis-

---

45. Muraoka, "So-called *dativus ethicus*," 497. Muraoka speculates that the centripe-tal Lamedh may have its origin in the "Lamedh of advantage and disadvantage (*dativus commodi et incommodi*)," but he maintains that "although ultimately derived from the Lamedh of advantage and disadvantage, on a synchronic level its centripetal usage must be kept apart from the ordinary Lamedh of advantage, for, whilst in the former function one can only say הלכתי לי אל ההר [I went/betook myself to the mountain], in the latter בניתי לי בית [I built myself a house] can be easily transformed to בניתי לך בית [I built you a house], בניתי לה בית [I built her a house], etc." (498; my insertions).

46. Again, the NIV reads "whatever," although this is neither necessary nor best in con-text. In any case, it is obvious that a *specific* military engagement is in view.

47. On this three-stage process (designation, demonstration, confirmation), see Long, *Art of Biblical History*, 209–10.

48. On this literary device, see Sternberg, *Poetics of Biblical Narrative*, 186–88.

course level—and, thus, moves beyond mere *linguistic* understanding to *literary* understanding.

Literary Competence

The concept of (ancient) literary competence has already been introduced, and so this section focuses on how we can become more competent in the two dominant literary genres of the OT, namely, narrative and poetry. Our aim will be to explore some of the "conventions" of biblical narrative and poetry (especially those that may differ from our expectations of these genres in our own cultures) and to offer guidelines for interpreting OT narrative and poetry literarily.[49]

Narrative

Just what is a narrative? Attempts at definition abound, but it is difficult to isolate the "definitive definition." Longman provides a useful starting point by observing that "narrative may be distinguished from other prose forms like the essay or the report by its storylike nature. Quite simply, narrative prose tells a story."[50] Powell takes the definition a step further:

> Narratives have two aspects: story and discourse. *Story* refers to the content of the narrative, what it is about. A story consists of such elements as events, characters, and settings, and the interaction of these elements comprises what we call the plot. *Discourse* refers to the rhetoric of the narrative, how the story is told. Stories concerning the same basic events, characters, and settings can be told in ways that produce very different effects.[51]

Perhaps a good way to grasp the point of the last statement is to reflect on portrait painting as an analogue to (historical) storytelling. Several portraits of a prominent individual may be quite accurate (that is, true to the subject) and yet quite different from one another. The differences reflect the creative choices that every portrait artist must make: the angle from which to view the subject, the light to be cast on the subject, the overall composition of the painting, the palette of colors in executing the portrait, the style of rendering (highly detailed or "broad

---

49. It would be useful to break down these large genre categories into more particular literary types, but space will not permit us to do so. For discussion of the literary types and forms of the OT, one should consult treatments such as G. Fee and D. Stuart, *How to Read the Bible for All Its Worth*, 2d ed. (Grand Rapids: Zondervan, 1993); D. B. Sandy and R. L. Giese Jr., eds., *Cracking Old Testament Codes: A Guide to Interpreting the Literary Genres of the Old Testament* (Nashville: Broadman & Holman, 1995); G. L. Klein, ed., *Reclaiming the Prophetic Mantel: Preaching the Old Testament Faithfully* (Nashville: Broadman, 1992).

50. "Biblical Narrative," in *A Complete Literary Guide to the Bible*, ed. L. Ryken and T. Longman III (Grand Rapids: Zondervan, 1993), 69–70.

51. *What Is Narrative Criticism?* 23.

brush"), and so on. Because no single portrait can be a full record of its subject, those wishing to gain a well-rounded impression of the subject welcome not only a multiplicity of portraits, but also the artists' own interpretations through their respective visions.

In reading the OT's narratives, therefore, it is vitally important to attend not only to *what* story is being told, but to *how* it is told. The interpretive capacity of narratives is to be welcomed, for, as Powell observes, "Revelation is given through the story, which remains with us today. We are, in fact, in a privileged position, for the story interprets the events for us in ways that we might never have grasped if we had simply been there to witness them transpire in history."[52] It would be an overstatement, of course, to say that "the medium is the message," just as it would be an overstatement to say that "the paint is the portrait," but the medium (narrative or paint) is the vehicle by which the message is conveyed. It is thus by gaining greater understanding of the narrative medium of the OT that we increase our competence as interpreters whose task is to discern the message.

Resources. Recent decades have witnessed a sharp increase in publications treating the poetics of biblical narrative. A number of book-length treatments offer guidance for beginning and intermediate students, the most influential perhaps by R. Alter.[53] At least one advanced treatise on Hebrew narrative is available, M. Sternberg's magisterial *Poetics of Biblical Narrative*.[54] A variety of essays also offer convenient and stimulating introductions to the workings of OT narrative.[55]

52. Ibid., 99.
53. R. Alter, *The Art of Biblical Narrative* (New York: Basic Books, 1981); other useful treatments include S. Bar-Efrat, *Narrative Art in the Bible*, trans. D. Shefer-Vanson (Sheffield: Almond, 1989); A. Berlin, *Poetics and Interpretation of Biblical Narrative* (Sheffield: Almond Press, 1983); D. M. Gunn and D. N. Fewell, *Narrative in the Hebrew Bible*, Oxford Bible Series (Oxford: Oxford University Press, 1993); T. Longman, *Literary Approaches to Biblical Interpretation*, Foundations of Contemporary Interpretation 3 (Grand Rapids: Zondervan, 1987); J. L. Ska, S.J., *"Our Fathers Have Told Us": Introduction to the Analysis of Hebrew Narratives*, Subsidia Biblica 13 (Rome: Editrice Pontifico Istituto Biblico, 1990).
54. Subtitled *Ideological Literature and the Drama of Reading* (see n. 25 above).
55. The following is but a small sampling: R. Alter, "How Convention Helps Us Read: The Case of the Bible's Annunciation Type-Scene," *Prooftexts* 3 (1983): 115–30; C. E. Armerding, "Faith and Method in Old Testament Study: Story Exegesis," in *A Pathway into the Holy Scripture*, ed. Philip E. Satterthwaite and David F. Wright (Grand Rapids: Eerdmans, 1994), 31–49; R. P. Gordon, "Simplicity of the Highest Cunning: Narrative Art in the Old Testament," *Scottish Bulletin of Evangelical Theology* 6 (1988): 69–80; V. P. Long, "Recent Advances in Literary Method as Applied to Biblical Narrative," chap. 1 in *The Reign and Rejection of King Saul*; R. E. Longacre, "Genesis as Soap Opera: Some Observations about Storytelling in the Hebrew Bible," *Journal of Text and Translation* 7, no. 1 (1995): 1–8; Prickett, "Status of Biblical Narrative"; P. E. Satterthwaite, "Narrative Criticism: The Theological Implications of Narrative Techniques," *NIDOTTE* 1.125–33.

The intent of each of these works is to push the reader toward greater understanding of OT narrative *discourse* and thus toward a firmer grasp of the messages—or, to use our technical term, the *truth claims*—of the biblical narratives. There are, of course, as Alter points out, "elements of continuity or at least close analogy in the literary modes of disparate ages," so that we can to some extent prepare ourselves to read OT narratives by reflecting on narrative traits in general— such things as plot, point of view, characterization, and so forth. Alter is right to insist, however, that we will become much better readers of biblical narratives if we adopt a "self-conscious sense of historical perspective" toward the "stubborn and interesting differences" between our narrative modes and the Bible's.[56]

While adequate treatment of the distinctive characteristics of biblical narrative is hardly possible within the confines of this chapter, we may at least consider a few basic features.

General traits of OT narrative. OT narratives are scenic, not in the sense of detailed descriptions of the physical setting or scene, but, rather, scenic in the way that a stage play involves scenes. Like a stage play, the OT narratives do more showing than telling. That is to say, the reader is seldom explicitly *told* by the narrator how this or that character, or this or that action, is to be evaluated (though this does occasionally occur). Instead, the reader is *shown* the characters acting and speaking, and is thereby drawn into the story and challenged to reach evaluative judgments on his/her own. In other words, the reader gets to know and understand the characters in the narrative in much the same way as in real life, by watching them and listening to what they say. The scenic character of OT narrative leads quite naturally to a second dominant trait.

OT narratives are subtle. As implied already, OT narrators are generally reticent to make their points directly, preferring to do so more subtly. To this end, they employ an array of indirect means in developing the narrative's characterizations and in focusing reader attention on aspects of the narrative that comprise its persuasive power. Mention of physical details, for instance, is seldom if ever random. If we read that Esau was hairy, Ehud left-handed, Eglon fat, and Eli dim-sighted, we should anticipate (though not insist) that such details in some way serve the characterizations or the action of the story. Sometimes the words or deeds of one character serve as indirect commentary on those of another. When Jonathan, for instance, remarks that "nothing can hinder the LORD from saving, whether by many or by few" (1 Sam. 14:6 NIV), this casts doubt on the validity of Saul's excuse in the preceding chapter—"the men were scattering" (13:11 NIV).

56. Alter, "How Convention Helps Us Read," 117–18.

OT narratives are succinct. Perhaps in part because of the constraints of writing in a scenic, or episodic, mode, biblical narrators tend to be very economical in their craft. They accomplish the greatest degree of definition and color with the fewest brushstrokes. Although written, the biblical literature is nevertheless "geared toward the ear, and meant to be listened to at a sitting. In a 'live' setting the storyteller negotiates each phrase with his audience. A nuance, an allusion hangs on nearly every word."[57] Narrations as succinct as the biblical texts invite close attention to detail. Moreover, the biblical narrators are masters in drawing special attention to key elements in their texts. They use all manner of repetitions to great advantage—words and word stems (e.g., *Leitworte*), motifs, similar situations (sometimes called "type-scenes"), and the like. The effect of repetition is often to underscore a central theme or concern in a narrative, as, for instance, in the repetition of the phrase "listen to the voice/sound" in 1 Samuel 15: as the chapter opens, Saul is exhorted to "listen" to the Lord's "voice" (v. 1) and to destroy all the Amalekites (man and beast); later he claims to have done so (v. 13). Samuel responds by asking about the "voice" of the sheep and cattle to which he is "listening" (v. 14); Samuel and Saul debate whether Saul has or has not "listened to the voice" of the Lord (vv. 19–20); when Saul seeks to excuse his failure to listen—claiming to have spared livestock only in order to sacrifice to the Lord—Samuel responds that "listening to the voice" of the Lord is vastly more important than sacrifice (v. 22); and Saul begrudgingly concedes that he has "listened to the voice" of the people (v. 24). While the attentive reader can surely judge from the "framing timbers" of this passage that Saul's (dis)obedience is a central theme, attention to the "plaster" and "wallpaper" (the texture) of the passage underscores and enriches this insight.[58]

Our discussion to this point only begins to scratch the surface of OT narratives. Students and working pastors are encouraged to consult the works noted earlier, especially by Alter, Longman, and Sternberg, for further guidance. Most helpful at this point might be a listing of questions or issues that will prime good narrative interpretation.

Checklist for interpreting OT narrative. In his recent book on the Bible's narrative art,[59] Jan Fokkelman offers a useful list of ten (groups of)

57. E. L. Greenstein, "Biblical Narratology," *Prooftexts* 1 (1981): 202.

58. See V. P. Long, "First and Second Samuel," in *A Complete Literary Guide to the Bible*, ed. Leland Ryken and Tremper Longman III (Grand Rapids: Zondervan, 1993), 165–81; esp. 170–72, where this and other examples of key-word style and also wordplays are described.

59. J. Fokkelman, *Vertelkunst in de bijbel* (Zoetermeer, Netherlands: Boekencentrum, 1995). After completion of this chapter, an English translation became available: *Reading Biblical Narrative*, trans. Ineke Smit (Louisville: Westminster John Knox, 1999).

questions designed to facilitate careful and competent reading of biblical narratives.[60]

1. Who is the *hero?* What are the grounds for your decision (think
    about criteria such as presence, initiative, who undertakes the
    quest)?
2. What constitutes the *quest?* What is the hero after, that is to
    say, what is the desired objective? Does the hero succeed, and
    if not, why not?
3. Who are *the helpers* and *the antagonists?* Persons as well as fac-
    tors, situations, or characteristics should be considered. Are
    there *attributes* (objects) present? What is their contribution?
    Do they have a symbolic value?
4. Do you sense the presence of *the narrator* anywhere in the text?
    This is relevant above all where he offers information, com-
    mentary, explanation, or evaluation from his perspective. Can
    you indicate the writer's form of speech? Where is the writer
    less detectable (for example, through his structuring or compo-
    sition)? Does he allow himself to speak at strategic points in the
    text?
5. Does the narrator hold to the *chronology* of the events and
    processes themselves? If not, where does he diverge, and why
    do you think he does so? Develop an impression of the rela-
    tionship between narrative time and narrated time. [Narra-
    tive time refers to the pace of the narrative presentation, while
    narrated time refers to the actual time taken by the event
    being described.]
6. Where are the gaps in *narrated time?* Are there instances of
    speeding up, retarding, retrospectives, or prospectives? Assum-
    ing that they are introduced by the writer at the right moment,
    why do they stand where they do? What is their relation to the
    context?
7. Is the *plot* clear, or is the unit you are reading without plot in
    that it is a part of the larger narrative? What is the macroplot
    that controls the larger narrative?
8. Where are the *dialogues?* Are they numerous? Are dialogues
    omitted where you might expect them? What factors guide the
    speakers—what self-interests, what background, what desires,
    what expectations? *Congruence:* Do the words of the character

60. I would like to thank Peter Williams and my longtime friends Kees and Doris
Minnaar for checking my translation of the Dutch. Remaining infelicities are my own
responsibility.

agree with his or her deeds? If not, why not? Are there elements
in the text that emphasize or suggest that the *writer* supports or
applauds his character?

9. What word choices strike you? What are the other characteristics of *style or structure?* Take them seriously, ponder them, and ask a question such as: What does this contribute to the plot, or to the typing of the characters?

10. *Limits:* what means were used to mark out a unit? (Consider the aspects of time, space, beginning/ending of action, appearance or disappearance of characters.) Can you *partition* the text (divide into smaller units)? On the basis of what signals do you make the partition? Try to find still other signals or indicators of another division. To what extent does the division illuminate theme or content?[61]

Simply asking and pursuing answers to these and similar questions will greatly enhance one's understanding of the Bible's masterfully written narratives.

Pros and cons of narrative criticism. Without doubt, there are great advantages in adopting a competent literary approach to OT narratives. As noted earlier, unless we read texts correctly as literature, we can hardly expect to perceive their truth claims correctly (historical, theological, or otherwise). In addition to this necessity of approaching biblical literature literarily, other benefits of narrative criticism include the following:

- It pays close attention to the text of Scripture rather than moving too quickly to extrinsic concerns.
- It provides a platform for discussion among Bible readers who may disagree about the text's truth value but who can still debate its truth claims.
- It sometimes offers necessary corrections to other exegetical methods, as when a proper literary reading undercuts a source-critical division of a text by offering a more plausible explanation of the textual phenomena upon which the division was based.
- It often restores a text's "voice," which may have been silenced through textual fragmentation, and in so doing it allows the text's message(s) to resound more clearly.[62]

61. Fokkelman, *Vertelkunst,* 214–15.
62. For a fuller listing of the benefits of narrative criticism, see Powell, *What Is Narrative Criticism?* 85–91.

Despite these obvious merits, narrative criticism does raise some serious questions:[63]

- Is the discovery of unity in a text truly a matter of evidence or merely the interpreter's preference? Has the literary reader simply found what he or she wished to find? This is an important issue that should be faced squarely—although it should also be remembered that those who discover disunity may also be finding what they wished to find.
- Is it appropriate to use modern literary terms and concepts in analyzing ancient literature? The answer is a qualified yes. Just as concepts such as *nouns, verbs, adjectives*, and so on seem useful in analyzing the grammar of ancient languages for which they may not have been native concepts, concepts such as *plot, characterization, narrative time, omniscient narration*, and so on can be useful in analyzing ancient literatures for which such terms were not native. But this leads to a related question.
- Since terms such as those above are often associated with fiction, can they be applied appropriately to the biblical texts, which do not present themselves as fiction? Again, a qualified yes seems in order. After all, one can use analytical categories such as composition, color, technique, and so on (often used in the description of *non*-representational art) to talk about the artistic aspects of a portrait (representational art).
- Perhaps most serious, does a literary approach tend to undermine the historical import of texts? The answer is "not necessarily," though in practice this sometimes happens.

Because of the vital link between history and faith, a few words on this fourth issue are necessary. In some quarters of biblical scholarship, it is popular to downplay the significance of historical questions, and to insist that we should not ask of a biblical narrative, "Did this actually happen?" The question, it is argued, should be, "Is this true to life/Is this true artistically?"[64] There may be a time to set aside historical questions in order to focus on literary artistry. But to leave aside historical concerns entirely and interminably is misguided in dealing

63. Cf. ibid., 91–98.

64. So Prickett ("Status of Biblical Narrative," 32), who objects strongly to such a view, arguing that it is "fundamentally untenable" and based on "certain assumptions about both 'history' and 'realism' that are essentially nineteenth century in origin and which can no longer be sustained in the face of recent changes in the way historians now understand their task" (33; cf. idem, *Words and the Word: Language, Poetics, and Biblical Interpretation* [Cambridge: Cambridge University Press, 1988], 76–78, 174–95).

with texts that appear to make historical truth claims—as misguided as focusing on the artistry of a portrait to the exclusion of any interest in the *historical* subject of which the portrait is a representation. A healthier approach is to recognize that "a symbiotic relationship exists between narrative and historical approaches to the text."[65] Just as sensitivity to artistic technique can prove useful in deriving historical information from a portrait, sensitivity to literary technique can prove useful in deriving historical information from biblical narratives.[66]

To exemplify this last point, we return to our discussion of the story of Saul's rise. As noted earlier, it is commonplace to regard the narratives of 1 Samuel 8–12 as *not* supplying a coherent, sequential story. One of the features of the text that has contributed to this assessment is that Samuel's order in 10:8 (i.e., that Saul should go to Gilgal and wait seven days for his arrival) does not come back into view until 13:8, after several intervening episodes. This has led to the general verdict that competing traditions of Saul's rise to power must have been juxtaposed in 1 Samuel 8–12, but with little success in crafting a sensible, sequential narrative. In our earlier discussion of Samuel's charge to Saul in 10:7 to "do what your hand finds to do," we saw that Samuel apparently had something specific in mind—an attack on the Philistine outpost mentioned in 10:5. When the time comes in chapter 10, however, Saul fails to act. That the narrator does not explicitly point out Saul's failure at this point was explained above on the basis of the *literary* device called "gapping." Saul's failure to execute the first step (10:7) in his twofold charge means that the second step, the rendezvous with Samuel in Gilgal (10:8), is deferred until such time as step one shall be accomplished. Not until 13:3 does Jonathan attack the Philistine outpost, thus accomplishing step one, and Saul repairs to Gilgal in keeping with step two. Once it is recognized that Saul's faltering at the time of his anointing caused a delay in the fulfillment of his first charge (which would, by the way, have brought Saul to public attention and led to his confirmation as king), then room is made for the intervening episodes. Thus, the *story* makes very good sense as it stands and, as such, improves its chances of being taken seriously as *history*. Without going into further detail,[67] the point is simply that an improved *literary* reading leads in this instance to an improved *historical* understanding. A similar argument could be made regarding the relationship of *literary* and *theological* understanding in this passage.

---

65. Powell, *What Is Narrative Criticism?* 98.

66. For more adequate discussion of these and related matters, see Long, *Art of Biblical History*, chaps. 2 and 3 and passim.

67. For full discussion, see Long, *Art of Biblical History*, chap. 6.

Poetry

Our discussion of *narrative*, the first of the OT's two broad genre categories, began with the observation that defining narrative continues to be a matter of debate. As we come now to *poetry*, a similar observation is in order, though perhaps to an even greater degree. Two of the most influential recent books on OT poetry—James Kugel's *The Idea of Biblical Poetry: Parallelism and Its History*[68] and Robert Alter's *The Art of Biblical Poetry*[69]—cannot even agree on whether it is accurate to speak of "poetry" in the Bible. Kugel prefers to think of a continuum of literary style in the Bible, with "heightened" rhetorical style on one end and "unheightened" style on the other. But he prefers not to use the term *poetry* for the former and *prose* for the latter, since Hebrew has no term for poetry per se, and to use the term might lead to confusion. Much depends, of course, on just how one defines poetry. Alter assumes a very basic definition: "the best words in the best order."[70] Kugel never offers an explicit theoretical definition of poetry,[71] although he does define prose as "common speech on its best behavior." This is not entirely unlike Alter's definition of poetry, save for the difference between "common speech" and uncommon speech (i.e., Alter's "the best words"). It seems fair enough to continue to speak of biblical "poetry"—defined, let us say, as "uncommon speech on its best behavior." But we must recognize that biblical "poetry" exists not as an absolute category, but along a continuum with the more poetic (heightened) on one end and the more prosaic (unheightened) on the other. Further, we must remember that biblical poetry may not share our notions of what constitutes poetry (end rhyme, meter, and so on). We shall try to sharpen our literary competence in dealing with poetry below, but first a word about available resources.

Resources. In terms of book-length treatments of Hebrew poetry, alongside the two titles by Alter and Kugel mentioned above are Adele Berlin's *The Dynamics of Biblical Parallelism*[72] and W. G. E. Watson's *Classical Hebrew Poetry*.[73] To these can be added a number of other use-

---

68. New Haven: Yale University Press, 1981.

69. New York: Basic Books, 1985.

70. Alter, *Art of Biblical Poetry*, x.

71. He does at one point observe that Western/classical poetry is characterized by its "regularity, its establishing of some sort of pattern of units—lines—whose characteristics are continuously reproduced" (Kugel, *Idea of Biblical Poetry*, 69). It may be that this definition is tacitly assumed in Kugel's campaign against the use of the term *poetry* for what we find in the Bible.

72. Bloomington: Indiana University Press, 1985.

73. Sheffield: JSOT Press, 1984.

ful volumes.[74] Because discussions of Hebrew poetry can be quite complex, beginning students may wish first to consult some of the briefer treatments, such as Alter's chapter, "The Medium of Poetry," in *The World of Biblical Literature*, Adele Berlin's concise *Anchor Bible Dictionary* entry on "Parallelism," Tremper Longman's "The Analysis of Poetic Passages" in *Literary Approaches to Biblical Interpretation*, or the like.[75]

General traits of OT poetry. In Tremper Longman's essay, mentioned above, he highlights three traits that characterize biblical poetry: terseness, parallelism, and imagery.[76] These three provide a useful beginning for discussing the essence of OT poetry.

Terseness. Like most poetry, Hebrew poetry tends to be compact in its expression. This is not to say that a Hebrew poem is necessarily short (Psalm 119 runs to 176 verses!), but rather that the individual clauses (or *cola*; sg. *colon*) that make up the individual poetic lines within the poem are themselves terse, consisting typically of three words/terms or major stresses, though sometimes two or four. The

74. For example, L. Alonso Schökel, *A Manual of Hebrew Poetics*, Subsidia Biblica 11 (Rome: Editrice Pontificio Istituto Biblico, 1988); D. Freedman and F. M. Cross, *Studies in Ancient Yahwistic Poetry* (Missoula, Mont.: Scholars, 1975); S. A. Geller, *Parallelism in Early Biblical Poetry* (Missoula, Mont.: Scholars, 1979); M. O'Connor, *Hebrew Verse Structure* (Winona Lake, Ind.: Eisenbrauns, 1980); D. L. Petersen and K. H. Richards, *Interpreting Hebrew Poetry*, Guides to Biblical Scholarship (Minneapolis: Fortress, 1992); S. Weitzman, *Song and Story in Biblical Narrative: The History of a Literary Convention in Ancient Israel*, Indiana Studies in Biblical Literature (Bloomington: Indiana University Press, 1997).

75. R. Alter, "The Medium of Poetry," in *The World of Biblical Literature* (New York: Basic Books, 1991), 171–90; A. Berlin, "Parallelism," *ABD* 5.155–62; T. Longman, "The Analysis of Poetic Passages," in *Literary Approaches to Biblical Interpretation*, Foundations of Contemporary Interpretation (Grand Rapids: Zondervan, 1987), 119–34. The following is a brief sampling of other short treatments: A. Cooper, "On Reading Biblical Poetry," *Maarav* 4 (1987): 221–41; J. Gammie, "Alter vs. Kugel: Taking the Heat in Struggle over Biblical Poetry," *Bible Review* 5, no. 1 (1989): 26–33; E. L. Greenstein, "How Does Parallelism Mean?" in *A Sense of Text: The Art of Language in the Study of Biblical Literature* (Papers from a symposium at The Dropsie College for Hebrew and Cognate Learning, 11 May 1982), Jewish Quarterly Review Supplement (Winona Lake, Ind.: Eisenbrauns, 1983), 41–70; W. W. Klein, C. L. Blomberg, and R. L. Hubbard, "General Rules of Hermeneutics—Old Testament Poetry," in *Introduction to Biblical Interpretation* (Dallas: Word, 1993), 215–55; M. C. A. Korpel and J. C. deMoor, "Fundamentals of Ugaritic and Hebrew Poetry," *Ugarit Forschung* 18 (1986): 173–212; F. Landy, "Recent Developments in Biblical Poetics," *Prooftexts* 7 (1987): 163–78; T. Longman III, "Biblical Poetry," in *A Complete Literary Guide to the Bible*, ed. L. Ryken and T. Longman III (Grand Rapids: Zondervan, 1993), 80–91; G. T. M. Prinsloo, "Analysing Old Testament Poetry: Basic Issues in Contemporary Exegesis," *Skrif en Kerk* 12 (1991): 64–74.

76. See also his treatment of these three traits in the aforementioned essay, "Biblical Poetry" (see previous note).

most common poetic line comprises two clauses (a bicolon), but one-clause lines (monocola) and three-clause lines (tricola) are not uncommon. The terseness of Hebrew poetry, however, as Kugel points out, is "far more than the concision and compression of expression that one associates with poetry."

> It is more reminiscent of "telegraph style" ("Urge support tax reform package for increase housing starts 1980") or the elliptical language of some popular sayings ("Red sky at morning, sailor take warning"), in which some of the signposts of ordinary discourse have been stripped away.[77]

Among the "signposts of ordinary discourse" sometimes omitted in Hebrew poetry are:

> the *definite article* "the" (e.g., "Take-the-side of [the] needy and [the] orphan / [the] poor and [the] downtrodden protect," Ps. 82:3);

> the *relative particle* "that, which" ("[The] stone [that] the builders rejected / became [the] head of [the] corner," Ps. 118:22);

> *personal suffixes* ("I praise the Lord with all [my] heart . . . ," Ps. 111:1);

> the *conjunction* "and" (not a single "and" appears in the Hebrew of Psalm 93); and so forth.[78]

Although such elements are not always omitted, interpreters must be aware of this "poetic license," lest they draw wrong conclusions from the absence of this or that element (e.g., assuming that an item is *necessarily* indefinite simply because a definite article is not present), or lest they fail to recognize that a Hebrew poem may be more open-ended than a given English translation might suggest—since such lacking elements must often be supplied in translation.

A further type of omission that deserves mention is the *ellipsis* of a word or a phrase found in one clause from subsequent clauses, in which it must be assumed. In Psalm 33:12, for example, "Blessed is . . ." begins the first colon and is lacking in the second, although it must be assumed: "Blessed is the nation whose God is the Lord, [blessed is] the people he chose for his inheritance." Similarly, "Blessed is the man who . . ." of Psalm 1:1 is followed by three parallel cola (the translation

77. Kugel, *Idea of Biblical Poetry*, 87.
78. For discussion of these and other grammatical omissions, see ibid., 87–94.

below is woodenly literal, and hyphens are used to join English words that represent a single Hebrew term or combination):

Blessed [is] the-man who
   does-not-walk in-the-counsel of-the-wicked,
   and-in-the-way of-sinners does-not-stand,
   and-in-the-seat of-mockers does-not-sit.

Parallelism. The above verse offers a fine example of a second general feature of biblical poetry, namely, parallelism. It is no exaggeration to speak of parallelism as "the most prominent rhetorical figure of ancient Near Eastern poetry."[79] The classic definition of biblical "parallelism of members" (*parallelismus membrorum*) was provided by Bishop Robert Lowth in the eighteenth century:

> The correspondence of one verse or line with another, I call parallelism. When a proposition is delivered, and a second is subjoined to it, or drawn under it, equivalent, or contrasted with it in sense, or similar to it in the form of grammatical construction, these I call parallel lines; and the words or phrases, answering one to another in the corresponding lines, parallel terms.[80]

Beginning with this definition, we may highlight several important features of parallelism. First, parallelism involves, of course, some kind of correspondence between elements in the poem. Lowth cites *semantic* parallelism (involving the sense) and *grammatical* parallelism (involving grammatical structures). Second, parallelism may exist on several levels. One clause (colon) may parallel a second clause (colon), in which case we may speak of *internal* (i.e., innerlinear) parallelism, since it exists within a single poetic line (or bicolon). Or one full poetic line (c.g., a bicolon) may parallel a second, in which case we speak of *external* (i.e., interlinear) parallelism. If each *term* within a clause or line has a parallel in another, we have complete parallelism, and when only some *terms* have parallels, we have *incomplete* parallelism. The following examples illustrate how these descriptors can be applied. It should be noted, however, that applying labels to Hebrew poetry is not an end in itself, but is meant to sharpen obervational skills and to facilitate discussion.

79. So Berlin, "Parallelism," 155.
80. *Isaiah: A New Translation, with a Preliminary Dissertation and Notes, Critical, Philological, and Expository*, 17th ed. (1778; London: William Tegg, 1868), viii. Cf. also R. Lowth, *Lectures on the Sacred Poetry of the Hebrews*, trans. G. Gregory, new edition with notes (Latin original, 1753; Andover, Mass.: Codman Press, 1829).

Psalm 103:9 *Internal/Complete*
Not-forever does-he-contend / and-not-perpetually is-he-angry //

Psalm 24:1 *Internal/Incomplete*
The-Lord's (is) the-earth and-its-fullness /
the-world and-those-who-dwell in-it. //

Isaiah 1:10 *External/Complete*
Hear the word of the Lord, / you rulers of Sodom! //
Give ear to the teaching of our God, / you people of Gomorrah! //[81]

In addition to the labels already applied, each of the above examples qualifies, in traditional Lowthian terms, as *synonymous parallelism.* Subsequent to Lowth's pioneering work, it became common to distinguish three types of semantic parallelism: *synonymous* (in which essentially the same thought is repeated in different words); *antithtetic* (in which the same thought is repeated using contrasting terms; e.g., "A wise son gladdens a father / but a foolish son grieves his mother //," Prov. 10:1); and *synthetic* (in which the thought introduced in the first colon or line is simply carried forward in the second; e.g., "The-fool has-said in-his-heart, / There-is-no God //," Ps. 14:1a). Not surprisingly, these Lowthian categories have been criticized, the first two for being essentially the same, and the last for being little more than a "catchall" into which lines not fitting the first two categories can be tossed.

Seminal challenges have come from James Kugel and Robert Alter, in the works already noted. According to Kugel, the genius of the so-called parallelism of Hebrew poetry is not really "paralleling" at all, but "seconding." By its very "afterwardness," *B* (Kugel's term for the second colon in an *A / B* bicolon) "will have an *emphatic* character: . . . its very reassertion is a kind of strengthening and reinforcing," which often involves "going one better." The exegetical significance of this insight is well illustrated by Kugel's commentary on Isaiah 1:3:

An ox knows his master, / and an ass its masters' trough; //
Israel does not know, / my people does not understand. //

Kugel writes:

If biblical parallelism were merely a repetition, the meaning of this verse would be: an ox knows its owner, and an ass its masters' trough; Israel does not know, my people does not understand. Any reader would, of

81. For more discussion and examples, see N. K. Gottwald, "Poetry, Hebrew," in *The Interpreter's Dictionary of the Bible*, ed. G. A. Buttrick et al. (New York and Nashville: Abingdon, 1962), 3.829–38; esp. 830–34.

course, be aware that some sort of unflattering comparison is being made. But if, in place of mere restatement, one allows B some independent existence, this series of clauses presents itself as a kind of progression. How is the first clause different from the second? The same verb, "know, obey," governs both halves. The animal of the first was hardly considered the most praiseworthy of beasts: nevertheless "ox" is in several respects considered superior to its frequent pair, "ass." More important, parallel to the "owner" of the first is "masters' trough" in the second. The cumulative effect of these differences is the establishment of a climactic descent: "An ox knows its owner, and *even* an ass"—who may not be very obedient or attentive—at least knows where to stand to be fed, i.e., knows "his masters' trough; but Israel does not know,"—or obey, even this much; in fact—"my people does not understand at all."[82]

Robert Alter's approach, though similar in some respects to Kugel's, was developed independently, and thus serves as some confirmation of the general thesis—namely, that the relationship between semantically parallel lines is not one of *stasis* but of *dynamic movement:* "The system of versification as a whole definitely encourages dynamic interplay between versets [cola] in which feelings get stronger, images sharper, actions more powerful or more extreme."[83] Simply put, if the traditional understanding of parallelism of members was something like $A = B$, the new understanding is $A < B$.[84] The exegetical payoff of this newer insight is sometimes considerable, as can be illustrated by returning to Psalm 1:1.

> Blessed [is] the-man who
>   does-not-walk in-the-counsel of-the-wicked,
>   and-in-the-way of-sinners does-not-stand,
>   and-in-the-seat of-mockers does-not-sit.

The three semantically parallel cola show a progression in each of the parallel terms: walk fi stand fi sit (suggests progressive *involvement*); counsel fi way fi seat (suggests progressive *identification*); wicked fi sinners fi mockers (suggests progressive *iniquity*).

While this new thinking on the dynamic character of parallelism is helpful, it is not all one needs to say about the essence of OT poetry. Semantic parallelism is not always present. Indeed, no single aspect—meaning, syntax, rhythm—is always present. Rather, as Benjamin Hrushovski puts it (cited approvingly by Alter), biblical poetry exhibits

82. Kugel, *Idea of Biblical Poetry*, 9.
83. Alter, *Art of Biblical Poetry*, 23.
84. For discussion, see T. Longman III, *How to Read the Psalms* (Downers Grove, Ill., and Leicester, England: InterVarsity, 1988), 95–98.

a "free-rhythm . . . based on a cluster of changing principles."[85] Hrushovski gets it about right when he describes the basis of biblical verse as a "semantic-syntactic-accentual rhythm."[86]

Imagery. The third general trait of biblical poetry, and indeed of most poetry, is imagery. Insightful discussions of the Bible's use of imagery, or figurative language, are provided by Longman in several places,[87] and we only highlight a few points. Imagery involves the use of figurative language to create a picture (or some other sensory perception) in the mind of the reader. An image is not to be taken literally; God is not literally a "shield" or a "rock" (2 Sam. 22:31–32). Rather, God is like a shield and like a rock *in some respect.* (If the similarity is expressly stated, using "like" or "as," the figure is called a *simile;* otherwise, we have a *metaphor.*) Confronted by such imagery, the reader is to ask *in what way* God is like a shield and a rock; God is protective like a shield, but is not made of leather or metal; God is strong and immovable like a rock, but has no crystalline structure. Because images incorporate both similarities and dissimilarities to that which they represent, their effect is "distanciation" or "defamiliarization," which prompts the reader to reflect on "old truths in new ways."[88] While some images function on the basis of similarity, others function on the basis of association. The poet may use one word to represent another closely associated with it, for example, *throne* for *kingship* (this is called *metonymy*), or he may use a part to represent the whole, for example, "He will guard the feet of his saints" (1 Sam. 2:9 NIV, in which "feet" represents the saints themselves and all their comings and goings; "part for the whole" is called *synecdoche*). Psalm 1 uses striking botanical images to contrast the "blessed" man who delights in God's instructions with the wicked man. The former is "like a tree (trans)planted by a canal, which yields its fruit in season, and whose leaves do not wither" (v. 3; my translation), while the latter is "like chaff, which the wind blows away." The first is stable, well-nourished, fruitful, and enduring. The second is worthless, weightless, and soon gone.

The two similes in Psalm 1 suggest (as we shall see in a moment) a further feature of Hebrew poetry that must be mentioned—namely, its use of sounds.

Sound. Hebrew poets apparently gave little attention to end-rhyme (popular in modern Western poetry), perhaps because the inflectional

---

85. Alter, *Art of Biblical Poetry*, 8.
86. "Prosody, Hebrew," in *Encyclopaedia Judaica* (New York, 1971), 13.1200–1202.
87. Longman, "Analysis of Poetic Passages," 128–32, and "Biblical Poetry," 84–86.
88. Longman, "Analysis of Poetic Passages," 132.

endings and attached suffixes of the Hebrew language would have made rhyming all too easy.[89] They did, however, delight in the sounds of words and exploited sounds to good rhetorical effect. The blessed man of Psalm 1 is *kĕʿēṣ* ("like a tree"), while the wicked are *kamōṣ* ("like chaff"). While the similar sound of the two expressions may be coincidental, in some instances the selection of words for their sound qualities is clearly intentional, as in Isaiah 22:5a and 24:16b.[90]

> *kî yôm mĕhûmâ ûmĕbûsâ ûmĕbûkâ*
> For it is a day of tumult, trampling, turmoil.

> *wāʾōmar rāzî-lî rāzî-lî ʾôy lî*
> *bōgĕdîm bāgādû ûbeged bōgĕdîm bāgādû*
> And I said, I waste away, I waste away! Woe is me!
> Traitors betray, with treachery traitors betray.

In the above instances, something of the evocative power of sounds can be captured in English translation, but more often than not, this aspect of biblical poetry can be enjoyed only by reading the texts in Hebrew.[91]

Our discussion of general traits of biblical poetry has so far focused mostly on line-level features. Before moving to a "checklist for interpreting OT poetry," we should think briefly about poetical structures above the level of individual lines. Some speak of strophes or stanzas, but it is probably better to speak simply of "sense units."[92]

Sense Units. A convenient description of "sense units" as the major subdivisions of a poem is provided by Klein, Blomberg, and Hubbard.[93] They explain that "just as a house may have one or more rooms, so a poem has at least one sense of unity, but may have many more of varying sizes." The criteria for recognizing sense units include: "(1) changes in content, grammar, literary form, or speaker; (2) the concentration of keywords in a section; and (3) the appearance of refrains or repeated statements."[94] The sense units in Psalm 1 may be analyzed in various ways (the following are but two possibilities).

89. On past attempts to discover rhyme in the Bible, see Kugel, *Idea of Biblical Poetry*, 233–51.

90. Cited by Watson, *Poetry*, 232 and 239, respectively.

91. For further discussion of the "phonological aspect" of Hebrew poetry, see Berlin, *Dynamics of Biblical Parallelism*, 103–26.

92. So Klein et al., *Introduction to Biblical Interpretation*, 252; following Petersen and Richards, *Interpreting Hebrew Poetry*, 60–61.

93. *Introduction to Biblical Interpretation*, 252–55.

94. Ibid., 252.

Option one: Psalm 1 as two sense units:

	His way contrasted with the wicked (v. 1)
The blessed (vv. 1–3)	His delight in God's law (v. 2)
	A botanical simile: tree (v. 3)
	A botanical simile: chaff (v. 4)
The wicked (vv. 4–6)	Their distress before judgment (v. 5)
	Their way contrasted with the righteous (v. 6)

Option two: Psalm 1 as three sense units:

How the righteous contrasts with the wicked (vv. 1–2)
   The contrast symbolized in botantical terms (vv. 3–4)
How the wicked contrast with the righteous (vv. 5–6)

A checklist for interpreting OT poetry. The following list is meant to be suggestive, not exhaustive. Pursuing these questions, or questions like them, should help one come to terms with the major issues in literary interpretation, mentioned earlier in this chapter—namely, genre and setting, topic and theme, structure and unity, texture and artistry.

1. How do you recognize the text before you as *poetry?* Look especially for terseness, parallelism, and imagery, but be alert also to *self-designations* such as "song," "psalm," "prophecy," and so on. Notice the *graphic layout* on the page, both in Hebrew and in translation.
2. What *false steps* does the recognition that the text is poetic enable you to avoid? Remember, for example, that "poetic license" allows *omission of grammatical features* that would be expected in prose. Remember also that poetry employs a high degree of *imagery, hyperbole*, and so forth, which should not be taken literally.
3. What *images* does the poem use? Why were these particular images chosen? What is the main point they convey?
4. What *parallelisms* does the poem display, line by line? Is there dynamic progression or intensification within each poetical line, or between more than one line, or in the poem as a whole? How do intensifying structures, if present, further the message of the poem?

5. How does the poet exploit the *sound* of words (often only apparent in Hebrew, although sometimes captured in English renderings)? How do the sounds (the phonology) of the poem add to its beauty, contribute to its mood, and so on?
6. What is the *mood* of the poem? Is there a shift in mood? If so, what is the progression?
7. What is the *structure* of the poem? Does it seem unified? Can it be divided into "sense units"? How would you outline the poem?
8. Does the poem conform in structure, mood, and/or language to a specific *formal* type, such as a psalm (e.g., lament, thanksgiving, hymn, royal, wisdom), a proverb, a prophecy (e.g., judgment speech, oracle of salvation), and so on? If so, how closely does the poem conform to the basic format, and how and why does it depart from it?
9. What is the poem's central *topic?* Can you summarize what the poem says about the topic in one thematic sentence?
10. Why was the poem, or why might it have been, originally written? How was it intended to enlighten, encourage, challenge, or move its original audience? How do we need to be similarly enlightened, encouraged, challenged, or moved?

Conclusion: Literary Reading as a Hermeneutical Duty

We began the present chapter asking whether the OT should be considered "literary." Assuming a definition of *literature* broad enough to include utilitarian literature, we answered the first question in the affirmative. We next asked what a proper literary reading requires and concluded that it requires readers who are competent (linguistically and literarily) and cooperative (willing to take the Bible on its own terms). We then looked at a basic four-part plan for reading and explicating a text literarily, and we finally moved to consider specific competencies that improve literary understanding. Our focus fell particularly on the two overarching genres of the OT: narrative and poetry.

In the course of our discussion, the reader may have been prompted to ask why divine wisdom would choose to place the divine word in sometimes challenging literary forms. Could not a simpler, briefer set of unambiguous propositions have served to teach us the truth about God, God's deeds, and our place in relation to God?

Why God Gave Us Literature

According to Abraham Kuyper, "The rationale for the diverse literary forms in Scripture is that revelation strikes all the chords of the soul, and not just one, e.g., the rational one." Similarly, if we may adapt a comment from C. S. Lewis, the stories and poems of the Bible to some degree elude "our systematizing intellect" so as to demand "a response from the *whole* person."[95] Perhaps it is this capacity of literature to invade the heart as well as to inform the head that has prompted wise preachers to welcome the newer literary approaches as a "breath of fresh air in homiletics."[96] Recent years have seen a growing number of works that explore the symbiotic relationship between competent literary reading of Scripture and compelling biblical preaching— preaching that evokes a response in its hearers.[97] The evocative power of biblical poetry—in the Psalms, in Job, and so on—is well recognized. But narrative, too, has its effects and demands its response.

> OT narrative style suggests a distinctive view of God's dealings with human beings and seeks from its readers a response to the claims of this God. It depicts the grandeur of God's purposes, underlines the worth of men and women made in God's image, and respects its readers by seeking their active engagement in the process of interpretation.[98]

The Role of the Reader: Good Faith and True Faith

In principle, all readers can show good faith if they approach the text cooperatively and competently, that is, if they are willing to be honest with the text and to understand it on its own terms. Good faith, however, is no guarantee of true faith. True faith, in the biblical sense, requires that readers allow the text to invade their lives and to change them. To use our now familiar distinction between truth claim and truth value, readers approaching the text in good faith may well grasp the text's truth claims, but true faith requires that readers also acknowledge the truth value of those claims and submit themselves to

95. Both Kuyper and Lewis are quoted in Vanhoozer, "Semantics of Biblical Literature," 78; the actual focus of Lewis's comment is the teaching style of Jesus.

96. So S. Greidanus, "Preaching and the New Literary Studies of the Bible," *Calvin Theological Journal* 28 (1983): 121–30; quote from p. 121; cf. also idem, *The Modern Preacher and the Ancient Text: Interpreting and Preaching Biblical Literature* (Grand Rapids: Eerdmans; Leicester, England: InterVarsity, 1988); idem, "Redemptive History and Preaching," *Pro Rege* 19, no. 2 (1990): 9–18.

97. On narrative see, for example, S. D. Mathewson, "Guidelines for Understanding and Proclaiming Old Testament Narratives," *Bibliotheca Sacra* 154 (1997): 410–35; on poetry see G. L. Klein, "Preaching Poetry," in *Reclaiming the Prophetic Mantel*, 71–92; on other OT genres see, in addition to the preceding volume, Sandy and Giese, *Cracking Old Testament Codes*.

98. P. E. Satterthwaite, "Narrative Criticism: The Theological Implications of Narrative Techniques," *NIDOTTE* 1.125–33; quote from p. 132.

them. Thus true faith involves not simply the intellect, but the will. True faith allows the text, as it were, to read the readers.

It must be added that while, in principle, the exercise of good faith should enable perception of a text's truth claims, in practice true faith often plays a role even in the intellectual sphere. Anselm's saying—*credo, ut intelligam* (I believe, that I may understand)—aptly summarizes the relationship between faith and reason. Where one is standing, so to speak, affects what one is able to see as well as what one is willing to accept. Readers who most nearly share the faith of those who composed the texts will be in the best position to understand them, provided that they avoid prejudgments that would blind them to the actual phenomena represented. The challenge of Scripture to its readers, if we may borrow from Augustine, is *crede, ut intelligas* (Believe, in order that you may understand).[99] Faithful reading, like faith itself, is a gift of God. And just as believers are called to grow in faith, they are called to grow in faithful reading. Learning to read the OT literarily is an important step in that growth process.

99. On both Anselm and Augustine, see R. A. Muller, *Dictionary of Latin and Greek Theological Terms Drawn Principally from Protestant Scholastic Theology* (Grand Rapids: Baker, 1985), 86.

four

Old Testament History and Sociology

JOHN BIMSON

All texts reflect something of the world in which they were written. As a consequence, we are unlikely to achieve a valid or plausible interpretation of a text without some understanding of the world that gave rise to it. This remains true of biblical texts, even when we read them in search of truths that transcend time and culture. Indeed, we are more likely to discern those things that have universal relevance when we understand a text's cultural setting. "Texts reflect their culture, and to read them apart from that culture is to invite a basic level of misunderstanding."[1] Exploring the historical and sociological background of an Old Testament text is a vital aspect of understanding its world.

Before going further, something must be said about the definition of *sociology*, especially as it relates to *anthropology*. The two terms have come to be used almost interchangeably, and satisfactory distinctions are difficult to pin down. This is partly because the terms are used differently on opposite sides of the Atlantic,[2] and partly because older definitions no longer hold. For example, it used to be said that anthropol-

1. W. Randolph Tate, *Biblical Interpretation: An Integrated Approach*, 2d ed. (Peabody, Mass.: Hendrickson, 1997), 4. For Tate, a text's historical and sociological setting comprises the domain of *pragmatics*, which, together with semantics, makes up what he calls "the world behind the text." See ibid., xix–xxvi and 3–11.

2. See John W. Rogerson, *Anthropology and the Old Testament* (Oxford: Blackwell, 1978), 9–10.

ogy was the study of "primitive" or preindustrial societies, while sociology was concerned with modern, industrialized societies, but this distinction has broken down. A better distinction might be that anthropology studies human physical, cultural, and societal development, whereas sociology is the area of anthropology that studies how human societies organize themselves.[3] Even this allows for a substantial overlap, since both involve the study of social systems and processes. Broadly speaking, however, when applied to ancient societies, sociology can be said to involve the study of social institutions such as the family, political structures, legal procedures, and the religious cultus—not only their internal organization, but also the ways in which they relate to each other.[4]

Socio-anthropological approaches to the Old Testament have a surprisingly long history,[5] but there has been a rapid growth in application of the method since the 1960s. This has gone hand in hand with a change in the way archaeology is applied to the study of ancient Israel. Whereas the chief interest of biblical archaeologists was once in historical questions—for example, trying to establish when, or if, an event such as the fall of Jericho took place—now the aim is to reconstruct the societies of ancient Palestine and their environments. This is an interdisciplinary task involving regional surveys, studying shifts in settlement patterns, and detecting ecological change. The emphasis is on long-term trends rather than events. This approach, known as *contextual archaeology* (a term now replacing the older "new archaeology"), is exemplified by the recent massive volume, *The Archaeology of Society in the Holy Land*.[6] The relevance of all this to the Bible may seem tangential in comparison with the older approach—indeed, the label "biblical archaeology" has been eschewed by many of its practitioners—but the result can be a fuller and more nuanced picture of Israelite society against which to read the biblical text.

It cannot be denied, however, that contextual archaeology has often been portrayed as an alternative, rather than a complement, to the biblical text. In recent decades the Old Testament has been increasingly marginalized as a source for the study of ancient Israel. In the words of

3. Cf. Victor H. Matthews and Don C. Benjamin, *Social World of Ancient Israel, 1250– 587 BCE* (Peabody, Mass.: Hendrickson, 1993), xx–xxi.

4. In Britain these subjects have traditionally fallen under the heading of *social anthropology*, which is roughly equivalent to *cultural anthropology* in the United States; see John W. Rogerson, "Anthropology," in *A Dictionary of Biblical Interpretation*, ed. R. J. Coggins and J. L. Houlden (London: SCM, 1990), 26.

5. See Rogerson, *Anthropology*, 1–21, and, more briefly, Matthews and Benjamin, *Social World*, xxi–xxiii.

6. Ed. Thomas E. Levy (London: Leicester University Press, 1995).

Niels Peter Lemche, "The study of ancient Israelite history is experiencing a crisis from which it will probably never fully recover."[7] It is important to understand the development of this crisis and to grasp its implications for both historical and sociological approaches to the Old Testament.

The Rise of Sociology and the Decline of Biblical History

Israelite Origins

From the 1930s to the end of the 1960s, the study of Israel's early history was dominated by debate between two rival approaches.[8] The approach associated with William F. Albright assumed the basic historicity of the Old Testament traditions and used archaeology to supplement and sometimes correct the biblical text.[9] The alternative, associated with scholars such as Albrecht Alt and Martin Noth, approached Israel's past via tradition history; it assumed considerable redaction of the biblical traditions and was consequently much more skeptical on matters of historicity, especially concerning the early periods.[10] In the 1970s, the Albrightian defense of the historicity of the patriarchal period came under heavy attack, as did its thirteenth-century B.C.E. scenario for the exodus and conquest.[11] These assaults provided an opportunity for a sociological approach to Israel's origins to move center stage.

In his seminal paper on the so-called peasant-revolt hypothesis, George Mendenhall used insights from anthropology and sociology

7. N. P. Lemche, "Early Israel Revisited," *Currents in Research: Biblical Studies* 4 (1996): 9.

8. See J. Maxwell Miller, "Israelite History," in *The Hebrew Bible and Its Modern Interpreters*, ed. D. A. Knight and G. M. Tucker (Missoula, Mont.: Scholars, 1985), 19–22.

9. This is typified by John Bright, *A History of Israel*, 3d ed. (Philadelphia: Westminster, 1980), and G. Ernest Wright, *Biblical Archaeology*, 2d ed. (London: Duckworth, 1962).

10. For example, M. Noth, *Geschichte Israels*, 2d ed. (Göttingen: Vandenhoeck & Ruprecht, 1954; ET: *The History of Israel* [London: Black, 1960]), begins his reconstruction with the confederation of tribes in Palestine.

11. On the patriarchal period, see Thomas L. Thompson, *The Historicity of the Patriarchal Narratives: The Quest for the Historical Abraham*, BZAW 133 (Berlin and New York: de Gruyter, 1974); John Van Seters, *Abraham in History and Tradition* (New Haven and London: Yale University Press, 1975); for responses, see *Essays on the Patriarchal Narratives*, ed. Alan R. Millard and Donald J. Wiseman (Leicester, England: InterVarsity, 1980). On the exodus and conquest, see J. M. Miller, "The Israelite Occupation of Canaan," in *Israelite and Judaean History*, ed. John H. Hayes and J. Maxwell Miller (London: SCM, 1977), 213–84; John J. Bimson, *Redating the Exodus and Conquest*, 2d ed. (Sheffield: Almond Press, 1981), 30–73.

to refute the view that the early Israelites had been pastoral semi-nomads who subsequently became sedentary. This undermined Alt's reconstruction of a peaceful and piecemeal settlement, but Mendenhall's alternative theory also challenged the conquest model. Mendenhall's "Hebrews" were originally people who had withdrawn from the political structures of the Canaanite city-state system; the exodus involved "only a small group," and there was "no statistically important invasion" of Canaan. The importance of the exodus group lay rather in its religious ideology, which the dis-affected Canaanite peasantry found attractive.[12] The theory was later restated by Mendenhall,[13] and developed along distinctive lines by Norman K. Gottwald.[14]

As a result of some deserved and devastating criticism, the internal peasant-revolt model never became dominant,[15] but it was an important catalyst in the rise of sociological approaches employing analogical data to reconstruct Israel's early history. The resulting consensus was that Israel's origins had been entirely indigenous.[16] By the end of the 1990s, the dominant view was that Israel had emerged gradually through a complex process connected with the

12. George E. Mendenhall, "The Hebrew Conquest of Palestine," *Biblical Archaeologist* 25, no. 3 (1962): 66–87.

13. George E. Mendenhall, *The Tenth Generation: The Origins of the Biblical Tradition* (Baltimore: Johns Hopkins University Press, 1973).

14. Norman K. Gottwald, *The Tribes of Yahweh: A Sociology of the Religion of Liberated Israel, 1250–1050 B.C.E.* (Maryknoll, N.Y.: Orbis, 1979). For the main disagreements between Gottwald and Mendenhall, see Gottwald, *Tribes of Yahweh*, 599–602, and Mendenhall, "Between Theology and Archaeology," *JSOT* 7 (1978): 28–34; idem, "Ancient Israel's Hyphenated History," in *Palestine in Transition: The Emergence of Ancient Israel*, ed. David Noel Freedman and David Frank Graf, The Social World of Biblical Antiquity Series 2 (Sheffield: Almond Press, 1983), 91–103. See also M. L. Chaney, "Ancient Palestinian Peasant Movements and the Formation of Premonarchic Israel," in Freedman and Graf, *Palestine in Transition*, 39–90.

15. For criticisms, see, for example, N. P. Lemche, *Early Israel: Anthropological and Historical Studies on the Israelite Society before the Monarchy* (Leiden: Brill, 1985); I. Finkelstein, *The Archaeology of the Israelite Settlement* (Jerusalem: Israel Exploration Society, 1988). Gottwald continues to champion the model, but since 1985 he has abandoned the terms "peasant revolt" and "egalitarian society" as imprecise and misleading descriptions of premonarchic Israel; instead he has adopted the constructs of "agrarian social revolution" and "communitarian mode of production"; see Gottwald's response to W. G. Dever in *The Rise of Ancient Israel*, ed. Hershel Shanks (Washington: Biblical Archaeology Society, 1992), 70–71; and Gottwald, "Recent Studies of the Social World of Premonarchic Israel," *Currents in Research: Biblical Studies* 1 (1993): 179.

16. Mendenhall's statistically unimportant invasion, for most scholars, has lost its importance altogether; Israel's religious ideology is now widely regarded as a later internal development instead of an early formative influence contributed from outside.

collapse of Canaanite city-states at the end of the Late Bronze Age, c. 1200 B.C.E.[17]

While there are several variations on the theme, current theory can be summed up as follows. A number of different groups—sedentarizing nomads, bandits, farmers, economic refugees from the Canaanite cities—coalesced in the central highlands, and a new society emerged, based on subsistence farming. A huge increase in the number of small villages in the highland areas at the start of the Iron Age provides the material evidence for this new agrarian and egalitarian society, which eventually became Israel. Continuing debate consists of trying to "fine-tune" this model rather than to challenge it, with issues of ethnicity and the role of nomads in the settlement process being the biggest bones of contention.[18]

It is important to recognize that, during the last two decades, a major shift has taken place in the role of sociological approaches to the Old Testament. Mendenhall, in effect, used insights from anthropology and sociology to supplement or modify the biblical traditions, in much the same way that the Albright school previously had used archaeological evidence.[19] But during the 1980s and 1990s, the old synthesis of biblical tradition and archaeology was replaced by a synthesis of ar-

17. For some milestone treatments, see Lemche, *Early Israel*; idem, *Ancient Israel: A New History of Israelite Society* (Sheffield: Sheffield Academic Press, 1988); Robert B. Coote and Keith W. Whitelam, *The Emergence of Early Israel in Historical Perspective*, Social World of Biblical Antiquity Series 5 (Sheffield: Almond Press, 1987); Finkelstein, *Archaeology of the Israelite Settlement;* idem, "The Great Transformation: The 'Conquest' of the Highlands Frontiers and the Rise of the Territorial States," in *The Archaeology of Society in the Holy Land*, ed. Thomas E. Levy (London: Leicester University Press, 1995), 349–65; I. Finkelstein and Nadav Na'aman, eds., *From Nomadism to Monarchy: Archaeological and Historical Aspects of Early Israel* (Jerusalem: Yad Izhak Ben-Zvi, 1994); William G. Dever, "How to Tell a Canaanite from an Israelite," in Shanks, *Rise of Ancient Israel*, 27–56; idem, "Will the Real Israel Please Stand Up? Archaeology and Israelite Historiography: Part 1," *BASOR* 297 (1995): 61–80.

18. See Dever, "How to Tell a Canaanite from an Israelite"; idem, "The Identity of Early Israel: A Rejoinder to Keith W. Whitelam," *JSOT* 72 (1996): 3–24; idem, "Archaeology, Ideology, and the Quest for an 'Ancient' or 'Biblical' Israel," *Near Eastern Archaeology* 61, no. 1 (1998): 39–52; Finkelstein, "Great Transformation"; idem, "Pots and People Revisited: Ethnic Boundaries in the Iron Age I", in *The Archaeology of Israel: Constructing the Past, Interpreting the Present*, ed. Neil Asher Silberman and David B. Small, JSOTSup 237 (Sheffield: Sheffield Academic Press, 1997), 216–37; Lemche, "Early Israel Revisited"; Keith W. Whitelam, "The Identity of Early Israel: The Realignment and Transformation of Late Bronze–Iron Age Palestine," *JSOT* 63 (1994): 57–87; idem, "Prophetic Conflict in Israelite History: Taking Sides with William G. Dever," *JSOT* 72 (1996): 25–44.

19. It is interesting to note that Mendenhall's peasant-revolt hypothesis of Israel's origins became part of Bright's synthesis in the second and third editions of his *History of Israel* (see 3d ed., 137–43).

chaeology, sociology, and anthropology in which the Old Testament text played little or no part.

The Rise of the Monarchy

Study of the rise of the Israelite monarchy has also attracted social science approaches. While the Books of Samuel give a vivid picture of some of the events and personalities involved, they offer few clues as to why the transition to monarchy occurred. Since anthropologists are interested in the process of state formation, the rise of the monarchy is a question to which their theories have proven readily applicable.

Since the 1980s, a number of scholars have argued that the circumscription theory of state formation provides the best model for understanding the rise of the state in Israel.[20] When agricultural land is limited by natural barriers such as seas, deserts, and mountains, *environmental circumscription* occurs; this leads to internal conflict over available resources, with one group eventually gaining military and organizational superiority. Alternatively, warfare can create circumscription by imposing pressures on the environment, in which case *social circumscription* occurs. The main point is that states generally form when at least one of these conditions obtains; they do not form when groups have the liberty to withdraw to other areas. Agricultural land in ancient Palestine was clearly circumscribed environmentally, and the Bible speaks of Philistine and Ammonite military pressure as well (1 Sam. 9:16; 12:12). Israel Finkelstein has synthesized circumscription theory with archaeological evidence from the Iron Age I period to show how population increase, intensification of agricultural activity, and interregional trade (giving rise to advanced administration) were all likely components in the process.[21]

It should be emphasized that circumscription theory does not necessarily displace the factors implied in the biblical account; rather, it fills out the picture and places the beginning of the monarchy in the context of long-term processes.

James W. Flanagan has applied the anthropologists' model of a chiefdom (an intermediate stage of development between tribe and state) to the rule of Saul: on this view Saul is best understood as a chief rather than a king, ruling a less complex polity than a state.[22] The tran-

---

20. For the seminal statement of the theory see R. Carneiro, "A Theory of the Origin of the State," *Science* 169 (1970): 733–38. For its application to the rise of the monarchy in Israel, see, for example, Chris Hauer, "From Alt to Anthropology: The Rise of the Israelite State," *JSOT* 36 (1986): 3–15; Coote and Whitelam, *Emergence of Early Israel*, 143–66.

21. I. Finkelstein, "The Emergence of the Monarchy in Israel: The Environmental and Socio-economic Aspects," *JSOT* 44 (1989): 43–74.

22. James W. Flanagan, "Chiefs in Israel," *JSOT* 20 (1981): 47–73.

sition from chiefdom to kingship and full statehood occurred under David and Solomon.[23]

The chiefdom model has been widely adopted as a tool for understanding the transition to monarchy.[24] However, its application has recently been modified by Christa Schäfer-Lichtenberger, who argues from the biblical evidence that organization under Saul had moved beyond chiefdom and possessed the typical features of "an inchoative state." She further argues that under David we can recognize features of "the transitional state" and "the typical early state" (all three concepts borrowed from political anthropologist Henri Claessen).[25] Alongside this development we should note John Rogerson's challenge to the widespread assumption that premonarchic Israel was a segmentary society (that is, one in which there is no centralization of power, but rather a number of groups with equal status). Rogerson argues that Israel should rather be seen as an association of small chiefdoms. "If this is correct, the emergence of the monarchy can be seen as the eventual dominance of one chief over the rest, rather than as a shift from the horizontal to the vertical distribution of power."[26]

In these explanations of the rise of the monarchy, we do not find the same ready dismissal of the biblical material as we do in the case of Israel's origins. In effect, the treatments summarized above still represent a synthesis of biblical narratives and social science models, akin to Mendenhall's approach to Israel's emergence in Canaan. This reflects a widespread assumption that, from the time of David onward, the biblical narrative derives to some degree from contemporary sources. However, in recent years this assumption has increasingly been challenged.

For example, Thomas L. Thompson's *Early History of the Israelite People* (1992) surveys the history of Palestine from the point of view of climate change, ecology, and settlement data, and concludes that in the tenth century B.C.E. Judah was too sparsely populated to have been a state; hence, the united monarchy of David and Solomon could not

23. Chris Hauer, "David and the Levites," *JSOT* 23 (1982): 33–54; idem, "From Alt to Anthropology: The Rise of the Israelite State," *JSOT* 36 (1986): 7–8.

24. For example, F. S. Frick, *The Formation of the State in Ancient Israel*, Social World of Biblical Antiquity Series 4 (Sheffield: JSOT Press, 1985), 69–97, 191; Finkelstein, "Emergence of the Monarchy in Israel," 48; cf. J. Maxwell Miller and John H. Hayes, *A History of Ancient Israel and Judah* (London: SCM, 1986), 137–43.

25. Christa Schäfer-Lichtenberger, "Sociological and Biblical Views of the Early State," in Fritz and Davies, *Origins of the Ancient Israelite States*, 96–105; cf. F. S. Frick, "Social Science Methods and Theories of Significance for the Study of the Israelite Monarchy: A Critical Review Essay," *Semeia* 37 (1986): 21.

26. John W. Rogerson, "Was Early Israel a Segmentary Society?" *JSOT* 36 (1986): 18; cf. D. Fiensy, "Using the Nuer Culture of Africa in Understanding the Old Testament: An Evaluation," *JSOT* 38 (1987): 73–83.

have been a historical reality. Instead, he proposes that Israel and Judah emerged later and separately as nation-states, Israel in the ninth century B.C.E., Judah not until the seventh century B.C.E.[27] Even the biblical account of the Babylonian exile is not to be treated as historical.[28]

Philip R. Davies offers a new view of the formation of the Old Testament documents within the context of Thompson's alternative historical reconstruction. He suggests they should be seen as the products of scribal "colleges" operating in Jerusalem in the late Persian and Hellenistic periods. While this does not rule out all historical content, it reduces it to a minimum: "There is no reason to doubt that a list of reigns, including one or two incidents, should have been preserved in Jerusalem (then Mizpeh?), and recovered to serve as the basis for the largely fictitious historiographical narratives that were built upon it."[29] Even the Prophetic Books were supposedly produced in this context, perhaps as scribal exercises, and then deliberately set "in the fictitious past . . . burgeoning all around the scribal school."[30]

If the arguments of the "minimalists" (as Thompson, Davies, Lemche, Coote, Whitelam, and others have been dubbed)[31] are correct,

27. Thomas L. Thompson, *Early History of the Israelite People from the Written and Archaeological Sources* (Leiden: Brill, 1992), 401–15; N. P. Lemche and Thomas L. Thompson, "Did Biran Kill David? The Bible in the Light of Archaeology," *JSOT* 64 (1994): 16–20; cf. David Jamieson-Drake, *Scribes and Schools in Monarchic Judah: A Socio-archaeological Approach*, Social World of Biblical Antiquity 9, JSOTSup 109 (Sheffield: Sheffield Academic Press, 1991); N. P. Lemche, "From Patronage Society to Patronage Society," in *The Origins of the Ancient Israelite States*, ed. Volkmar Fritz and Philip R. Davies, JSOTSup 228 (Sheffield: Sheffield Academic Press, 1996), 106–20.

28. Thompson, *Early History*, 122–23, 339–51; idem, *The Bible in History: How Writers Create a Past* (London: Cape, 1999), 217–25; for a reply see Richard S. Hess, "Recent Studies in Old Testament History: A Review Article," *Themelios* 19, no. 2 (1994): 11–13.

29. Philip R. Davies, *In Search of "Ancient Israel,"* JSOTSup 148 (Sheffield: Sheffield Academic Press, 1992), 122; cf. previously John Van Seters, *In Search of History: Historiography in the Ancient World and the Origins of Biblical History* (New Haven and London: Yale University Press, 1983), 311, 319. On the late date, see Thompson, *Early History*, 123, and most fully N. P. Lemche, "The Old Testament—A Hellenistic Book?" *Scandinavian Journal of the Old Testament* 7 (1993): 163–93; and, for a reply, A. Hurvitz, "The Historical Quest for 'Ancient Israel' and the Linguistic Evidence of the Hebrew Bible: Some Methodological Observations," *VT* 47, no. 3 (1997): 301–15.

30. Davies, *In Search of "Ancient Israel,"* 124; for a critique see Hess, "Recent Studies," 13.

31. I place this label in quotation marks because the scholars to whom it is applied have never accepted it. Gary N. Knoppers, "The Vanishing Solomon: The Disappearance of the United Monarchy from Recent Histories of Ancient Israel," *JBL* 116, no. 1 (1997): 20, argues that these scholars should actually be called historical nihilists, since they do not so much reduce historical content to a minimum as deny it altogether. This is certainly true of the early monarchy period that Knoppers is discussing, but not so applicable when considering Old Testament history as a whole.

there is plainly no future for biblical history. In a wry reflection written from the perspective of the mid-twenty-first century, Davies delivers the verdict that the end of the twentieth century saw the genre's demise: "The epoch of biblical history is over, and for the moment that seems permanent," says his alter ego, writing in 2048.[32] Some are celebrating already. "From now on the discussion of peoples, societies and cultures—including whatever may be designated 'Israel'—will need to advance largely without the biblical text. . . ."[33]

History or Story: How Should We Read Old Testament Narratives?

With archaeology and social science theories providing the "real" history, what are we to make of the biblical text? Lemche welcomes the changed perspective, since "the interpretation of the text of the Old Testament . . . has to a large extent been liberated from historical considerations," and biblical narrative can at last be "studied as what it is—a narrative."[34]

This, of course, is not new. The advance of radical skepticism has all along been accompanied by a move in literary studies of the Old Testament to replace *history* with *story* as a category for understanding biblical narrative.[35] In many respects it is indeed a move to be welcomed. Focusing our attention on the text provides a corrective to the view that saw events in Israel's history, rather than the Bible itself, as the locus of revelation.[36] The problem comes when it is insisted that the story has (and needs) no contact with history, as when Ramsey argues: "The telling of a story does not in and of itself constitute a claim that the events narrated actually happened. The story has a world of its own, whether based on actual events or not. *As a story* it is not dependent on its correspondence with actual historical realities."[37]

32. Philip R. Davies, "The Future of 'Biblical History,'" in *Auguries: The Jubilee Volume of the Sheffield Department of Biblical Studies*, ed. D. J. A. Clines and S. D. Moore (Sheffield: Sheffield Academic Press, 1998), 140.

33. Keith W. Whitelam, "The Identity of Early Israel: The Realignment and Transformation of Late Bronze–Iron Age Palestine," *JSOT* 63 (1994): 76.

34. Lemche, "Early Israel Revisited," 9.

35. R. J. Coggins, "History and Story in Old Testament Study," *JSOT* 11 (1979): 36–46; James Barr, *The Scope and Authority of the Bible* (Philadelphia: Westminster, 1980), 1–17.

36. See G. Ernest Wright, *God Who Acts: Biblical Theology as Recital* (London: SCM; Chicago: Regnery, 1952), esp. 126–27, and the comments of John Goldingay, *Approaches to Old Testament Interpretation*, 2d ed. (Leicester, England: Apollos, 1990), 66–77.

37. G. W. Ramsey, *The Quest for the Historical Israel: Reconstructing Israel's Early History* (London: SCM, 1982), 123, emphasis in original.

Thompson has long held that the biblical narratives are not to be read as historiography. He defines *historiography* as "a specific literary genre relating to critical descriptions and evaluations of past reality and events, in contrast to more fictional varieties of prose,"[38] and can find nothing of this genre in the Old Testament. In fact, he thinks that the earliest example of historiography within the biblical tradition is the lost Hellenistic work of Jason of Cyrene, employed by the author of 2 Maccabees. In Thompson's view, therefore, "Salvation history did not happen; it is a literary form . . . ,"[39] and there is a great gulf fixed between this literary form and history. He lays stress on the fact that there is no word for history in biblical Hebrew and believes that the Old Testament writers made a distinction between history, which they viewed as "illusory—like the whole of this material and accidental world," and reality, which could only be evoked through metaphor: "Events in time are distortions. True reality is unknowable, transcendent of experience. Tradition is important in order to bring understanding: to evoke truth, not to recount it."[40]

But how do we know the biblical writers operated with this distinction? It does not emerge from any studies of literary form, and many scholars take a very different view. Miller concludes that

> the biblical writers were very conscious of history, and the Bible itself may be looked upon as largely historical in format and content. It is not history written for the sake of history, of course, and not history of the sort one would read in a modern history book. . . . Nevertheless, the theological messages that the biblical writers sought to convey are so thoroughly intermeshed with their perceptions of history that it is difficult to separate one from the other.[41]

However, if we are to defend the historiographical nature of biblical narrative, we must answer some specific objections. Three have recurred in recent debate and will be addressed briefly in turn.

1. The problem of ideology. It is frequently claimed that Old Testament narratives are ideologically tendentious and, thus, their goal can-

---

38. Thompson, *Early History*, 373.

39. Thompson, *Historicity of the Patriarchal Narratives*, 328; cf. p. 3: "As literary tradition, no part of Genesis can be assumed to be history unless its literary character can first be shown to be historiographical."

40. Thomas L. Thompson, "Historiography of Ancient Palestine and Early Jewish Historiography: W. G. Dever and the Not So New Biblical Archaeology," in Fritz and Davies, *Origins of the Ancient Israelite States*, 41; cf. Thompson, *Early History*, 372–83.

41. J. Maxwell Miller, "Reading the Bible Historically: The Historian's Approach," in *To Each Its Own Meaning: An introduction to biblical criticisms and their application*, ed. S. McKenzie and S. Haynes (London: Chapman, 1993), 14.

not be to present history.[42] The charge of bias is not to be denied. What is at issue is whether narratives with didactic or propagandistic purposes can also be viewed as history-writing.

The issue has been addressed in detail by Lawson Younger and Alan Millard.[43] Younger demonstrates that a definition of history that excludes ideological, propagandistic tendencies is unrealistically narrow. The ideal of history as an objective recording of events as they actually happened is a distortion that dies hard (especially, it seems, among biblical scholars). But once it is appreciated that all history writing embodies the historian's interpretations, which are never impartial, and often didactic, it is evident that a text does not have to be unbiased in order to fall into the category of history-writing.[44]

2. The question of aesthetics. It is further argued that Old Testament narratives are not history-writing because they display too much concern with literary artistry;[45] specifically, they display traits usually associated with fictional narratives—plot, dialogue, point of view, characterization, and so on.

On one level, this is a charge that the biblical narratives are simply the wrong genre to be history-writing. This depends on an essentialist view of genre that has been thoroughly critiqued.[46] In fact, historiography is not (as Thompson claims) a literary genre in its own right, but can encompass many genres, including some we normally associate with fiction. Meir Sternberg has demonstrated that ideology, history, and literary aesthetics all combine in Hebrew narratives,[47] a stance which John Goldingay approvingly sums up by affirming: "They are more than history, not less than history."[48] In other words, rather than

42. Gösta W. Ahlström, *The History of Ancient Palestine* (Sheffield: Sheffield Academic Press; Minneapolis: Fortress, 1993), 375–76.

43. K. Lawson Younger, *Ancient Conquest Accounts: A Study in Ancient Near Eastern and Biblical History Writing*, JSOTSup 98 (Sheffield: Sheffield Academic Press, 1990), 31–35; Alan R. Millard, "Story, History, and Theology," in *Faith, Tradition, and History: Old Testament Historiography in its Near Eastern Context*, ed. Alan R. Millard, James K. Hoffmeier, and David W. Baker (Winona Lake, Ind.: Eisenbrauns, 1994), 54–60.

44. Younger, *Ancient Conquest Accounts*, 33; see also John Goldingay, "'That You May Know That Yahweh Is God'—A Study in the Relationship between Theology and Historical Truth in the Old Testament," *Tyndale Bulletin* 23 (1972): 82–84; Garnett H. Reid, "Minimalism and Biblical History," *Bibliotheca Sacra* 155 (1998): 407–8.

45. See Davies, *In Search of "Ancient Israel,"* 12–13.

46. See Younger, *Ancient Conquest Accounts*, 27–30 and 37–41.

47. Meir Sternberg, *The Poetics of Biblical Narrative* (Bloomington: Indiana University Press, 1985), 1–57.

48. John Goldingay, *Models for Interpretation of Scripture* (Grand Rapids: Eerdmans; Carlisle, Pa.: Paternoster, 1995), 32.

viewing Old Testament narratives as fiction that happens to look like history, we would do better to see them as history written like fiction.[49]

However, the idea that biblical narrators should be viewed as literary artists rather than writers of history also betrays a misunderstanding of the historian's technique. It rests on a false assumption that history is an untold story that the historian simply discovers and tells; in fact, the historian *constructs* history from a particular point of view, and in doing so may employ the devices of a literary artist to impose form on the past and to draw out its perceived meaning. One upshot of this is that there may be "no difference *in form* between an imaginary story and a historical narrative."[50]

3. History or mythology? Speaking of the Exodus narratives, Gösta W. Ahlström says: "Since the biblical text is concerned primarily with divine actions, which are not verifiable, it is impossible to use the exodus story as a source to reconstruct the history of the Late Bronze and Early Iron I periods. The text is concerned with mythology rather than with a detailed reporting of historical facts. As soon as someone 'relates' a god's actions or words, mythology has been written."[51]

To illustrate that modern standards of historicity did not function in the ancient Near East, Ahlström cites Egyptian royal inscriptions describing Ramesses II's battle with the Hittites at Kadesh; in truth, this battle was probably a near-disaster for the Egyptians, but it is depicted in reliefs and texts as a resounding victory for Pharaoh and the god Amon because "the 'god-king' cannot be a loser."[52] However, what this example equally shows is that real historical events were often presented in a religious (and ideological) wrapping. No one doubts that Ramesses II fought the Hittites at Kadesh in his fifth year (Hittite sources also refer to the event), and historians use his inscriptions critically to reconstruct the course of the battle.[53]

49. Whereas Robert Alter, *The Art of Biblical Narrative* (London: Allen & Unwin, 1981), 24, adopts the term "historicized fiction" to describe biblical narrative, W. Randolph Tate prefers "'storicized' history" (Tate, *Biblical Interpretation*, 83). The phrase occurs in Tate's treatment of Hebrew narrative as "mimetic narrative," which "may be historical without being history in the modern sense."

50. Younger, *Ancient Conquest Accounts*, 38, with further discussion on 41–44; see also J. Tracy Luke, "Abraham and the Iron Age: Reflections on the New Patriarchal Studies," *JSOT* 4 (1977): 36–37; Goldingay, *Approaches*, 196; Millard, "Story, History, and Theology," 47–50.

51. Gösta W. Ahlström, *Who Were the Israelites?* (Winona Lake, Ind.: Eisenbrauns, 1986), 46; cf. Ahlström, *History*, 28.

52. Ahlström, *History*, 29.

53. For example, Robert Drews, *The End of the Bronze Age: Changes in Warfare and the Catastrophe ca. 1200 B.C.* (Princeton: Princeton University Press, 1993), 130–34.

References to a deity, even to divine intervention and causation, should therefore be seen as cultural or religious encoding; they tell us nothing about the historicity of the event so encoded.[54] To claim, as Ahlström does, that the involvement of a deity renders an account "mythological or ideological, rather than factual,"[55] is to introduce an unhelpful dichotomy. It is true that religious statements are not open to historical investigation (e.g., the statement that God appeared to Moses and commanded him to lead the Israelites out of Egypt), but that is not to say that other aspects of the exodus narrative cannot be investigated historically, or that it could not in principle be a historical source.[56]

We may conclude that tendentious ideology, divine intervention, and sophisticated literary techniques are not incompatible with genuine historiography. That all are features of biblical narrative in no way militates against such narrative being historiographical in character. But there is far more at stake here than the generic label we place on biblical narrative. The crucial issue is that of historical reference.

Responding to various literary and structuralist approaches, Goldingay emphasizes that the stories in the Old Testament are not merely works of human imagination, but a witnessing tradition: "As witness, their stories have reference, not merely sense. . . . If the stories lacked any historical reference they would arguably also lack sense; they would self-deconstruct. To seek to understand biblical stories in their own right leaves quite open the possibility that they need to have, and do have, some historical reference in order to 'work' as stories."[57] This means that when Ramsey writes of the Bible employing "the narrative form of testimony," while also insisting that the events in Old Testament stories need not have happened, he is emptying the word *testimony* of real meaning.[58] If truth is to be found only in a story *as story*, it is hard to see how biblical narrative can retain its power as testimony (or witness).[59]

54. See Millard, "Story, History, and Theology," 42–43; on "cultural or religious encoding," see Younger, *Ancient Conquest Accounts*, 36.

55. Ahlström, *History*, 29.

56. The converse of this is also important: proving that an event in biblical narrative actually happened does not by itself validate the faith perspective that the narrative embodies.

57. Goldingay, *Models for Interpretation*, 32; for fuller discussion of this subject, see his essays, "'That You May Know That Yahweh Is God,'" and "The Patriarchs in Scripture and History," in *Essays on the Patriarchal Narratives*, ed. A. R. Millard and D. J. Wiseman (Leicester, England: InterVarsity, 1980), 11–42, esp. 36–40.

58. Ramsey, *Quest for the Historical Israel*, 123.

59. See further Goldingay, *Approaches*, 195–96; also Reid, "Minimalism and Biblical History," 396–403.

This is not to insist, however, that there must be *an exact correspondence* between the narrative and the facts of history (the fundamentalist fallacy). Recent emphasis on the literary artistry of Old Testament narrative has brought the creativity of its writers into sharp focus. There can be little doubt, for example, that when the writer of 1–2 Kings reports private conversations between individuals he is using his imagination to portray character and motivation; or that the speech of the Rabshakeh in 2 Kings 18 has been written to bring out the theological significance of Judah's confrontation with Assyria (should trust be placed in human resources or in Yahweh?). On the other hand, we should still credit the Kings writer with "a deep concern for what actually happened, in that he seeks to trace the working-out of the will and word of God precisely in what happened in Israel's history."[60]

In summary, the category of story is important but insufficient as an approach to much Old Testament narrative: "The historical 'having happened-ness' of the story matters."[61]

History and Exegesis: The Conquest of Canaan

We have seen how the exodus and conquest narratives have been sidelined in recent research, in favor of a very different view of Israel's origins based on socio-anthropological theory and archaeology. These narratives have been regarded as unhistorical on various grounds, but chief among them has been the claim that archaeology does not support the account of an Israelite conquest of Canaan. It is also frequently asserted that the conquest narratives are late writings with a clear theological/ideological intent. Focusing on the Book of Joshua, I suggest an approach that insists on these narratives having real historical reference, while also taking into account literary form and ancient Near Eastern context.

It is now widely accepted that the archaeological picture of the close of the Late Bronze Age (c. 1200 B.C.) does not include the destruction of cities as portrayed in Joshua 1–12. Indeed, the sites of some of the cities featured in these chapters have not even yielded evidence of oc-

60. Goldingay, "'That You May Know That Yahweh Is God,'" 85. (For a somewhat different view of Rabshakeh's speech, see Millard, "Story, History, and Theology," 60–63.) Not every Old Testament text requires historical reference in order to "work" as a story. Goldingay excludes the Book of Job from the category of historical writing because it makes its primary claims on the basis of creation rather than history ("'That You May Know That Yahweh Is God,'" 80–81), and the story of Jonah arguably has theological validity without historical veracity. Issues of genre naturally come into play here.

61. Goldingay, "How Far Do Readers Make Sense? Interpreting Biblical Narrative," *Themelios* 18, no. 2 (1993): 5.

cupation at that time. The site of et-Tell (assumed to be the Ai of Joshua 7–8) is especially notorious in this respect, having apparently been abandoned from roughly 2400 B.C.E. to 1150 B.C.E.[62] The late Joseph A. Callaway, who conducted the third series of excavations at et-Tell (1964–70), came to the conclusion that there was no truth in the biblical picture of a violent conquest of Canaan in Joshua 1–12:

> The research at Ai compels us, in my opinion, to review and evaluate the Deuteronomistic History's presentation of Israel's origins and to ascertain more realistically its relevance for today's world. Foremost among the items that should be reviewed is the "preaching" of holy war in Joshua 1–12 which, taken literally for centuries by conservative and fundamentalist Christians, has made Bible-belt church members in particular the most militant segment of our population in every war we have fought. Who can conceive the waste of resources and life, as well as the damage to the social and religious fabric of our society, that wrong interpretation of the conquest of Ai, and of Canaan, has wrought![63]

Notice that the phrase "wrong interpretation of the conquest of Ai, and of Canaan" refers not to our interpretation of the biblical text, but to the interpretation found *within* the biblical text. In effect, Callaway welcomes the discrepancy between archaeological evidence and Joshua 7–8, because archaeology permits us to replace Israel's violent conquest of Canaanite cities with a more palatable, less "damaging" account of Israel's origins in Canaan.

In response, it could be said that (*a*) et-Tell may not actually be the site of Ai,[64] and (*b*) even if it were, Callaway's interpretation of the evidence is not the only one possible.[65] However, the more fundamental issue raised is that of the two histories, one to be found in the biblical narratives and the other—very different—history produced by modern re-

62. On the date, see Finkelstein, *Archaeology of the Israelite Settlement*, 72.

63. Joseph A. Callaway, "Ai (et-Tell): Problem Site for Biblical Archaeologists," in *Archaeology and Biblical Interpretation: Essays in Memory of D. Glenn Rose*, ed. Leo G. Perdue, Lawrence E. Toombs, and Gary L. Johnson (Atlanta: John Knox, 1987), 97. Callaway came to believe that Israel had emerged from a melting pot of different groups, including some refugees from slavery in Egypt, but also Canaanite farmers displaced from the coastal plain by newcomers such as the Philistines. Hence his view is, in essence, similar to those outlined earlier in this chapter as forming the current consensus.

64. John J. Bimson and David Livingston, "Redating the Exodus," *BAR* 13, no. 5 (1987): 46–51; David Livingston, "Further Considerations on the Location of Bethel at El-Bireh," *PEQ* 126 (1994): 154–59. For an up-to-date summary of the possibilities, see David M. Howard, *Joshua*, The New American Commentary 5 (Nashville: Broadman and Holman, 1998), 178–80.

65. Richard S. Hess, "Early Israel in Canaan: A Survey of Recent Evidence and Interpretations," *PEQ* 125 (1993): 126.

search. It is an issue previously debated in connection with von Rad's view of salvation history, but that is raised even more acutely by the "minimalism" controversy. It is important to stress that, for a reader of the Bible concerned with exegesis, the discovery of underlying historical facts is no substitute for (and must never be confused with) understanding the biblical narrative itself. On the other hand, this understanding must be held together with the importance of historical rootedness.

I have argued elsewhere that current reconstructions based on archaeology and socio-anthropological models ultimately fail to explain Israel's origins.[66] If the proliferation of Iron Age villages in the central highlands marks the beginning of the process by which Israel emerged, we should not find any extrabiblical reference to Israel until that process was well underway. Yet we do have such a reference on the well-known stele of Merneptah, on which the pharaoh boasts: "Israel is laid waste, his seed is not."[67] This inscription is dated to 1207 B.C.E. (adopting the low dates currently favored for Egypt's Nineteenth Dynasty). The earliest Iron Age highland villages probably date from two or three decades later. In other words, Israel existed *before* the shift to new settlement patterns that supposedly brought Israel into being.[68]

Some "minimalists" have tried to deny any connection between the Israel of Merneptah's stele and Israel in the Old Testament. Most recently, Thompson has stated: "Apart from the obvious difficulty that the Egyptian stele reports that 'Israel's seed' had been destroyed and 'was no more,' it does not correspond with the highland Israel or any biblical Israel."[69] But when the traditional hyperbolic language of pharaonic inscriptions is taken into account (and there are many other ex-

66. J. J. Bimson, "Merneptah's Israel and Recent Theories of Israelite Origins," *JSOT* 49 (1991): 3–29.

67. J. A. Wilson's translation in *ANET* 376–78.

68. In response to my argument, Richard Hess (*Joshua: An Introduction and Commentary*, Tyndale OT Commentaries [Leicester, England: InterVarsity, 1996], 142), refers to Adam Zertal, "Israel Enters Canaan: Following the Pottery Trail," *BAR* 17, no. 5 (1991): 28–47, in which it is claimed that Iron Age settlements in eastern Manasseh began as early as the middle of the thirteenth century B.C.E. For critiques of Zertal's settlement theory and his dating criteria, see William G. Dever, "How to Tell a Canaanite from an Israelite," in Shanks, *Rise of Ancient Israel*, 27–56; James Weinstein, "Exodus and Archaeological Reality," in *Exodus: The Egyptian Evidence*, ed. Ernest S. Frerichs and Leonard H. Lesko (Winona Lake, Ind.: Eisenbrauns, 1997), 88–89. The objections to my reading of Merneptah's inscription in Frank Yurco, "Merneptah's Canaanite Campaign and Israel's Origins," in Frerichs and Lesko, *Exodus*, 27–55, do not affect the argument I am putting forward here.

69. Thomas L. Thompson, *The Bible in History: How Writers Create a Past* (London: Cape, 1999), 79. See previously Keith W. Whitelam, "Recreating the History of Israel," *JSOT* 35 (1986): 45–70; R. B. Coote, *Early Israel: A New Horizon* (Minneapolis: Fortress, 1990), 86; Thompson, *Early History of the Israelite People*, 311.

amples on Merneptah's "Israel stele"), the "obvious difficulty" amounts to nothing. There are no grounds for denying a link between the Israel mentioned by Merneptah and biblical Israel, except that such a link is inconvenient for the "minimalist" position.[70]

In light of the weakness of current theory, the biblical picture of Israel's emergence in Canaan in Joshua 1–12 deserves fresh historical investigation. I have argued at length elsewhere that the archaeological evidence for a conquest is greatly strengthened if the events are dated to the fifteenth century B.C.E. instead of the thirteenth century, and that such a date is supported by the few chronological notes within the OT itself.[71] Richard Hess, on the other hand, has tried to defend a historical conquest within the more favored thirteenth-century B.C.E. setting.[72] This is not the place to discuss the thorny issue of date; suffice it to say that to draw negative conclusions on the basis of the archaeological evidence is a superficial and hasty approach to a complex question that deserves more rigorous methodology and much more research.

But what of the argument that the conquest narratives in Joshua 1–12 are late, Deuteronomistic theological products?[73] A number of writers have offered responses to this assertion, showing that many of the features of these chapters are paralleled by the motifs and forms of other conquest accounts produced during the second millennium B.C.E. by the Egyptians,[74] the Assyrians,[75] and the Hittites.[76] These parallels not only undermine the criteria for a late date, but they also make it doubtful that certain features in Joshua 1–12 should be attributed to a Deuteronomistic hand.

While this evidence shows forcefully that the conquest narratives need not be late, it does not necessarily demonstrate that they are early.[77] However, possible dating criteria have been investigated by

70. See Hess, "Recent Studies," 12.

71. Bimson, *Redating the Exodus and Conquest*; idem, "The Origins of Israel in Canaan: An Examination of Recent Theories," *Themelios* 15, no. 1 (1989): 4–15; idem, with D. Livingston, "Redating the Exodus," *BAR* 13, no. 5 (1987): 40–53, 66–68. See also Bryant G. Wood, "Did the Israelites Conquer Jericho? A New Look at the Archaeological Evidence," *BAR* 16, no. 2 (1990): 44–58.

72. Hess, "Early Israel in Canaan," 125–42; see also Hess, *Joshua*, 139–43.

73. For example, John Van Seters, "Joshua's Campaign of Canaan and Near Eastern Historiography," *Scandinavian Journal of the Old Testament* 4, no. 2 (1990): 1–12.

74. Younger, *Ancient Conquest Accounts*, 165–94; James K. Hoffmeier, "The Structure of Joshua 1–11 and the Annals of Thutmose III," in Millard, Hoffmeier, and Baker, *Faith, Tradition, and History*, 165–79.

75. Jeffrey J. Niehaus, "Joshua and Ancient Near Eastern Warfare," *JETS* 31 (1988): 37–50; Younger, *Ancient Conquest Accounts*, 61–124.

76. Younger, *Ancient Conquest Accounts*, 125–63.

77. Ibid., 262.

Hess, who lists nine items in the Book of Joshua (seven of them in Joshua 1–12) that "cannot otherwise be explained than, or can best be explained, by tracing their origin to the second millennium B.C."[78] Among Hess's strongest evidence for this claim are the names of peoples, places, and individuals. If these are valid, then whatever date is given to the final form of the book, it must be seen as "preserving authentic and ancient sources."[79]

The antidote to theological misappropriation of the conquest narratives is not to jettison them in favor of a more appealing, modern hypothesis of Israel's origins (as advocated by Callaway), but to read them in their ancient Near Eastern context. Examples of this approach will now be offered.

Comparisons with ancient Near Eastern texts suggest that, in Joshua 1–12, phrases such as "all Israel," "the whole land," "no survivors," and "totally destroyed" are hyperbolic; they are examples of the stereotyped syntagmas that characterize ancient conquest accounts. This has several implications. First, an account that uses these hyperbolic syntagmas "is not meant to be interpreted in a wooden, literal sense," and such language actually "argues against the notion of a complete, total conquest."[80] This goes a long way to resolving the apparent difficulty that Joshua 13:1–7 contradicts the previous chapters by depicting a conquest that is only partial (and that remains partial even after the victories of Caleb in chaps. 14–15).[81]

Second, there are no longer any grounds for seeing Judges 1 as a rival account that depicts Israel's settlement in Canaan as a more piecemeal and incomplete process (and one more compatible with an Altian infiltration theory). In a separate study of Judges 1, Younger argues that the concept of a unified Israel permeates that chapter as much as it does Joshua 1–12. The truth is simply that both accounts are selective and reflect a particular point of view. "While the conquest account in Joshua narrates in a partial and selective manner the initial victory that 'softened up' the land, the partial, selective account of Judges 1 narrates

78. Hess, *Joshua*, 26.

79. Ibid., 31; for more detailed treatments see Richard Hess, "Asking Historical Questions of Joshua 13–19: Recent Discussion Concerning the Date of the Boundary Lists," in Millard, Hoffmeier, and Baker, *Faith, Tradition, and History*, 191–205; idem, "Fallacies in the Study of Early Israel: An Onomastic Perspective," *Tyndale Bulletin* 45 (1994): 345–53; idem, "Non-Israelite Personal Names in the Book of Joshua," *CBQ* 58, no. 2 (1996): 205–14; idem, "Issues in the Study of Personal Names in the Hebrew Bible," *Currents in Research: Biblical Studies* 6 (1998): 169–92.

80. Younger, *Ancient Conquest Accounts*, 247.

81. For other aspects of this problem, and some literary approaches to their solution, see Hess, *Joshua*, 284–86.

the failure to subjugate that land later. . . . Both are highly stylized narrations re-presenting or imposing structures on their 'historical' referents."[82] Neither the historian nor the exegete is called upon to prefer one account over the other. It is not a matter of deciding which account is likely to be earlier and more genuinely historical. The first task for the exegete is to discern the distinctive emphases and the underlying authorial intentions.

A third implication of Younger's study illustrates this concept further. When the conquest narratives in Joshua 9–12 are placed alongside comparative historical material, they are seen to contain an ideology that Younger classes as "imperialistic." This recognition challenges the view that these chapters are a stylized account of an ideological clash between egalitarian Israel and a city-based aristocracy.[83] The transmission code adopted in Joshua 9–12 would seem to contradict the message presupposed by such a view.[84] However, we must beware of throwing out the baby with the bathwater. That premonarchic Israel lacked social stratification seems highly likely on the basis of the archaeology of the Iron Age I highland settlements. The idea that early Israel was ideologically at odds with Canaanite society is therefore defensible. What is extremely doubtful is that Joshua 9–12 reflects in any sense a social revolution. In describing the ideology of Joshua 9–12 as imperialistic, however, we must also keep in mind that it is the imperium of Israel's holy, redeeming, and promise-keeping God that is the focus, not human kingship.

This brings us to Hess's work on the boundary descriptions contained in Joshua 13–21. Comparing these with boundary descriptions found in Late Bronze Age treaties from Ugarit and the Hittite capital, Hattusas, Hess suggests that all these documents had a similar purpose. Because the ancient Near Eastern examples occur in treaties, they define a legal relationship between the parties involved; in the Book of Joshua, the boundary descriptions occur in the context of formal covenant ceremonies (chaps. 8 and 24). "In the case of the biblical text, God establishes a covenant with Israel and uses the boundary descriptions to define the fulfillment of promises made to the nation's ancestors."[85] The covenant context, like the treaty context of the extrabiblical examples, protected ownership of the land and laid down responsibilities. Therefore the boundary descriptions are not mere lists

---

82. K. Lawson Younger, "Judges 1 in Its Near Eastern Literary Context," in Millard, Hoffmeier, and Baker, *Faith, Tradition and History*, 227.

83. Cf. Gottwald, *Tribes of Yahweh*, 552–54, on Joshua 10:16–43.

84. Younger, *Ancient Conquest Accounts*, 253–56.

85. Hess, *Joshua*, 59; cf. idem, "Asking Historical Questions of Joshua 13–19," 203.

of names, interesting only to the historical geographer. They lead us to that rich vein of Old Testament theology that lies in Israel's relationship with the land—a vein helpfully explored in recent years by Christopher Wright.[86]

Finally we must say something about the related themes of "holy war" and "the ban." There is no easy solution to the problems these terms create for modern readers, but the comparative literature does help to put them in context. First it should be noted that the theme of "holy war," so often identified in the Book of Joshua, is an inappropriate concept. It is clear from numerous ancient Near Eastern texts that all wars fought in that cultural milieu were thought of as led and brought to success by the national deity (or, in the case of defeat, viewed as a sign of divine wrath). There were no "holy wars" distinct from "secular wars." In the language employed, the Old Testament's way of speaking about war is no different from that of its neighbors.[87]

The ban, that is, the concept of devoting a whole town and its inhabitants to a deity by destruction (ḥrm, Josh. 2:10, 6:17, and so on), was likewise not peculiar to Israel. It is attested in Egypt, Assyria, and Moab. In line 17 of the Moabite Stone (ninth century B.C.E.), King Mesha of Moab uses the same Semitic root to refer to the destruction of the town of Nebo (at that time in Israelite hands): ". . . taking it and slaying all, seven thousand men, boys, women, girls and maid-servants, for I had devoted them to destruction for (the god) Ashtar-Chemosh."[88] The ban was therefore another aspect of a political ideology that Israel shared with its neighbors.

However, when we read the Book of Joshua in its canonical context, we discover that Israel's actions during the conquest of Canaan were far from being the nation's regular practice in war. It is clear from the rules for warfare in Deuteronomy 20:10–18 that an enemy city was normally offered terms of peace; if it surrendered, its inhabitants became subject to forced labor. If there was resistance followed by a successful siege, the male population (i.e., the city's fighting force, real and potential) was killed, the rest being taken alive as booty. It is also clear that the ban was not meant to serve the interests of a crude nationalism, for in Deuteronomy 13:12–17 we find the same principle of total destruc-

86. Christopher J. H. Wright, *Living as the People of God: The Relevance of Old Testament Ethics* (Leicester, England: InterVarsity, 1983); idem, *God's People in God's Land: Family, Land, and Property in the Old Testament* (Exeter, N.H.: Paternoster, 1990). See also E. W. Davies, "Land: Its Rights and Privileges," in *The World of Ancient Israel: Sociological, Anthropological, and Political Perspectives*, ed. R. E. Clements (Cambridge: Cambridge University Press, 1989), 349–69.

87. See Younger, *Ancient Conquest Accounts*, 258–60.

88. See *ANET* 320.

tion applied to any *Israelite* town that abandoned the worship of Yahweh for that of other gods.

In summary, then, understanding the text in relation to its historical rootedness does not mean uncovering the historical events to which the text refers (which is often not possible in any case). While historical reference is an important aspect of many Old Testament narratives (those that fall within Goldingay's category of a witnessing tradition), the exegete who approaches the text historically will attempt primarily to discover its message in the light of its ancient context, including comparative literature. It is rarely possible to know with certainty when a text was written or underwent its final redaction, but in the Book of Joshua we have reasons to think that it contains material dating back to the second millennium B.C.E. Some features often considered late may in fact be original to these early sources. The aims of the writer in adopting various forms (such as the transmission code of ancient conquest accounts) must be carefully assessed. For example, we might conclude that one aspect of the "imperialistic" ideology conveyed by Joshua 9–12 is an emphasis (particularly appropriate to premonarchic Israel) on the kingship of Yahweh, and the covenant forms that parallel ancient Near Eastern treaties can also be read in this light.

Sociology and Exegesis: Limitations and Gains

As already noted, sociological approaches to the biblical text have burgeoned in recent decades.[89] In addition to their use in reconstructing Israel's emergence and the rise of the monarchy, they have been brought to bear on the study of prophecy,[90] Israelite family structure,[91]

89. For general outlines and discussion, see Robert R. Wilson, *Sociological Approaches to the Old Testament* (Philadelphia: Fortress, 1984); Thomas W. Overholt, *Cultural Anthropology and the Old Testament* (Minneapolis: Fortress, 1996).

90. For example, Robert P. Carroll, *When Prophecy Failed: Reactions and Responses to Failure in the Old Testament Prophetic Traditions* (London: SCM, 1979); Robert R. Wilson, *Prophecy and Society in Ancient Israel* (Philadelphia: Fortress, 1980); D. L. Petersen, *The Roles of Israel's Prophets*, JSOTSup 17 (Sheffield: JSOT Press, 1981); Bernhard Lang, *Monotheism and the Prophetic Minority*, SWBA 1 (Sheffield: Almond Press, 1983); Thomas W. Overholt, *Channels of Prophecy: The Social Dynamics of Prophetic Activity* (Philadelphia: Fortress, 1989); Joseph Blenkinsopp, *Sage, Priest, Prophet: Religious and Intellectual Leadership in Ancient Israel* (Louisville: Westminster John Knox, 1995).

91. For example, Gottwald, *Tribes of Yahweh*, 285–92; James D. Martin, "Israel as a Tribal Society," in Clements, *World of Ancient Israel*, 95–117; Leo G. Perdue et al., eds., *Families in Ancient Israel* (Louisville: Westminster John Knox, 1997).

the role of women in Israelite society,[92] and matters of purity and holiness in the cult.[93]

Broadly speaking, sociological approaches can be employed in two ways. First, they can help explain how events or institutions mentioned in the text came about. We have already seen a prime example in the case of Israel's transition to monarchy. Second, they can help us reconstruct and explore the context from which a biblical text arose. Both applications can be fruitful, but we should be wary of the method's limitations, especially the danger of theory taking over where facts are on thin ground. Dever reminds us that *models* as used in the social sciences are "abstractions, not drawn from the data but imposed upon them in order to manipulate those data experimentally, that is, heuristic devices."[94] The danger is that this procedure will be inverted; a model may be used to infer data that do not in fact exist.

An example already discussed is the "peasant-revolt" model of Israelite origins.[95] On a smaller scale we may note the treatment of Israelite midwifery by Matthews and Benjamin. On the basis of analogues from other societies, these authors assert that it was a midwife's task to certify pregnancy after sexual intercourse: "The first confirmation of fertilization was the bleeding caused by the rupture of the woman's hymen during intercourse. Midwives inspected the bedclothes for blood stains and then presented them to the woman's parents as evidence (Deut. 22:15)."[96] However, in Deuteronomy 22:15 a woman's parents present the bloodstained bedclothes to the town elders as evidence of their daughter's premarital virginity. Presumably Matthews and Benjamin envisage a midwife having previously presented the bedclothes to the parents, but the passage says nothing about midwives, and this portrayal of the midwife's role finds no support in this or any other biblical text. Whether midwives acted this way in ancient Israel therefore remains unknown.

92. For example, Carol C. Meyers, *Discovering Eve: Ancient Israelite Women in Context* (Oxford: Oxford University Press, 1988); Grace I. Emmerson, "Women in Ancient Israel," in Clements, *World of Ancient Israel*, 371–94.

93. Mary Douglas, *Purity and Danger: An Analysis of the Concepts of Pollution and Taboo* (London: Routledge & Kegan Paul, 1966); Philip J. Jenson, *Graded Holiness: A Key to the Priestly Conception of the World*, JSOTSup 106 (Sheffield: Sheffield Academic Press, 1992). The impact of Douglas's work can be seen in a number of recent commentaries on Leviticus.

94. Dever, "Philology, Theology, and Archaeology," 300.

95. See the sharp comments on methodology by John Hayes, "On Reconstructing Israelite History," *JSOT* 39 (1987): 9.

96. Matthews and Benjamin, *Social World of Ancient Israel*, 69.

In short, caution is always called for when bringing sociological approaches to bear on the Old Testament text. Having said that, when proper controls are observed, the insights can be enormously fruitful. One benefit for exegesis is best explained in terms of historical and cultural distancing. Thomas G. Long tells of one of his students who returned from a trip to the Holy Land with his preaching in "profound disarray."

> This student returned deeply impressed with the differences between the historical circumstances of the Bible and his own situation. "I used to preach about Abraham and Sarah," he said, "as if they were people who could have lived on my street, who grew up in our neighbourhood, who could have been comfortable at worship in our church. I now know that Abraham and I inhabit different worlds, and the gulf between us is unimaginably vast. I don't know what to say in the pulpit any more about somebody like Abraham."[97]

As Long goes on to say, the student's confusion stemmed from a problem that is common in biblical preaching—an attempt to bridge the gap of history too quickly, by simply substituting our world for the biblical world. In fact, the student had experienced something essential for faithful exegesis, the *distancing* that must take place between us and the biblical text if we are to avoid the error of drawing superficial and misleading parallels. Only when this distancing has occurred can there be valid fusion of our world and the world of the text.[98]

Abraham and Sarah did not live like us, but knowing how they did live can make their story relevant in new ways. For example, an appreciation of ancient Near Eastern laws and customs concerning adoption and concubinage brings into focus the temptations they faced to take the fulfillment of God's promise into their own hands. This in turn brings Abraham's walk of faith, often faltering and with not a few false turns, more vividly to life. "A proper appreciation of the social and historical dimension of the patriarchal narratives thus leads to a more accurate understanding of Genesis' theological contribution."[99]

Furthermore, only when the peculiarities of ancient Israelite society are properly understood can we begin to undertake what Gottwald

97. Thomas G. Long, "The Use of Scripture in Contemporary Preaching," *Int* 44, no. 4 (1990): 345.

98. See Tony C. Thiselton, "Understanding God's Word Today," in *Obeying Christ in a Changing World*, vol. 1: *The Lord Christ*, ed. John Stott (Glasgow: Fountain, 1977), 90–112.

99. Martin J. Selman, "Comparative Customs and the Patriarchal Age," in Millard and Wiseman, *Essays on the Patriarchal Narratives*, 129.

calls normative social hermeneutics—that is, separating those aspects of Israelite society that reflect abiding ethical principles.[100]

Sociological Approaches and the Book of Amos

A look at some aspects of the Book of Amos will illustrate a few of the available insights. Amos was a Judean prophet called to address the social ills of the northern kingdom in the reign of Jeroboam II (786–746 B.C.E.?), a king whose military successes recovered lost territory for Israel (2 Kings 14:25–28). It is often assumed that a combination of tribute and the control of trade routes also brought a strong economic recovery at this time, and that Amos's attacks on the inequalities of Israelite society (e.g., Amos 5:11; 6:4) were directed against new developments that followed. However, archaeology and sociology have both sharpened awareness that the division between economic classes had probably appeared much earlier as a consequence of the change to monarchy.[101]

In Gottwald's view, Israel came into existence through the rejection of Canaanite kingship, and therefore monarchy in Israel must be seen as a "counterrevolutionary establishment."[102] However, we do not have to agree with the theory of Israel's revolutionary origins to accept that the monarchy must have brought profound changes to Israelite society, many of them detrimental (as Samuel had warned: 1 Sam. 8:10–18). While premonarchic Israel was not without its wealthy tribal sheikhs (Judg. 12:8–9, 13–14), the excavated villages of the early Iron Age suggest a society largely without social stratification. By contrast the archaeology of the time of the monarchy (Iron Age II) attests the urbanization and increasing stratification of Israelite society.[103] It is against such profound and long-term changes that the message of Amos must be read.

---

100. N. K. Gottwald, "Sociology,"*ABD* 6.79–89. For possible approaches, see Christopher J. H. Wright, *Walking in the Ways of the Lord: The Ethical Authority of the Old Testament* (Leicester, England: Apollos, 1995), 13–45 and 147–78.

101. J. K. de Geus, "Die Gesellschaftskritik der Propheten und die Archäologie," *ZDPV* 98 (1982): 50–57; Chris Wright, *Walking in the Ways of the Lord*, 280–82; Joseph Blenkinsopp, "The Family in First Temple Israel," in Perdue et al., *Families in Ancient Israel*, 85–92.

102. Norman K. Gottwald, *The Hebrew Bible: A Socio-literary Introduction* (Philadelphia: Fortress, 1985), 289.

103. See John S. Holladay, "The Kingdoms of Israel and Judah: Political and Economic Centralization in the Iron IIA–B (ca. 1000–750 BCE)," in Levy, *Archaeology of Society in the Holy Land*, 368–98; and Dever, "Social Structure in Palestine in the Iron II Period on the Eve of Destruction," in ibid., 416–30.

These changes included major shifts in economic power. The pre-monarchic peasants had mostly been free landowners whose inherited plots (which they both cultivated and lived on) were inalienable in Israelite law. However, kings needed land, both for their own revenue and to make land grants to their retainers. The state therefore became a threat to rural Israelite families as it found means of taking their land away from them.[104] In addition, through royal favors and the rise of a wealthy merchant class, there emerged a small elite with the power and ability to buy land, leading to the growth of large estates (*latifundialization*, in the social science literature). This reflects a further economic shift from a subsistence to a market economy, as the large estates could be used to grow vines and olives as commercial crops.[105]

The growth of large estates would have been a major cause of poverty in Israel, eroding the basic household unit, the "father's house(hold)" (*byt ʾb*),[106] and turning peasant farmers into tenants or landless laborers with no security (people whose plight is vividly described in Job 24:5–11). It is not surprising that Isaiah denounced those "who join house to house, who add field to field" (5:8), and when Amos refers to the "great houses" (*bāttîm rabbîm*, 3:15) that will be brought to an end, he may also have large estates in view, for in texts from Ugarit the Akkadian *bītu* can mean house and land, or simply land, as well as a residence.[107]

When Amos 5:11 refers to grain exacted from the poor, it points to the creation of a class of tenant farmers. A possible translation of that verse is: "Because you make tenants out of the weak and take tribute of corn from him . . ."[108] When tenants became unable to pay (e.g., because of a poor harvest), they had to sell themselves into debt bondage. Provision was made for this in Israelite law, with controls for the protection of the poor (Lev. 25:39–40). But those controls were evidently flouted in Amos's time, and people were sold into full slavery (Amos 2:6).[109]

At the root of these ills is the destruction of the "kin group" (*mšpḥh*), which played a vital role in the hereditary system of land tenure.[110] The laws in Leviticus 25 envisage the poor working off debts owed to wealthier kinsmen, who effectively became the patrons in a debtor-

104. Blenkinsopp, "Family in First Temple Israel," 89.

105. D. N. Premnath, "Latifundialization and Isaiah 5.8–10," *JSOT* 40 (1988): 49–60.

106. Gottwald, *Tribes of Yahweh*, 285–92; Lawrence E. Stager, "The Archaeology of the Family in Ancient Israel," *BASOR* 260 (1985): 1–35; Wright, *God's People in God's Land*, 53–55.

107. Premnath, "Latifundialization," 55.

108. Bernhard Lang, *Monotheism and the Prophetic Minority*, SWBA 1 (Sheffield: Almond Press, 1983), 124.

109. See ibid., 126; Matthews and Benjamin, *Social World*, 202.

110. Wright, *God's People in God's Land*, 48–53.

creditor relationship. "Once this network is broken, the creditor no longer acknowledges any responsibility for his debtor and uses him as a source of income. The debtor . . . becomes a depersonalized object to be exploited."[111] Similarly, the law for the redemption of estranged land by a wealthy kinsman (Lev. 25:25–28), originally designed to prevent its loss from the family, was misused to permit the appropriation of land by people who had no obligations to the original owners.

These exploiters of the poor were the urban wealthy, living lives of conspicuous consumption and extravagant luxury (Amos 6:1–8). Archaeologically, the lifestyle of the wealthy in Amos's time is well-documented.[112] In fact, most archaeological evidence relates to the rich and powerful in society, because it was they who lived in substantial houses, owned ivory-decorated furniture, and were literate. The lives of the poor are harder to reconstruct, because they owned less and what they did own was less enduring. But the evidence of burials suggests an existence marked by hard labor, poor diet, disease, and a shortened life expectancy.

From the coastal fortress of Mesad Hashavyahu, not far from Yavneh-yam, comes an ostracon that throws some light on judicial practices and the poor. However, it is not from the time of Amos, being dated to the late seventh century B.C.E. (the reign of Josiah, when the fortress was under Judean control). Its fourteen lines of Hebrew, written in ink, are a complaint by a farm laborer that one of his garments had been impounded unjustly. Since literacy among laborers is unlikely, the complaint was presumably recorded by a scribe:

> Let my lord commander hear the case of his servant! As for thy servant, thy servant was harvesting at Hazar-susim(?). And thy servant was (still) harvesting as they finished the storage of grain, as usual before the Sabbath. While thy servant was finishing the storage of grain with his harvesters, Hoshiah son of Shobai came and took thy servant's mantle. (It was) while I was finishing with my harvesters (that) this one for no reason took thy servant's mantle. . . .[113]

The word used for the confiscated garment is *bgd*, the same word used in Amos 2:8, in which the prophet accuses his self-indulgent audience of lying down "on garments taken in pledge."[114]

111. Lang, *Monotheism*, 125.
112. Philip J. King, *Amos, Hosea, Micah—An Archaeological Commentary* (Philadelphia: Westminster, 1988), 64–68, 139–49.
113. See *ANET* 568.
114. The legal background to this charge is provided by Exodus 22:25–26 [26–27] (in which the word for the garment is *slmh*, but the same item of outer clothing is clearly intended). See further Matthews and Benjamin, *Social World*, 203–4.

The ostracon therefore reflects, albeit indirectly, the hardships and injustices that were everyday life for the poor in the time of Amos. Although we do not know the outcome of the case, the ostracon at least shows that the reaper had his complaint heard and recorded, which means that the poorer classes had access to the legal system in this provincial fortress. In Amos's Israel, the poor regularly had justice denied them (2:6–7; 4:1; 5:7; 6:12; 8:4–6). His repeated references to justice (or its absence) "in the gate" (bšʿr, 5:10, 12, 15) relate to malpractice in Israel's legal system, since the city gate was where business was transacted and disputes of all kinds were settled (cf. Gen. 23:10, 18; 2 Kings 7:1; Job 29:7–17; Ps. 127:5; Prov. 22:22). For this reason some modern translations (e.g., NIV) render šʿr as "court," which is somewhat misleading since the city gate was the setting for a wide range of activities (cf. 1 Kings 22:10).

Some fortified Iron II cities had substantial gate areas in which public gatherings could have been held, but even an unwalled village probably had an official entry point where commercial and legal business was carried out. Alternatively, a threshing floor sometimes served as a place for public decision making and legal transactions. In 1 Kings 22:10, we find Ahab of Israel and Jehoshaphat of Judah "sitting on their thrones, arrayed in their robes, at the threshing floor at the entrance of the gate of Samaria; and all the prophets were prophesying before them." In the Ugaritic *Tale of Aqhat*, King Danel is portrayed "sitting before the gate, beneath a mighty tree on the threshing floor, judging the cause of the widow, adjudicating the case of the fatherless."[115]

Traditionally, such business was presided over by the elders of each village and city (Deut. 22:15; Ruth 4:1–12; Prov. 31:23). The elders were probably the senior men from a community's land-owning households.[116] While the legal system was in such hands, judicial power was diffused and disputes were settled locally. But the monarchy brought changes in this sphere as well.[117] As more provincial landowners were dispossessed and lost their status as elders, power passed to the urban elite and became centralized. These people introduced new legislation that legalized their oppression of the poor (Isa. 10:1–2).

In Judah, there was (at least in theory) a central court of appeal headed by the king or his representative and held at the main gate of Jerusalem (2 Sam. 15:2–4). (This provides the background to the story of Solomon's judgment in 1 Kings 3:16–28 and the picture of the king as righteous judge and defender of the poor in Ps. 72:1–4.) We hear

---

115. See *ANET* 151.
116. On elders and the judiciary, see Matthews and Benjamin, *Social World*, 121–24.
117. Wright, *Walking in the Ways of the Lord*, 281–82.

nothing of a similar arrangement in Samaria, but if it existed it was evidently ineffectual by Amos's time.

How well did Amos know the laws and legal processes of his day? Gottwald suggests that, even if Amos had never seen written laws, he had probably witnessed them in action in "the living integrity of village life." "These laws were more or less faithfully practiced before his eyes in villages like Tekoa, as they were grotesquely ignored and overridden in the governing circles of Israel."[118] While we should be wary of idealizing life in the villages of this period (we know next to nothing about it), there is probably some truth in this statement, especially when we remember that gates were public places. Indeed, need for public scrutiny was probably the original reason that legal and other disputes were settled there; hole-and-corner deals were excluded—at least in theory— by the number of witnesses who could easily be gathered (see Gen. 23:10; Ruth 4:9–11). But in Amos's time bribery had corrupted the system (5:7), and those who spoke openly against malpractice were victimized (5:10, 13).

Hans Walter Wolff envisages Amos receiving formal teaching from the elders of Tekoa: "The instruction of ancient Israel, in the form of clan wisdom, had been taught to him by the clan elders in the gate."[119] This conclusion must be treated with caution. It rests on Amos's use of certain forms of speech, which may not in fact have been confined to a particular class in Israelite society.[120] But if Amos's connection with clan wisdom is doubtful, a link with the court wisdom of Proverbs is even less likely. The vocabulary used for the poor in Proverbs is quite different from that employed by Amos and other prophets, and conveys a different attitude to poverty. From the evidence of Proverbs, J. David Pleins concludes that the social world of its authors was that of a ruling elite.[121] We can therefore be fairly sure that Amos did not belong to such a class, though the term *nōqēd* used in Amos 1:1 suggests he was a wealthy stockbreeder rather than an ordinary shepherd (the same term is used in 2 Kings 3:4 of Mesha, king of Moab, who reared sheep on a massive scale). In fact Amos's social status and background are far from clear, as the further clues provided in 7:14–15 are not easily reconciled with his designation in 1:1.[122]

118. Gottwald, *Hebrew Bible*, 357–58.

119. Hans W. Wolff, *Joel and Amos*, Hermeneia (Philadelphia: Fortress, 1977), 91.

120. See the comments on proverbial speech in Abdulla M. Lutfiyya, *Baytin, a Jordanian Village: A Study of Social Institutions and Social Change in a Folk Community* (London: Mouton, 1966), 52.

121. J. David Pleins, "Poverty in the Social World of the Wise," *JSOT* 37 (1987): 61–78.

122. See A. Graeme Auld, *Amos*, Old Testament Guides (Sheffield: JSOT Press, 1986), 37–40.

These observations on the Book of Amos illustrate a few of the insights afforded by sociological approaches. Such studies do not, of course, provide a finished exegesis of the text, for they work further back on the "production line" of hermeneutics. What they do is illuminate the situations from which the message of Amos emerged and provide a context in which the exegete can work. The resultant "distancing" can provide a safeguard against overly hasty conclusions, sharpening our understanding of institutions peculiar to ancient Israel. While historical and sociological approaches to the text are inevitably indirect, they are nonetheless important in enabling us to do justice, to love kindness, and to walk humbly with our God.

Appendix

The Early Israelite Monarchy: A Further Reply to the "Minimalist" Case

The "minimalist" denial that the united monarchy of David and Solomon had any historical existence has been challenged by many biblical scholars and archaeologists. What follows is a brief summary of some of the evidence against the "minimalist" view.

Extrabiblical evidence for the existence of David and his dynasty came to light in July 1993 when excavations at Tel Dan uncovered a fragment of an Aramaic stele. In this inscription, an unnamed king or general boasts of having killed a king of Israel and a king of "the House of David" (*byt dwd*). This phrase has been reasonably interpreted as a reference to the state of Judah ruled by the dynasty of David (in the same way that we find Israel referred to in Assyrian inscriptions as "the house of Omri").[123]

Two smaller pieces of the same stele were found during the 1994 excavations.[124] With the joining of these to the fragment found in 1993 it became clear that the inscription named the defeated Israelite and Judean kings as Joram (Jehoram) and Achazyahu (Ahaziah) respectively. We may be fairly certain that the inscription is an Aramean propagandistic account of the defeat of Jehoram and Ahaziah at Ramoth-gilead, and their subsequent deaths (2 Kings 8:28–9:28), and that the king whose victory it celebrates is therefore Hazael. André Lemaire has argued that the surviving fragments are part of a "summary royal inscription" that went on to deal with further military ventures and that was "probably engraved in the second part of Hazael's

123. Avraham Biran and Joseph Naveh, "An Aramaic Stele Fragment from Tel Dan," *IEJ* 43 (1993): 81–98.
124. Avraham Biran and Joseph Naveh, "The Tel Dan Inscription: A New Fragment," *IEJ* 45 (1995): 1–18.

reign, c. 826–805/3 BCE."[125] The "minimalists" have gone to extraordinary lengths to avoid the implications of this inscription,[126] but there is now no good reason to doubt that a dynasty claiming descent from David was ruling Judah by the ninth century B.C.E. at the latest.[127]

Several scholars have argued from archaeological evidence that the beginning of the Iron Age II period (1000–750 B.C.E.) in Palestine saw a degree of urbanization and centralization that points strongly to the formation of a state in the tenth century B.C.E.[128]

Against the claim that the Old Testament books were composed (not merely edited) in the late Persian and Hellenistic periods, Dever refers to numerous "convergencies" between biblical texts and archaeological evidence from the Iron Age, which suggest to him that the texts include genuine historical material contemporaneous with the events they purport to describe.[129] For example, he notes that many details in the description of Solomon's temple (1 Kings 6–9) can now be illustrated by the archaeology of "Bronze and Iron Age temples and their furnishings elsewhere in the southern Levant. A later writer who had never seen the temple could not possibly have given such accurate, detailed descriptions."[130]

125. André Lemaire, "The Tel Dan Stela as a Piece of Royal Historiography," *JSOT* 81 (1998): 3–14.

126. For example, N. P. Lemche and Thomas L. Thompson, "Did Biran Kill David? The Bible in the Light of Archaeology," *JSOT* 64 (1994): 3–22, and references there.

127. See further Gary N. Knoppers, "The Vanishing Solomon: The Disappearance of the United Monarchy from Recent Histories of Ancient Israel," *JBL* 116, no. 1 (1997): 36–40; Lemaire, "Tel Dan Stela," provides an extensive bibliography.

128. See John S. Holladay, "The Kingdoms of Israel and Judah: Political and Economic Centralization in the Iron IIA–B (ca. 1000–750 BCE)," in Levy, *Archaeology of Society in the Holy Land*, 368–98; Volkmar Fritz, "Monarchy and Re-urbanization: A New Look at Solomon's Kingdom," in Fritz and Davies, *Origins of the Ancient Israelite States*, 187–95; Dever, "Philology, Theology, and Archaeology," 301–3; Knoppers, "Vanishing Solomon," 19–44. We should note, however, a recent proposal that Iron Age II strata conventionally associated with Solomon's reign (tenth century B.C.E.) should be downdated to the following century: for example, Finkelstein, "The Archaeology of the United Monarchy: An Alternative View," *Levant* 27 (1996): 177–87. So far this remains a minority view. For recent debate on the archaeology of Jerusalem, see Margreet Steiner, "The Archaeology of Ancient Jerusalem," *Currents in Research: Biblical Studies* 6 (1998): 143–68, and the reply by Jane Cahill, "David's Jerusalem: It Is There," *BAR* 24, no. 4 (1998): 34–41.

129. Dever, "Philology, Theology, and Archaeology," 301–2; cf. idem, "Social Structure in Palestine in the Iron II Period on the Eve of Destruction," in Levy, *Archaeology of Society in the Holy Land*, 427–29.

130. Dever, "Philology, Theology, and Archaeology," 302. Cf. Alan Millard, "Does the Bible Exaggerate King Solomon's Wealth?" *BAR* 15, no. 3 (1989): 20–34, in which Millard defends the biblical descriptions of Solomon's wealth by showing that they are paralleled by other accounts of tribute and temple/palace decoration in the ancient world, and by archaeological evidence from Egypt. See also A. R. Millard, "Texts and Archaeology: Weighing the Evidence; The Case of King Solomon," *PEQ* 123 (1991): 19–27.

Nadav Na'aman argues from extrabiblical texts that the writer of 1–2 Kings made use of written sources (though he thinks they were sparse) when compiling his history of the tenth to ninth centuries B.C.E.[131] For the later monarchy, Hayes points out that the evidence of the biblical text "has proven to be surprisingly trustworthy. Akkadian sources mention or allude to a dozen Israelite/Judean kings—Omri, Ahab, Jehu, Jehoash, Menahem, Hoshea, Ahaz, Hezekiah, Manasseh, Jehoiakim, Jehoiachin, and Zedekiah. The information gleaned from these sources correlates quite well with the biblical traditions and requires no major adjustments in the biblical presentation, such as a reordering of the kings."[132]

In summary, we can conclude that the extreme skepticism of the "minimalists" is strongly contradicted by facts on the ground.[133]

131. N. Na'aman, "The Contribution of Royal Inscriptions for a Re-evaluation of the Book of Kings as a Historical Source," *JSOT* 82 (1999): 3–17; see also idem, "Sources and Composition in the History of David," in Fritz and Davies, *Origins of the Ancient Israelite States*, 170–86.

132. Hayes, "On Reconstructing Israelite History," 7.

133. In addition to discussions cited above, debate between "minimalists" and scholars with opposing views can be found in *The Fabric of History: Text, Artifact, and Israel's Past*, ed. Diana V. Edelman, JSOTSup 127 (Sheffield: Sheffield Academic Press, 1991); *The Origins of the Ancient Israelite States*, ed. Volkmar Fritz and Philip R. Davies, JSOTSup 228 (Sheffield: Sheffield Academic Press, 1996).

five

Traditions, Intertextuality, and Canon

Craig C. Broyles

The context of a biblical passage includes more than its literary context within a biblical book, and more than the historical and sociological contexts to which it originally referred and to which it originally spoke. Besides being part of a literary work and of an original historical situation, a passage also belongs to generations of believing communities who are defined by shared traditions and sacred texts. A passage is not merely literature or merely history; it also defines the community's purpose, values, and reason for being. The community has an existential stake in what the passage means.

These affiliated traditions and texts both narrow the range of possible meanings for any given passage and open possibilities for new associations and overtones of meaning. They restrain a passage's range of meanings, because its meanings must be generally consistent with those of other sacred texts and traditions. But traditions and texts also import meanings as the given passage links with other texts and traditions and their meanings.

157

Traditions

In common usage, a *tradition* is any belief or custom passed from generation to generation. In OT studies, these beliefs and customs are sacred, normative, and generally associated with particular persons, events, places, institutions, symbols, or rituals. A sampling of OT traditions includes creation, the ancestors, exodus, Sinai covenant and law, theophany, wilderness, conquest and Yahweh war, judges, Zion, divine kingship, Davidic kingship, day of Yahweh, wisdom, and apocalyptic. In addition, there are various traditions related to worship (i.e., the "cult"): the ark, tabernacle, temple, festivals, sacrifice, liturgies, and priests and Levites.

A way of illustrating the role of traditions in the formation of the OT is to say that as believers today use scriptural texts, OT writers generally used traditions. For example, the Psalms and the Prophets usually do not cite passages from the Pentateuch, although they frequently use the same motifs and traditions. Creation traditions surface in Psalm 74:12–17; 89:9–12; Isaiah 51:9–10a; they echo not Genesis 1–2 but the ANE tradition of divine kingship, in which the deity creates order after battling the chaotic forces of the waters. The theophanic tradition of the God of the thunderstorm is frequent in the Psalms and Prophets (Ps. 18:7–15; 29:3–10; 93:3–4; 97:2–6; Jer. 10:10–13; Amos 9:5–6; Mic. 1:2–4; Hab. 3:3–15), but it usually bears no direct connection to the Sinai theophany (Exod. 19:9, 16–20; 24:15–18). Wilderness traditions appear in Hosea 2:14–15 and Jeremiah 2:1–3, but, unlike the Book of Numbers, this period is portrayed as wholly positive, depicting Israel as a youth "devoted" and "singing" to Yahweh. Even the so-called historical psalms (Psalms 77; 78; 105; 106; 135; 136) differ from the pentateuchal narratives. The Egyptian plagues are presented in a different order, and some are omitted (78:43–51; 105:27–36). Psalm 106 presents a different sequence of Israel's rebellions (vv. 7–33). Here Israel was sinful even in Egypt (v. 7; cf. Ezek. 20:8). The Sinai laws are sometimes mentioned in these psalms (though omitted entirely in Psalms 135; 136), but Israel's meeting with Yahweh on Sinai is strangely omitted from the narrative sequence (78:5, 7, 10, 37, 56; 105:45; cf. Deut. 26:5–10). In Psalm 78, the northern tribes and the exodus-wilderness traditions are, in fact, superseded by the southern tribe of Judah and the David and Zion traditions.

By no means do these observations indicate contradictions within the Bible; rather, they illustrate that biblical writers do not build their case on fixed, written texts but on a variety of fluid traditions. After all, we should not expect to see clear references to pentateuchal texts until Josiah's discovery and public reading of "the book of the law" (apparently some form of Deuteronomy; see 28:61; 29:21; 30:10; 31:26) in the late preexilic period (2 Kings 22:8, 11), and Ezra's public reading of "the book of the law of Moses" in the postexilic period (Neh. 8:1, 3). The issue is not one of composition (as though Deuteronomy were first written in the seventh century and the Pentateuch was a product of the exile) but of publication or dissemination. This explains why the eighth-century prophets especially (Amos; Hosea; Isaiah 1–39; Micah) do not make explicit appeal to the Pentateuch or the "covenant." Even if they had access to these texts themselves, the people would have been ignorant.

Identifying Traditions

A tradition may be identified by a constellation of motifs (e.g., recurring phrases) that center on notable persons, events, places, institutions, symbols, or rituals. These motifs may also show affinity to particular genres or literary forms (e.g., the wisdom tradition and proverbs). Because a tradition is, by definition, handed down through the generations, we should give some attention to the social circles (e.g., the royal court, sages, Levites, the Jerusalem temple, the family) and institutions that transmit the tradition (e.g., the exodus tradition and the institution of Passover). Where possible we may also consider their geographical provenance (e.g., whether from northern Israel or Judah, whether from Jerusalem or "the people of the land").

In Isaiah 40–55, for example, we hear echoes from the Psalms. What alerts us to their presence are parallels of both terminology and literary form (i.e., genre). While the echoes are clear, we cannot be certain that these passages in Isaiah 40–55 are actually citing the extant psalms of the Bible (hence these are not necessarily instances of "intertextuality"). The 150 psalms in the Psalter are but a selection of those used during the centuries of Israel's worship.[1] The most we can say with reasonable certainty is that Isaiah 40–55 echoes the kind of liturgical psalms in the Book of Psalms. There are allusions to lament or prayer psalms in the "trial speeches against Israel," in which Yahweh explains that the nation's lamentable condition is a deserved, deliberate judgment on their sin (Ps. 44:10–11 and Isa. 42:22, 24; Ps. 44:12 and Isa. 50:1). There are allusions to prayer psalms in the "proclamations of salvation," in which Yahweh responds to the lament with a promise of salvation (Ps. 44:12–13 and Isa. 52:3, 5; Ps. 44:24 and Isa. 49:14; Ps. 74:3–8; 79:1, 7 and Isa. 49:17, 19). There are allusions to hymnic psalms, es-

---

1. There are a number of psalms outside the Book of Psalms (e.g., Judg. 5:1–31; 1 Sam. 2:1–10; Jon. 2:3–9; Isa. 38:10–20; Exod. 15:1–18, 21; Deuteronomy 32; the laments of Job). The Prophets recite or imitate psalms that did not find their way into the Psalter (e.g., Jeremiah's "confessions"; Mic. 7:8–20; Hab. 3:1–15).

pecially those of Yahweh's kingship, at key points in the structure of Isaiah 40–55 (Isa. 40:5 and Ps. 97:6; Isa. 40:26, 28 and Ps. 147:4, 5; Isa. 40:30–31 and Ps. 103:5; 147:10–11; Isa. 42:10 and Ps. 96:11; 97:1; 98:7; Isa. 52:10 and Ps. 98:3; Isa. 55:10–11 and Ps. 147:15–19; Isa. 55:12 and Ps. 96:11–12; 98:8).

So what do we gain from this exercise? Is there a theological or spiritual "payoff"? Why could we not simply comment on the content of Isaiah 40–55 itself? By comparing Scripture with Scripture—here Isaiah and the Psalms—it becomes clear that Yahweh is a responsive deity. The many laments and complaints in the Psalms, which have no answer there, are answered in the Prophets. God is one who provides reasonable answers to complaints (as in the trial speeches), and God is one who promises hope (as in the proclamations of salvation), lest God's people despair. We also learn that Isaiah 40–55 not only endeavors to provide a message of salvation (i.e., a content), but this section also endeavors to awaken a response of praise among Yahweh's worshipers in the exile (i.e., a literary form). Thus, the medium is part of the message. The prophet is interested not merely in theology and prediction, but also in worship. Had we studied these passages in Isaiah 40–55 in isolation we would have missed that Yahweh's prophetic word here is part of a continuing dialogue between Yahweh and his now exiled people.

Attention to traditions and the varying perspectives they offer may help us to appreciate theological diversity within a single literary work. We may also see that a passage's traditional context is as important as its literary context as we endeavor to elucidate its meaning and significance. The Joseph narrative, for example, has a decidedly different flavor from the preceding narratives about Abraham, Isaac, and Jacob.

First, it differs in overall literary form. It forms more of a continuous, coherent narrative that focuses on a particular theme, in which if any scene or chapter were missing, the reader would notice a puzzling gap. No single chapter makes sense without the rest. While the stories about Abraham, Isaac, and Jacob are certainly connected sequentially, we may not notice a gap had some of their stories been omitted (e.g., the thrice-told motif of wife as sister in Genesis 12; 20; 26; the stories about Lot in Genesis 14; 18:16–19:38). These stories deal with a variety of themes.

Second, the characterization of Joseph is more focused: he is portrayed as the ideal wise man. After Joseph interprets Pharaoh's dream and volunteers a plan of action, Pharaoh himself announces, "There is no one so discerning and wise (*ḥākām*) as you" (Gen. 41:39). This scene exemplifies Proverbs 22:29: "Do you see those who are skillful in their work? They will serve kings." Joseph's counsel to his brothers, "Do this and you will live, for I fear God" (Gen. 42:18), not only embodies the motto of the wise, namely "the fear of the LORD" (Prov. 1:7; 9:10), it also echoes that "the fear of the LORD leads to life" (Prov. 19:23 NASB; cf. 14:27). Indeed, Joseph's imprisonment and subsequent appointment by Pharaoh illustrates Proverbs 15:33: "The fear of the Lord is instruction in wisdom, and humility goes before honor" (cf. 22:4). Joseph's flight from Potiphar's wife exemplifies the avoidance of the "loose woman" (Proverbs 5; 7).

Third, the Joseph story differs in theological and religious perspective. While God acts or speaks in virtually every story of Genesis 12–36, God is more of an offstage character in the Joseph story.[2] There are no references to religious, ritual acts (such as sacrifice or "calling on the name of the LORD"). The Joseph story is a very human story, in which people drive the action, dialogue, and plot. The clearest reference to divine providence is found in the mouth of Joseph (esp. 45:4–8; 50:20). His speech reveals that while humans plan and act, God's overriding purpose prevails. His claim echoes a key motif of Proverbs: "The human mind plans the way, but the LORD directs the steps" (16:9; cf. 16:33; 19:21; 20:24; and Rom. 8:28). Hence, in the Joseph story we see that God is in control when people are least aware of it. We see the mystery of God at work in human decisions and actions.

In light of the above observations, while the Joseph story certainly continues the narrative and chronological sequence of Genesis 12–36, it has more in common with the traditions and perspective found in OT wisdom literature than it does with those found in the Pentateuch. Some interpreters may not wish to go as far as Gerhard von Rad, who suggests that the Joseph narrative is from a different hand entirely than the rest of Genesis.[3] But these comparisons at least help us appreciate the varying perspectives and theological claims represented in a single literary work. We might think Joseph a spiritual inferior to his ancestors, but we learn that God works as providentially in Genesis 37–50 as God did in chapters 12–36. The ways of God cannot be attributed to a

2. The claims of God's providence are more of a general nature (e.g., "Yahweh was with Joseph," Gen. 39:2; God "blesses," 39:5; cf. also 41:25, 28, 32; 45:5–7; 50:20). The closest we get is Pharaoh's dream. But even here the ability to interpret dreams is also a characteristic of the wise, as in the case of Daniel. Genesis 46 is an exception, but literarily it forms part of the Jacob cycle. In the "Succesion Narrative" (2 Samuel 9–20; 1 Kings 1–2), the human drama is similarly in the foreground and Yahweh in the background.

3. "The Joseph Narrative and Ancient Wisdom," *The Problem of the Hexateuch and Other Essays* (London: SCM, 1966), 292–300.

single scheme. God works dramatically for some people and behind the scenes for others.

Thus we see that proximate literary passages may reflect different traditions. The defining context for a passage should not be limited to its literary context. We may, in fact, discover unexpected links within the biblical canon. Sensitivity to traditional context may reveal diversity and deeper theological insight.

Transformed OT Traditions

After identifying a tradition presupposed by a passage, we may discover that the tradition has been transformed or given a distinct twist from its regular, cultural usage. Genesis 15 records a "covenant" ceremony between Yahweh and Abraham (v. 18), but it offers no explanation for the mysterious ritual sacrifice described in verses 9–10 and the "smoking fire pot and a flaming torch" that "passed between these pieces" in verse 17. Insight comes from an unexpected source, namely a judgment oracle in Jeremiah 34:18. The normal pattern in this strange ritual is that the human participants wish on themselves the fate of the dissected animals should they break their part of the covenant. But in Genesis 15 a mysterious "smoking fire pot" passes between the dissected sacrifices. The implication is that Yahweh, not the human party to the covenant, thereby invokes the curse on himself! The Abrahamic covenant is thus presented as a conditional covenant, like the others, but the punishment for its infraction falls on God, not the human party.

Transformed ANE Traditions

Examinations of biblical traditions may reveal that some are not distinctively Israelite but shared within the wider ancient Near Eastern culture. Archaeologists and biblical scholars have noted the close parallels in form and content between OT covenants and ANE "suzerainty treaties." In particular, Deuteronomy, or "the book of the law," which presents itself as a covenant document (Deut. 29:21; 31:26; Josh. 8:34; 2 Kings 22:8, 11; 23:2–3, 21), parallels the outline of Hittite treaties: preamble (Deut. 1:1–5); historical review (1:6–3:29); stipulations (general in 4:1–11:32, and specific in 12:1–26:19); list of witnesses (esp. 31:19–22, 26–28; 31:30–32:1); and blessings and curses (28:1–68).[4] These observations bring to light that covenant is not a notion "dropped from heaven," but a helpful metaphor employed by the ulti-

---

4. A notable example may be found in *ANET* 203–5. The Deuteronomic curses, however, find closer parallels in an Assyrian treaty (see *ANET* 538–41).

mate communicator to reveal the binding relationship established with God's people. More specifically it is a legal metaphor, whereby a relationship is solidified by a binding contract. Although the notion of covenant/treaty is not unique to the OT, the parties of this covenant are unique in the ANE. Here we see not simply human parties (an overlord, or "suzerain," and a vassal) but a remarkable deity who binds himself to his people in a legal contract (somewhat analogous to a modern-day warranty or guarantee).

Other ANE traditions transformed in the OT are the related traditions of divine kingship, the God of the skies, and theophany (i.e., a dramatic appearance of a deity). The general impression we get in the OT regarding the Yahweh-versus-Baal and Israelite-versus-Canaanite conflicts is that of overt polemic. As exemplified par excellence in Elijah's challenge to the prophets of Baal (1 Kings 18), there is a clear either-or (v. 21). But once we recognize a pattern recurring in the OT and ANE, we see that the OT's engagement in this religious and cultural conflict was more than mere rejection. In effect, the OT sometimes uses the "language" or imagery understandable within the ANE to claim that divine, royal prerogatives belong to Yahweh alone.

In the Psalms and Prophets especially (e.g., Psalms 24; 29; 65; 74; 93; 104; Isa. 44:27–28; 51:9–10; Exodus 15), we see a recurring pattern of Yahweh's superiority to the waters, his acclamation as king, and reference to his temple-palace (denoted by *hêkāl*). This threefold pattern is fundamental to both the Baal Epic of the eastern Mediterranean (see esp. 2.iv.7–32; 4.vi.16–37)[5] and the Enuma Elish of Mesopotamia (4.31–134; 5.85–154; 6.50–104).[6] In each case, Yahweh, Baal, and Marduk appear as the god of the skies/storm to vanquish the god of the seas (called *yām, nĕhārôt, tĕhôm, mayim rabîm* in the OT, Yam-Nahar in the Baal Epic, and Tiamat in the Enuma Elish). Thus, in its exchange with Baalism and the Canaanites, the OT did not engage in mere rebuff, but was more creative than we might have imagined. Yahweh assumes this dramatic role of royal deity, but he is no near-equal to the seas; he achieves victory with considerable ease. In addition, Yahweh's intervention is not limited to the natural realm; these scenes (noted in the OT passages listed above) exemplify his saving intervention on his people's behalf in the historical realm, and his "righteousness" (i.e., his "putting things right") in the moral realm.

Yahweh's cherubim throne above the ark of the covenant (Exod. 25:18–22; 1 Sam. 4:4; 2 Sam. 6:2; 1 Kings 8:6–7) similarly reflects a

5. J. C. L. Gibson, *Canaanite Myths and Legends* (Edinburgh: T. & T. Clark, 1977), 43–45, 62–63.

6. *ANET* 66–67, 502–3, 68–69.

transformed tradition. At several non-Israelite sites, archaeologists have unearthed cherubim thrones, on which the local human monarch sits.[7] But the striking feature of Yahweh's cherubim throne is that his was "empty"—without idol representation. This symbol thus makes plain that Yahweh himself cannot be represented by any image. Moreover, the cherubim-ark shows how OT traditions may be embodied in a tangible symbol; they are not simply mental notions. Furthermore, we can see how a variety of traditions and divine roles can be linked in a single symbol. The cherubim-ark portrays Yahweh as king (Ps. 24:7–10; 97:1–2; 99:1, 5; 132:7–8, 14; Jer. 3:16–17; 1 Chron. 28:2); warrior (Num. 10:33–36; Joshua 6; Ps. 24:8; 68:1, 24; 80:1–3; 1 Chron. 28:18); and God of the skies (Ps. 68:1, 4, 7–9, 33; 97:2–6).[8]

Dynamic Traditions

When we think of theology, especially systematic or "dogmatic" theology, we tend to think of doctrines that are fixed and static. While doctrinal theology is certainly a valid and necessary pursuit, we must also reckon with the dynamic nature of OT traditions. Through Israel's changing circumstances and fluctuating faithfulness, and through Yahweh's progressive revelation, traditions developed, sometimes through evolution and sometimes through revolution.

This development is perhaps nowhere more evident than in the tradition of Davidic kingship. From the beginning, the OT is clear that human kingship was a foreign import (1 Sam. 8:5, 19–20) and that it was instigated by Israel's demand for an expedient solution to neighboring military threats (9:16; 12:12)—a demand that reflected their distrust and rejection of Yahweh (8:6–7; 10:17–19; 12:8–12). Yahweh does grant them a king but only as a concession (1 Sam. 8:7, 9, 22; 12:1, 13–25). Their first king brings some early successes (though in passages that call him *ngyd*, not *mlk*, 9:16; 10:1), but before long he defaults, and Yahweh rejects him (13:13–14; 15:17–29). Kingship is first seen in a positive light with Yahweh's choice of David, "a man after his own heart" (1 Sam. 13:14; cf. 16:7). Later, in response to David's wish to build Yahweh a "house," Yahweh, in a "dynastic oracle," promises to build David a house (2 Sam. 7:5–16), an oracle that

7. Othmar Keel, *The Symbolism of the Biblical World: Ancient Near Eastern Iconography and the Book of Psalms* (London: SPCK; New York: Seabury, 1978), 166–71; Tryggve N. D. Mettinger, *In Search of God: The Meaning and Message of the Everlasting Names* (Philadelphia: Fortress, 1988), 127–31.

8. For elaboration on the allusions to the cherubim-ark in these psalms, see Craig C. Broyles, *Psalms,* New International Biblical Commentary 11 (Peabody, Mass.: Hendrickson, 1999).

develops in various versions with divergent emphases. Some versions read as though the covenant is unconditional and even heighten the promises further (cf. 2 Sam. 7:13–16 and Ps. 89:28–37). In others it is explicitly conditional (1 Kings 6:12; 8:25–26; Ps. 132:11–12). The expectations of Yahweh's "anointed" (*mēšîaḥ*) develop further in the royal psalms sung at regular commemorative occasions (Psalms 2; 18; 20; 21; 45; 72; 89:1–37; 110; 132). But the historical reality of the Davidic monarchy presents us with a dismal failure that ends in exile, as seen through the Deuteronomistic lens (1–2 Kings). The prophetic lens sees the same result but is also able to foresee further. Isaiah (7:1–9:7; 11:1–5), Micah (5:1–5a), and Jeremiah (22; 23:5–6) all agree that the Davidic dynasty will be cut down, but then Yahweh will raise up a new son of David—a promise seen fulfilled in the pages opening the NT (Matthew 1). The David tradition takes a remarkable and surprising journey: it is rooted in rebellion, it withers in the exile, and it is resurrected and flowers in the Messiah Jesus. It is a classic case of Yahweh working evil for good.

The Zion tradition also illustrates the dynamism of OT traditions. As the "songs of Zion" (Psalms 46, 48, 76, 84, 87, 132:13–18) exemplify, at the heart of this tradition are Yahweh's claim to Zion as his dwelling and his commitment to protecting it. In the late eighth century, as Judah was vexed by the Assyrian empire, the political leadership in Jerusalem endeavored to break free by forming political coalitions with its neighbors, especially Egypt. The prophet Isaiah, however, maintained a contrary position throughout his ministry, largely on the basis of the Zion tradition. Yahweh dwells in Zion (Isa. 2:2–4; 8:18; 12:6), and he will protect his people there (14:32). In fact, even Egypt will bring tribute to Yahweh who dwells there (18:7). Later, Isaiah again affirms that Yahweh will shield Zion and fight against its aggressors (31:4–5, 9). Yahweh will arise to protect the righteous in Zion, "the city of our appointed festivals" (33:5–6, 10–16, 20–24). Isaiah faults these attempts at treaties and coalitions because their proponents disregard the God whose temple is on Mount Zion, and they fail to look to Judah's only real source of help (30:1–7; 31:1–3; 33:7–9). Judah's problem was that it failed to trust in Yahweh, whose temple was on Mount Zion. In 701 B.C.E., Isaiah's prophecies and the Zion tradition were demonstrably vindicated when he predicted that Sennacherib's attack against Jerusalem (which was tantamount to an attack on the Holy One of Israel) would fail because Yahweh will defend Zion (37:22–23, 32–35). After 185,000 of Sennacherib's forces suddenly die, Sennacherib retreats to Nineveh.

Nearly a century later in 609 B.C.E., however, after Egypt had killed King Josiah at Megiddo and made Judah their vassal (Jer. 26:1; cf. 2 Kings 23:29–35), Jeremiah warns, "Do not trust in these deceptive words: 'This is the temple of the LORD, the temple of the LORD, the temple of the LORD'" (7:4). The people "come and stand before . . . this house . . . and say, 'We are safe'" (v. 10 NIV). In the midst of foreign threat, the people affirmed their national security on the basis of Yahweh's residence in the city's temple. It would seem they had finally learned the lesson Isaiah had proclaimed earlier. We can well imagine that Josiah's widespread temple reforms in 622 B.C.E. (2 Kings 22–23) had also bolstered the people's feeling that they and their temple were indeed sanctioned by God. But to everyone's surprise, Jeremiah brands the phrase "this is the temple of the LORD" as "deceptive words"! Was the Zion tradition now invalid? Jeremiah goes on to explain: the people live in violation of the "Ten Words" (7:8–10). He thus clarifies that the promises related to Mount Zion are conditional on the covenant of Mount Sinai. We thus see that the biblical tradition that was crucial for one generation to hear became a stumbling block for the next. God will frustrate any attempt to box him in with a single theological perspective.

Similarly, later in the Babylonian exile, an oracle in Isaiah 43:16–21 alludes to the exodus out of Egypt and the "way in the sea." But it astonishingly warns the exiles, "Do not remember the former things, or consider the things of old." Up to this point remembering Yahweh's saving deeds had been an indispensable component of OT faith and its religious festivals (e.g., Exod. 13:3; Deut. 7:18; 8:2; 16:3; Ps. 105:5). But God's people are told to forget the first exodus, because Yahweh is "about to do a new thing," namely, to "make a way in the wilderness." In other words, he will perform a second exodus out of Babylonia, through the desert, back to their homeland. Again we see that old traditions can become new idols, but we also see that the old models can prefigure new saving acts.

The dynamism of OT traditions is exemplified in a positive way in the prophets' depiction of the restoration from exile as a renewal of the old traditions. There is to be a new exodus (Hos. 2:14–15; 11:11; Isa. 43:16–21; 48:20–21; 52:11–12); a new covenant (Jer. 31:31–34; 32:37–41; Ezek. 36:24–28); a new temple (Ezekiel 40–48); a new Zion (Mic. 4:1–3); and a new David (Isa. 9:1–7; 11:1–9; Ezek. 34:23–24; 37:24–28; Amos 9:11–15; Mic. 5:1–5).

It can also be enlightening to explore how varying traditions explore the same phenomenon. A telling example is the nature of Yahweh's presence at the temple. Some passages, especially preexilic texts, reflect the conception that God's very "face" (*pnym*, often translated "presence" in English versions) resides at the temple.[9] Later Deuteronomic passages prefer to speak of the temple as the dwelling place of Yahweh's "name" (Deut. 12:5, 11, 21; 1 Kings 8:16–20, 29, 44, 48; Jer. 7:10–14, 30). Later priestly passages speak of the temple as the place where Yahweh's "glory" is revealed, as seen especially in Ezekiel, who depicts Yahweh's rejection of Israel by the departure of his glory from the temple (10:4, 18–19), and Yahweh's reinstatement of Israel by the return of his glory to the temple (43:2–5). We thus see a growing awareness of the freedom of God—a necessity if Yahwism is to survive the Babylonian destruction of the temple.

Intertextuality

A passage's intertextual context includes any quotations, allusions, or echoes it may contain to other biblical passages. *Quotations* are explicit references to other texts; *allusions* and *echoes* are implicit. In any case, there must be some apparent signal or flag that distinctly points the reader/listener to another passage. While the traditional context is identified by connections of motif and subject (more fluid because they may have been shaped originally through oral transmission), the intertextual context is identified by literary connections (fixed because they are written). These intertextual connections thus add new layers of meaning to a given passage because elements of another passage are imported. In addition, the use that later passages make of earlier passages can provide windows into the earliest interpretations of biblical passages (sometimes called "inner-biblical exegesis").

Jeremiah 26:18 and Micah 3:12. An oracle from Micah 3:12 is explicitly quoted in Jeremiah 26:18. It appears in the context of Jeremiah's temple sermon, recorded in two accounts. The contents of the sermon itself are spelled out in greater length in Jeremiah 7:1–15 (discussed

9. Exodus 23:15, 17; 34:20, 23–24; Deuteronomy 16:16; 31:11; Psalm 42:2; 84:7; Isaiah 1:12—in the MT each of these passages contain the awkward phrase *rʾh pny* (Niphal), usually translated, "appear before" Yahweh. We should normally expect *lpny*, "before." Exodus 34:23–24 and Deuteronomy 16:16 indicate that *pny* ("face") was originally the direct object of the verb *rʾh* by the inclusion of the direct object marker *ʾt* before "face." In Psalm 42:3, a few manuscripts of the MT, the Syriac Peshitta, and the Targum, in fact, read, *ʾerʾĕʾeh* ("I see"). It thus appears that the original phrasing was "to see the face of God." To avoid the difficulty of claiming that humans could see the face of God and live (see Exod. 33:20), later scribes inserted the Niphal pointing without altering the consonantal text. We should note that each of these occurrences probably stems from the ancient "Book of the Covenant," which refers to the three major pilgrimage festivals by their agricultural names (Exod. 23:14–17). In some psalms, "seeking the face of God" meant visiting the temple (24:3, 6; 27:4, 8; cf. 11:7; 17:15).

briefly above), and its ensuing events are narrated in Jeremiah 26. In response to the sermon, "the priests and the prophets" (26:7, 8, 11, 16) instigate a commotion to have Jeremiah executed because he prophesies the destruction of "this house and this city" (vv. 6, 9, 12). From the proximity of "the king's house," "the officials of Judah" (vv. 10, 11, 12, 16) go to "the house of the LORD," where they convene a trial ("took their seat in the entry of the New Gate of the house of the LORD," v. 10). After "the priests and the prophets" indict Jeremiah and call for his execution (v. 11), he offers his defense, claiming "it is the LORD who sent me" (vv. 12–15). The key evidence for Jeremiah's defense is submitted by "the elders of the land" (vv. 16–19). They cite Micah 3:12, "Zion shall be plowed as a field; Jerusalem shall become a heap of ruins, and the mountain of the house a wooded height," and they remind the court that Hezekiah's response was one of repentance, not execution. They thus use this citation as a precedent on Jeremiah's behalf.

This case has profound implications for the nature of prophecy. When seen in isolation, there is nothing in Micah 3:9–12 to suggest that this oracle is conditional. It reads like a straightforward prediction— with no contingencies attached. But in view of Hezekiah's response and the oracle's nonfulfillment to the present day, these "elders" interpret it as a conditional threat. Its fulfillment was waived because Hezekiah did "fear the Lord and entreat the favor of the LORD," and Yahweh did "change his mind (*wayyināḥem*) about the disaster that he had pronounced against them." Thus, a judgment oracle may not predict an inevitable disaster but may be conditional on the recipients' response.

We also learn something about the social context of prophecy, especially of Micah's, and how texts and traditions are transmitted within particular social circles (discussed above under "Traditions"). The group that advocates on behalf of Jeremiah, who claims to have been sent by Yahweh, and that treasures Micah's prophecies are "the elders of the land." They represent "the people of the land," that is, the farmers of the rural countryside. They appear to have been a conservative segment of Judahite society who sought to preserve Yahwism and the rightful succession within the Davidic dynasty (2 Kings 11:14, 18–20; 21:24; cf. 14:21). Their fondness for Micah makes sense in light of the contents of his prophecy. Micah himself was from Moresheth (Mic. 1:1), twenty miles outside of Jerusalem. His prophecies are directed primarily against Jerusalem (1:1, 5), and his harshest oracles are against its "heads" and "rulers." Micah 3:1–4 even describes their oppression of "my people" in terms of cannibalism. The oracle of which our citation is a part (3:9–12) is addressed to the same elite group, those "who build Zion with blood," and it pronounces the utter leveling of Jerusalem. The book's final judgment oracle (6:9–16) is pronounced against "the city," especially its "wealthy," and threatens its "desolation" and the Deuteronomic curses (Deut. 28:30, 38–40). Moreover, Micah 2:1–5, although not explicitly addressed to Jerusalem and its elite, pronounces woe on those who defraud the people of their "fields" and "inheritance." Thus, Micah appears to have been an advocate on behalf of the farmers, the ancestral landholders, who sought to preserve traditional Yahwism and its parceling of the land to the wider society.[10]

Elijah and Moses. The story of Elijah's contest with the prophets of Baal at Mount Carmel is well known, as is the subsequent account of his flight to Mount Horeb and Yahweh's meeting with him. Elijah goes from the heights of victory over the prophets of Baal to the depths of fearing for his own life as Jezebel vows to execute him. In this meeting Yahweh appears not in the wind, earthquake, or fire, but in the "still, small voice" (1 Kings 19:12). The lesson usually drawn is that God may not always appear in the grand and magnificent, but may come in ways more subtle. While this is clearly a valid inference, we miss a key point of the story if we fail to hear echoes of Moses' experiences in Exodus 19–34. The stories' similarities invite comparison, so we hear in "stereo" more than we would if we merely read each story in its own right. Both Elijah and Moses go up to Mount Horeb/Sinai (1 Kings 19:8; Exod. 19:17, 20; 24:15–16; 33:6; 34:2, 4) without food for forty days (1 Kings 19:8; Exod. 24:18; 34:28) and wait in a cave (1 Kings 19:9; Exod. 33:21–22). Both claim, at least, to be the sole mediator (1 Kings 19:10; Exod. 19:3, 7–10, 20–21, 25; 20:21; 24:15, 18; 32:30; 33:5, 7–11; 34:2–4). To both, Yahweh announces that he will "pass by" (*ʿbr*, 1 Kings 19:11; Exod. 33:19, 22; 34:6). For Elijah there is a "wind" (1 Kings 19:11), and for Moses a thunderstorm (Exod. 19:16; 20:18). For Elijah there is "an earthquake" (1 Kings 19:11) and, for Moses, "the whole mountain shook violently" (Exod. 19:18). For both there is "fire" (1 Kings 19:12; Exod. 19:18; 24:17). For Moses there is the loud "sound (*qôl*) of a trumpet" (Exod. 19:16, 19; 20:18) and, implicitly, God's audible voice proclaiming the Ten Words (20:1, 19; Deut. 5:22–26 makes explicit reference to Yahweh's "loud voice [*qôl*]"). For Elijah, however, there is the "sound of a quiet whisper" (*qôl dĕmāmāh daqāh*, 1 Kings 19:12).

It would seem that Elijah, in his desperation, goes to Horeb to try to repeat Moses' experience, and, it appears, Yahweh plays along with him to make a point. But Yahweh does not appear to Elijah as he had

10. For futher discussion, see Joseph Blenkinsopp, *A History of Prophecy in Israel* (Philadelphia: Westminster, 1983), 121–22.

to Moses. Though Elijah goes to a sacred place where Yahweh had earlier revealed himself so dramatically, Yahweh is free to reveal himself differently, even to tease Elijah to make the point. God is not a computer, whereby a given input has a guaranteed output. God is a person, and free to act as his own person. God is faithful, but not predictable. And so Elijah must trust directly in the person of God—apart from sacred places and patterns that worked for others in another generation.

Isaiah 40–45 and Genesis 1. Though more subtle, there are echoes of Genesis 1:1–2:4 in Isaiah 40–45.[11] In this case, however, the earlier text is not merely a foil; the later text appears to clarify and qualify the earlier text, to avoid possible misunderstanding. The following chart illustrates the contrasts.

Genesis 1	Isaiah 40–45
"Now the earth was 'willy nilly' (*tōhû wābōhû*) and *darkness* (*ḥōšek*) was over the face of the deep" (1:2, lit.).	"I form light and create *darkness* (*ḥōšek*)" (45:7). "He did not create it a chaos (or *willy*, *tōhû*)" (45:18).
"Let us make humankind in our image, according to our *likeness*" (*dĕmût*, 1:26).	"To whom then will you liken God, or what *likeness* (*dĕmût*) compare with him?" (40:18; cf. 40:25; 46:5). "Who has directed the spirit of Yahweh, or as his counselor has instructed him . . . ?" (40:13). "I am Yahweh, who made all things, who alone stretched out the heavens, who by myself spread out the earth" (44:24).
"He rested on the seventh day from all the work that he had done" (2:2).	"Yahweh is the everlasting God, the Creator of the ends of the earth. He does not faint or grow weary . . ." (40:28).

(Cf. also Isa. 45:19: "I did not speak in secret, in a land of *darkness* (*ḥōšek*); I did not say to the offspring of Jacob, 'Seek me in chaos (*tōhû*).'") The contrasts are striking—almost to the point of refutation—and at the very least qualify the statements in the Genesis 1 account. While chaos may have been present at the beginning of creation, God did not create the world for this purpose. Darkness does not exist on its own, nor is it an independent entity rivaling God; rather it, like

11. The following observations are based on a Hebrew article by M. Weinfeld, described in M. Fishbane's *Biblical Interpretation in Ancient Israel* (Oxford: Clarendon, 1985), 325–26.

light, is a creation of God. Although there may be a sense in which humans uniquely reflect the divine, there is ultimately nothing in creation that compares to God. While God may use plural pronouns of royalty in Genesis 1, Isaiah 40–45 emphasizes that God performed creation alone, without counsel from any council. Although the Genesis account may claim that God "rested" (*šbt*), Isaiah 40 explains that God, in fact, has no need of rest. In this light, the divine "rest" in Genesis 1 must be interpreted as metaphoric.

Canon

A passage's canonical context moves us into a sphere wider than its literary context, which extends as far as its biblical book. Yet because the biblical canon is a literary anthology, both contexts are of the same kind; that is, they are literature. This property distinguishes the canonical context from the historical and sociological context, which presupposes some actual contact between the text and historical people and events. Similarly, the traditional context generally presupposes that biblical writers intentionally use traditions known within their communities. The canonical context, however, means simply that these texts are joined into the same written corpus, and does not presuppose previous "genetic" connections among them. Those who wrote or edited one text may or may not have intended to comment on others within the final literary canon, and they may or may not have been aware of others. By moving us outside a passage's original historical context and outside its transmission through later historical contexts, the canonical context allows us to take a synchronic perspective of the whole anthology. Other passages may serve as a commentary on our passage simply because they are part of the same literary corpus, not because they necessarily had any connection during their transmission history. At this level, the so-called meant-means dichotomy can be set aside.[12]

On the one hand, these observations make the Bible's unity all the more remarkable. How such a diverse collection can speak in harmony testifies to its divine authorship, redaction, and collection. There is ultimately one Voice in Scripture. On the other hand, we must be struck

---

12. "The canonical method . . . is concerned with the meanings each part of the text is constrained to have by its juxtaposition with all the others. Canonical meanings are a function of the shape of the canon and do not depend on our being able to reconstruct the minds of the canonizers. For the same reason, they have a certain permanence and timelessness that bypasses the problems of the cultural gap between ourselves and their 'original' authors . . ." (John Barton, *Reading the Old Testament: Method in Biblical Study* [London: Darton, Longman, and Todd, 1984], 90).

by the diversity of voices and perspectives in this anthology. The individual passages and books were incorporated into the canon without first smoothing out "rough edges" or by explicitly harmonizing potential discrepancies. (While the Bible may be "harmonized," it was never "homogenized." It includes four Gospels and not a singular *Diatessaron*. Chronicles was never meant to displace Samuel and Kings.) For example, in the early postexilic period, should Jerusalem have been rebuilt with walls (so Nehemiah) or without walls (so Zech. 2:1–5)? (See further below.) In the same period, should foreigners have been included in the community (so Isa. 56:3–8) or not (so Ezra 9–10)? As interpreters of this sacred collection, we become aware that we must seek to discern God's voice amid the choir of human voices and God's panoramic perspective among the singular, human viewpoints. The whole is more than the sum of its parts. This makes our task both fascinating and frustrating. Awareness of the canonical context takes us beyond the shortsightedness of "prooftexting," but it also means that a satisfying synthesis may elude us.

If we take seriously that God used human agents to write Scripture, then the Bible is not a "book dropped from heaven." But if we take seriously that God is its ultimate author, redactor, and collector, then this variety of perspectives is intentional. The scriptural canon thus becomes a model for the scriptural community: a diversity of perspectives does not mean that God is not speaking through each member.

Using Scripture to interpret Scripture: differing functions. The problem of discerning God's will from the OT and of using one passage to serve as commentary on another are well illustrated in Jesus' debate with the Pharisees on the issue of divorce (Mark 10:2–12 // Matt. 19:3–12). In Mark, the Pharisees take their lead from Deuteronomy 24:1–3, which they interpret as Moses' allowance for divorce. Jesus, however, takes his lead from Genesis 1:27; 2:24, which he uses to show that divorce is contrary to God's original institution of marriage. Is this a case in which Jesus subordinates Moses' words to God's? No, he does not dispense with Moses' words, but clarifies that Moses "wrote you this commandment . . . for your hardness of heart." (Deut. 26:16 clearly includes this commandment among those that "the LORD your God is commanding you to observe.") On what grounds does Jesus claim this commandment to be a concession? Although the Gospels do not provide us with his reasoning, a look at Deuteronomy 24:1–3 itself shows that it is "law," and "case law" in particular. Moreover, the particular segment to which the Pharisees appeal is found in the "if" clause. In other words, Deuteronomy 24:1 offers no endorsement of divorce; it merely admits it as a preexisting condition. The "then" clause attempts to put a hedge around this pre-existing, cultural evil. To elucidate God's ideal will, Jesus goes to narrative, especially to a narrative concerning "the beginning of creation," in which we see God's original, unspoiled intention expressed. Both OT passages are embraced as revelatory and authoritative, but each has its particular function and contribution. The Genesis narrative reflects God's ideal will, and the Deuteronomic law God's concessionary will and God's prescription for curbing further abuses. (This example also illustrates the importance of considering literary genre.) Thus, all Scriptures are not on the same plane; some may be subordinated to others.

God's values and priorities. In another instance in the Gospels, Jesus shows that some biblical passages are more revealing of God's priorities than others. He twice quotes Hosea 6:6 ("I desire mercy, not sacrifice," Matt. 9:13; 12:7; cf. Mic. 6:1–8), thus relativizing those portions of the OT that prescribe ritual observances, such as sacrifice, Sabbath, and avoiding the company of "sinners." From this one passage, Jesus understands that God places greater value on relationship than on "religion." Similarly, within the OT itself, we should note that for all the legislation in the Torah about ritual procedures and distinctions, the bottom line for God's decision to bring exile lies in the people's worship of other gods (the first of the Ten Words, Exod. 20:3) and their idolatry (the second of the Ten Words, Exod. 20:4; see 2 Kings 17:7–20; 21:3–15; 23:26–27). What provokes God to anger is faithlessness and misrepresenting the true God. Although God "had brought them up out of the land of Egypt from under the hand of Pharaoh" (2 Kings 17:7; cf. the prologue to the Ten Words, Exod. 20:2), they did not remain true to God. Contrary to much popular thinking today about the OT, it is defined primarily by relational categories, not by legal or "religious" categories.

Progressive revelation and trajectories. Another discovery we make when comparing Scripture with Scripture is that later passages may update earlier passages, either by clarification or by outright change. A comparison of the "Hebrew" slave laws in "the book of the covenant" (as identified in Exod. 24:7; see 21:1–11) and in the later "book of the law" (as identified in Deut. 29:21; 31:26; Josh. 1:8; 2 Kings 22:8, 11; see Deut. 15:12–18) reveals a striking development. Female slaves are now granted the same civil rights as the male slaves, namely freedom in the seventh year (esp. Deut. 15:12, 17). It may be that the original version reflects more closely some of the cultural norms common to the ANE, while the later version reflects the transformed norms of Yahwism. Were we to take the version found in "the book of the covenant" as God's final word, we would be sadly mistaken.

These observations bring to light that biblical laws may change. Theologically we can describe this as "progressive revelation." In this light, the Bible shows us patterns of how God speaks and works with people in particular situations. The Bible is a fixed text, but it reflects a process within itself and that sometimes goes beyond itself.

Diverse points of view and complementary perspectives. Scanning the OT canon may also reveal diverse points of view on certain issues. As already noted, the early postexilic period reflects several controversies. Around the year 520 B.C.E., Zechariah in a vision hears that "Jerusalem shall be inhabited like villages without walls, because of the multitude of people and animals in it. For I will be a wall of fire all around it, says the LORD, and I will be the glory within it" (2:4–5). But in 445 B.C.E., Nehemiah, in prayerful dependence on Yahweh, rebuilds Jerusalem's walls. He does so without reference to a specific directive or oracle from Yahweh. He simply decides to do it and prays that Yahweh "give success" (1:11; cf. 2:20), and he confesses that "the gracious hand of my God was upon me" (2:8, 18; cf. 6:16).

Did Nehemiah not know of Zechariah's prophecy, or did he simply choose the path of political pragmatism? These are historical questions and certainly interesting ones, although our limited sources may never reveal answers. But even if we could answer them, that both positions are included within the same scriptural canon begs the theological question of how they are to be reconciled. Here we need to respect the literary form or genre of each passage. As a prophetic oracle, Zechariah's claims must be interpreted according to the conventions of that genre. Such a prophecy may not be an inevitable *prediction* but a conditional *promise* (see esp. the discussion above on Mic. 3:12 and Jer. 26:17–19; note also Jon. 3:4, 3:10–4:2; Isa. 38:1–5). It provides a vision for what is ultimately possible under Yahweh. Thus, if the people do not respond appropriately in trust and obedience, the oracle may fall short of its intended fulfillment (as noted below in Isaiah 40–66).

Nehemiah 1–6, however, is historical narrative, and a memoir in particular (note the "I" form throughout). Instead of focusing on ultimate causes and possibilities, this genre reports on immediate exigencies and historical complexities and on the intrigue of human distrust and deviousness. Other portions of the OT canon make clear that prophetic calls to return from Babylonian exile to the land of Israel, and to enjoy an exodus more glorious than the first (Isa. 48:20–21; 52:11–12), largely went unheeded.[13] The Book of Isaiah admits that promises of Yahweh's personal return to Jerusalem (Isa. 52:7–10) remained unful-

13. Here we should note the relatively small return led by Zerubbabel in 538 B.C.E. As a result, around 520 B.C.E., Zechariah must issue another prophetic summons for the exiles to "flee from the land of the north" and to "escape to Zion" (2:6–7). Ezra participates in a second return in 458 B.C.E., and Nehemiah himself in a third return in 445 B.C.E.

filled because of the people's continued lack of repentance (59:1–20). Although Yahweh's promises regarding the restored Jerusalem are grand and glorious (e.g., Isaiah 54), the report that Nehemiah himself receives is that Jerusalem's inhabitants are "in great trouble and shame" (Neh. 1:3). In these circumstances, Yahweh apparently graciously blesses Nehemiah's efforts to build Jerusalem's walls. Thus, what initially appears to be an awkward discrepancy within the canon becomes a profound and comforting theological lesson. God offers God's people promises and possibilities that far exceed the imaginations of politicians and military strategists. But even if God's people fail to believe in God utterly, God remains with them to bless their efforts. Yahweh offers high ideals, but he is also a realist—and a faithful one at that.

six

The History of Religion, Biblical Theology, and Exegesis

ELMER A. MARTENS

Two disciplines, the history of Israelite religion and Old Testament theology, are integral to exegesis. The disciplines, as tools, are especially important as the interpreter moves toward putting the exegetical work on display and to applying the text. This essay sketches the nature of the two disciplines, briefly traces their ebb and flow over two centuries, and, by using examples from the various literary genres, elaborates on their usefulness for the interpreter.

Becoming Familiar with the Tools

The first tool, *history of Israelite religion*, has a well-worn feel, for it has been held in many hands. This tool is used to characterize Israel's religious life, not only the religion of officialdom but popular religion. Its descriptions focus on observable religious behavior as well as on the

177

ideology that stands behind this behavior. Historians, anthropologists, and social scientists who work in this arena have an interest in the origins of a belief or practice and in its development, and especially in tracing influences.[1] If, for example, the subject is monotheism, certain questions would be appropriate. Where does monotheism have its origin?[2] How are the different names applied to the deity to be understood? Are the terms *God* (Elohim) and *Lord* (Yahweh) to be equated, and, if so, by whom and at what stage in Israel's religious development? What influence did the Canaanite belief system, even the vocabulary (e.g., El), have on Israelite thinking?

Researchers seek to give an account of what went on in Israel religiously. Their sources of information include the Bible and archaeology. Archaeology works with artifacts and the literary works of surrounding cultures.[3] Since large use is made of the comparative method, materials from cultures surrounding Israel are also important. A self-conscious attempt is made to proceed scientifically and to treat Israelite religion objectively. Explanations for phenomena are deliberately presented on the human plane, without resort to gods or deity. A history of religion singles out the human factors in a religion, for the human side of history is the focus. For this reason, findings in anthropology and sociology are sometimes incorporated. One frequent assumption is that the movement in societies is from simple to complex. Partly because of this commitment to developmentalism, many hold that the detailed cultic laws in Exodus and Leviticus come late, rather than early in Israel's history. Literarily this means that the sources for this legislation should be dated late, and if they appear early it is because of later rearrangement and editing. When Genesis 1 is dated from a priestly source in exilic times, the interpretation can be expected to deal with the cultic concern of the seven-day week as giving identity to Israel. By contrast, an early date for the chapter points toward an agenda centering on cosmic beginnings.

1. See G. Fohrer, who cites four major influences affecting Israelite religion: Mosaic Yahwism, kingship, prophecy, and Deuteronomic theology. About the importance of this tool, Fohrer states: "Neither the exegesis nor the theology of the Old Testament can do without it [history of religion]" (*History of Israelite Religion* [Nashville, Abingdon, 1972], 22).

2. See Robert K. Gnuse, *No Other Gods: Emergent Monotheism in Israel*, JSOTSup 241 (Sheffield: JSOT, 1997). Cf. P. D. Miller, "God and the Gods: History of Religion as an Approach and Context for Bible and Theology," *Affirmation* 1, no. 5 (1973): 37–62.

3. For example, Jeffery H. Tigay, *You Shall Have No Other Gods: Israelite Religion in the Light of Hebrew Inscriptions* (Atlanta: Scholars, 1986). Cf. R. S. Hess, "Yahweh and His Asherah? Epigraphic Evidence for Religious Pluralism in Old Testament Times," in *One God, One Lord in a World of Religious Pluralism*, ed. A. D. Clarke and B. W. Winter (Cambridge: Tyndale House, 1991), 5–33.

Specialists in the history of Israelite religion have a distinctive contribution to make. By their descriptions, they "earth" the Scripture. An insidious danger is to think of Scripture in terms of the ethereal, the mystical, or the speculative. Beyond rooting religions in what is basic to human existence, these specialists ferret out the contours of a religion and help explain how the "pieces" within that religion contribute to an overall worldview. Using the comparative method, these scholars enable us to understand early and late Israelite views on a subject (e.g., covenant) and especially to pinpoint how Israelite religion was both similar to and different from other religions.[4]

The second tool, *Old Testament theology*, seems more unwieldy. Perhaps for that reason it is often a misplaced tool; it may even be ignored.[5] Biblical theologians work alongside biblical historians with the same data, such as dreams, sacrifice, and prayer, but their focus is different. Biblical theologians try to present the essential theological structure of Israel's beliefs. This structure, in turn, may point to what is said authoritatively about God, humanity, the world, and their interrelationships. They see their task as summarizing the material by carefully weighing what is of fundamental significance. The objective is to make clear the dynamic of a religion and especially to identify its normative aspects. The historian of religion, for example, may describe polygamy and trace its role in Israelite life; the biblical theologian is interested in the "authorized" understanding about marriage presented in the Bible. The historian of religion tells what was; the theologian describes what should be.

4. How Israelite religion differs from its contemporaries is exemplified in the title to Frank Cross's *Canaanite Myth and Hebrew Epic: Essays in History of the Religion of Israel* (1973; Cambridge: Harvard University Press, 1997). Cf. idem, *From Epic to Canon: History and Literature in Ancient Israel* (Baltimore and London: Johns Hopkins University Press, 1998). For extensive bibliography on the subject and for discussions about monotheism and the cult of the dead, see Bill T. Arnold, "Religion in Israel," in *The Face of Old Testament Studies*, ed. David Baker and Bill T. Arnold (Grand Rapids: Baker, 1999), 333–38.

5. If not altogether ignored, biblical theology is barely a factor in the other-wise helpful guide to exegesis by Robert B. Chisholm Jr., *From Exegesis to Exposition: A Practical Guide to Using Biblical Hebrew* (Grand Rapids: Baker, 1998). A different understanding of exegesis appears in *Theological Exegesis: Essays in Honor of Brevard Childs*, ed. Christopher Seitz and Kathryn Greene-McCreight (Grand Rapids and Cambridge: Eerdmans, 1999). For the importance of biblical theology for exegesis and with some suggestions about its use, see Walter C. Kaiser Jr., "Theological Analysis," in *Toward an Exegetical Theology: Biblical Exegesis for Preaching and Teaching* (Grand Rapids: Zondervan, 1981), 131–47; B. S. Childs, "Exegesis in the Context of Biblical Theology," in *Biblical Theology of the Old and New Testaments: Theological Reflection on the Christian Bible* (Minneapolis: Fortress, 1993), 323–47; and Moises Silva, *Explorations in Exegetical Method: Galatians as a Test Case* (Grand Rapids: Baker, 1996), 141–215.

Biblical theologians, while curious about extrabiblical sources, focus particularly on the Bible, its narratives, poetry, and didactic and prophetic material, in short, the content that spans Genesis to Chronicles (Hebrew order; Genesis through Malachi in the Alexandrian canon). Biblical theologians make use of biblical categories, such as redemption, covenant, and land, rather than philosophical categories of essence, ontology, and foundationalism. Biblical theologians also aspire to be objective in their research, although the issue of appropriate methodology is an ongoing debate. Other issues also surface. Is a theology to be presented diachronically (following the biblical plotline), synchronically (seizing on some governing concepts through which to arrange the material), or in a way that combines approaches? Is there one theology or multiple theologies? Can the claim for unity be substantiated?[6]

The contribution of Old Testament theology, a subset of biblical theology, is to present a theological framework for the Old Testament. By answering questions as to the "heart" of the Old Testament, and by sorting out what constitutes the dynamic in this literature, and especially, although this too is debated, by establishing what is normative, the individual texts can be helpfully "located." This means that individual texts can be assessed as to how they fit into the whole, the larger system of belief. Are they helpful summaries of a doctrine? Do they present a divergent viewpoint from the norm? The historian may detail practices of sacrifice, law, or holy war. The biblical theologian interprets how these topics are to be understood in the larger view of what God intends. Likewise, the historian describes the pessimism of Ecclesiastes, which holds that there is nothing new under the sun (Eccles. 1:9). The biblical theologian brings texts into play that assert that God *does* do new things (Num. 16:30; Isa. 43:19), and delineates how disparate views within the Scriptures are to be correlated, and how they fit in the larger theological structures.

The relationship between an isolated text and a full-fledged biblical theology is symbiotic, or, more cynically stated, circular. Individual texts contribute to the formulation of a summary theological statement on a given topic. Sometimes, however, it is the larger theology that assists in giving meaning to an individual text. So while texts constitute the theological grid, the grid in turn is a tool for interpreting the text.

Further discussion about the task and method for the two disciplines—history of Israelite religion and Old Testament theology—can

---

6. For a brief sketch on issues and for an extensive bibliography, see E. A. Martens, *Old Testament Theology*, IBR Bibliographies 13 (Grand Rapids: Baker, 1997), 37–60.

be found in relevant literature.[7] For now, the following chart, oversimplified to be sure, should help nevertheless in distinguishing between the two tools and their functions.

Distinctions between History of Religion and Biblical Theology

Item	History of Religion	Old Testament Theology
Subject matter	Phenomenon	Meaning
Practitioner	Historian, anthropologist	Theologian
Sources	Bible, archaeology, and so on	Bible
Assumption	From simple to complex	Revelation
Perspective	"Seen from below"	"Seen from above"
Emphasis	Variety	Unity (mostly)
Tendency	Stresses pluralities	Stresses normativity
Debated Issues	Development (progress)	Center
	How to relate Bible to ANE	Synchronic; diachronic
Results	Relative	Normative
Value	"Earth" the Scriptures	Apply the Scriptures
	Facilitate comparisons	Shape a community

Both historians and theologians work with the biblical text, but each proceeds along a different path, as the chart indicates. For the historian, the Bible serves as sourcebook; for the theologian, the Bible is Scripture, a canon for the faith community. The historian fleshes out identified practices and beliefs using data outside the Bible and traces Israel's religious journey, noting shifts and changes. Biblical theology deals with theological structures, occupies itself with the standard or normative, and points to the possible meaning and significance for present-day believers.

7. For example, Rainer Albertz's two articles in *Jahrbuch für Biblische Theologie* 10 (1995): 3–24, 177–87; and G. M. Tucker, "Old Testament Theology and Israelite Religion: Problems and Possibilities," *Colloquium* 22, no. 2 (1990): 1–11.

Understanding the Quarrel about the Tools

Before employing the tools it is best to examine what place these tools have had in the history of biblical interpretation. In one era (1870–1920) the rage was largely over one tool, history of religion. In a subsequent era (1930–90), the "other" tool, Old Testament theology, was widely championed, although texts in the history of religion were beginning to make a comeback. One reason for this ebb and flow is the change in cultural ethos. Our interest here is not to analyze, however, but to sketch the oscillating fortunes of these two disciplines.

The term *history of religion* was first used by R. Smend in 1893, but the project of writing a religious history of Israel was underway a century earlier as part of the Enlightenment. It was also this mind-set that generated biblical theology. The two specializations were not so far apart at the beginning. W. Vatke, for example, who produced a history of Israelite religion in 1835, also planned several volumes detailing the theology of the Old Testament, although only one appeared.

As a distinct study, the tool we call *biblical theology* has a beginning date of 1787. In Germany that year, Philipp Gabler presented a lecture in which he distinguished between reading the Bible from the vantage point of a systematic theology that was already in place, and a reading that had a zero baseline, theologically speaking, from which a systematized belief system would emerge. The latter method, known as biblical theology, has an inductive edge. Gabler proposed that to arrive at a "biblical" theology, similar texts should be grouped for comparison. From these texts as raw material, the interpreter would make a summary theological statement, taking care not to distort the material. Armed with the freshly touted tool of *reason*, the interpreter would next scrutinize the findings to determine what was universally valid. Rationalism and a propensity toward philosophy birthed this new approach in biblical study. The first work in biblical theology to limit itself to the Old Testament was produced by G. L. Bauer in 1796, with the subtitle, "A Summary of the Religious Concepts of the Hebrews." It was followed in the next sixty years by many other proposals of summary or synthesis.[8]

Soon after the middle of the nineteenth century, a change of enthusiasm occurred with a swing toward the history of Israel's religion. This increased interest in the history of Israelite religion resulted

8. See B. C. Ollenburger's essay, "From Timeless Ideas to the Essence of Religion," in *The Flowering of Old Testament Theology: A Reader in Twentieth-Century Old Testament Theology, 1930–1990*, ed. B. C. Ollenburger, E. A. Martens, and G. F. Hasel (Winona Lake, Ind.: Eisenbrauns, 1992), 3–19.

from aggressive archaeological activity in Mesopotamia, with such finds as ancient mythical stories of creation and the flood, and prophetlike activity at Mari on the Euphrates. Scholars, intrigued by the interrelationship between the religion of Israel and the religions of the surrounding regions, worked to give an account of Israel's religion, its phenomena, and its development. This surge of interest in Israel's religious story line (1870–1920) eclipsed the writing of Old Testament theologies. The few theologians who ventured to write felt it incumbent to preface their theologies with lengthy rehearsals of Israel's religion.[9]

But then a change set in. The pendulum swing was illustrated by a debate in the 1920s between two German OT scholars: O. Eissfeldt and W. Eichrodt. Eissfeldt's claim was that the history of religion was a scientific and objective study whose subject matter was knowledge. An Old Testament theology, more faith-oriented, was essentially subjective and, although necessary, could not be scientific. W. Eichrodt countered with the claim that biblical theology could employ the tools of historical investigation to arrive at the essence of Old Testament religion.[10] A large boost to the importance of theology came from Karl Barth in the 1920s. This European scholar, trained in questions of sources and history (knowledge), sounded a clarion call for the church to return to its witness (faith-based) about the transcendent God, the "Wholly Other." The times were changing; the gravitational pull began to come from theology.

The renaissance of biblical theology can be dated to the 1930s and particularly to W. Eichrodt's work, *Theology of the Old Testament*, later to be fueled by, among others, Gerhard von Rad.[11] By midcentury, an American, G. E. Wright, had produced a benchmark book in Old Testament theology.[12] By 1970 the golden age of biblical theology was losing its glow, or so thought B. S. Childs.[13] But Childs was mistaken; the 1970s saw the release of several notable Old Testament theologies in

9. For example, H. Schultz, *Old Testament Theology: The Religion of Revelation in Its Pre-Christian Stage of Development*, 2 vols. (Edinburgh: T. & T. Clark, 1892). The book was a translation from the second German edition of 1878.

10. For the two essays in English translation, together with an interpretive essay, see Ollenburger, Martens, and Hasel, *Flowering of Old Testament Theology*, 3–39.

11. W. Eichrodt, *Theology of the Old Testament*, trans. John A. Baker, 2 vols. (Philadelphia: Westminster; London: SCM, 1961, 1967). The German original appeared in three volumes between 1933 and 1939. G. von Rad, *Old Testament Theology*, trans. David M. G. Stalker, 2 vols. (New York: Harper & Row; Edinburgh: Oliver & Boyd, 1962, 1965).

12. G. E. Wright, *God Who Acts: Biblical Theology as Recital* (Naperville, Ill.: Allenson; London: SCM, 1952).

13. B. S. Childs, *Biblical Theology in Crisis* (Philadelphia; Westminster, 1970).

the English language.[14] The surge of scholarly activity slowed, however, toward the end of the century when ambiguity over matters of method and task became acute.[15]

Meanwhile, the dearth of books on the history of Israelite religion in the first half of the century had ended, as noted by P. D. Miller: "A perceptible shift began . . . in the 1960s, a revival of interest in the history of Israel's religion."[16] The translation of G. Fohrer's work in 1972[17] along with other works, notably the two-volume project of Rainer Albertz in the 1990s,[18] signaled an ascendancy of the discipline. The renewal was due, in part, to fresh archaeological finds, and also to a fresh agenda in biblical studies, marked by sociological and cultural concerns.[19] Among the advantages listed for the history of religion, largely over against biblical theology, Albertz cites the following: (1) religious statements are not separated from their historical background; (2) the discipline describes a dialogical process of struggle for theological clarification; (3) the continuity that history of religion sees is in the people of Israel itself, not in religious ideas appropriated by Christians; and (4) its comparative approach facilitates dialogue with other religions.[20]

In sum, the two hundred years of scholarly research are characterized by a seesaw relationship between the two disciplines. Much like the relationships between interest rates and the performance of the stock market, when one is up the other tends to be down. Twice in these two hundred years, Old Testament theology has enjoyed a sixty-year scholarly ascendancy (1797–1860; 1930–90). Once (1870–1920), and maybe for a second time (1990–), the history of religion has singularly captured the interest of biblical scholars.

14. For example, S. L. Terrien, *The Elusive Presence: Toward a New Biblical Theology* (San Francisco: Harper & Row, 1978); W. Zimmerli, *Old Testament Theology in Outline*, trans. D. E. Green (Atlanta: John Knox; Edinburgh: T. & T. Clark, 1978); R. E. Clements, *Old Testament Theology: A Fresh Approach* (Atlanta: John Knox, 1978); and W. C. Kaiser Jr., *Toward an Old Testament Theology* (Grand Rapids: Zondervan, 1978).

15. E. A. Martens, "The Flowering and Foundering of Old Testament Theology," *NIDOTTE* 1.172–84.

16. P. D. Miller, "Israelite Religion," in *The Hebrew Bible and Its Modern Interpreters*, ed. D. A. Knight and G. M. Tucker (Philadelphia: Fortress; Decatur, Ga.: Scholars, 1985), 201–37, at 204.

17. *History of Israelite Religion* (Nashville: Abingdon, 1972).

18. Rainer Albertz, *A History of Israelite Religion in the Old Testament Period*, trans. John Bowden, 2 vols. (Louisville: Westminster John Knox, 1994).

19. For example, N. Gottwald, *The Tribes of Yahweh: A Sociology of the Religion of Liberated Israel, 1250–1050 B.C.E.* (Maryknoll, N.Y.: Orbis, 1979); cf. Andrew J. Dearman, *Religion and Culture in Ancient Israel* (Peabody, Mass.: Hendrickson, 1992); J. Cheryl Exum and Stephen D. Moore, eds., *Biblical Studies/Cultural Studies: The Third Sheffield Colloquium*, JSOTSup 266 (Sheffield: JSOT, 1998).

20. Albertz, *History of Israelite Religion*, 1.16–17.

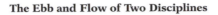

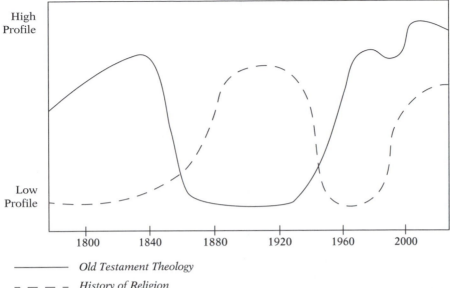

The Ebb and Flow of Two Disciplines

——————— *Old Testament Theology*

– – – – – *History of Religion*

Using the Tools

The tools described above—history of Israelite religion and Old Testament theology—come into play in the later stages of exegesis. Work on text transmission, word studies, and immediate context has been completed. The next move is from the cocoon of the text unit (even its immediate context) to the wider world of religious thought. This world of religious thought can be accessed, on the one hand, through books on the history of Israelite religion. The comparative method is helpful to compare early and late stages of a belief within Israel, Israelite belief and ancient Near Eastern religions, and—by extension—Israelite belief and world religions. Israel's religious thought can be accessed, on the other hand, through Old Testament theology, which provides systematic theological structures. Here the concern is not for what is, or what was, but for what should be under God. Scripture is not treated so much as a source document for Israel's history, but as a community's canon, or standard, that sets out God's will. Once the interpreter has a firm grip on what the text says in its own right, the interpreter lifts that text for inspection, so to speak, in the light of Israel's story (history of religion), and in the light of the full revelation of God (the Old and New Testaments as summarized in a biblical theology).

The interpreter has not finished the exegetical task until a particular text is "situated" historically and theologically. The principle of holistic interpretation is illustrated by looking at a carburetor and a food blender. Each can be examined in its own right. But they are not understood until their relative place in the whole—car or kitchen—is grasped. The principle of holistic interpretation will be illustrated by using our two tools in four genres: narrative (Genesis 3); legal material (Exodus 20); poetry (Psalm 8); and prophecy (Jeremiah 7).

The Interplay of Narrative, History of Religion, and Biblical Theology (Genesis 3)

For our purposes, we suppose that research on the text, the well-known story of "the fall," is complete. Now, either in preparation for an essay or a sermon, the larger question of significance becomes pressing.

Tracing the Story: History of Religion

To answer the question of significance, we begin with the history of religion. A check of the index in one of the texts on the history of religion puts us in touch with several topics, one of which is the tree of life. Another topic is immortality, a topic of importance for the Babylonians as shown in the Epic of Gilgamesh.[21] Still another topic is that of sin's origins—or, put another way, what went wrong?

Let us pursue the last question. In Israelite religion, the question of sin's origin is given one answer in Genesis 3. In the apocryphal books, but not elsewhere in the OT, reference is made to the Adam and Eve story. "O Adam, what have you done? Although you (alone) sinned, the fall was not yours alone, but ours too who descended from you" (2 Esdras 7:118). But elsewhere in the Pseudepigrapha, the explanation for "what went wrong" turns to Genesis 6, the cohabitation of the sons of God, called "watchers" or angels, with humans (1 Enoch). In this literature, responsibility for the perversion within the world is laid at the feet of angels from the heavenly realm.

Leaving Israel's religious history, we leapfrog to modern times to inquire about "what went wrong." Some African peoples, for example, have a story. There once was a golden age characterized by total harmony among all—gods, humans, animals, nature. God hovered nearby, just above the heads of the populace. In that culture it was the custom for women to pound manioc, a potatolike root, into flour by using a stick and a jar. Once in the distant past a woman used an inordinately long stick with which to pound. She did so with unusual vigor, poking

21. *ANET* 72–99.

the stick into God's heaven and disturbing him. God warned her repeatedly to stop. She refused. Then God went away and has never come back. Such stories point to the widespread acknowledgment that things are gravely out of joint. Such stories serve as conversational partners, help sharpen issues in interpretation, and give a cutting edge, a poignancy, to the Eden story.

Taking the Measure: Biblical Theology

If the first tool opens a range of interpretations, the second tool, Old Testament theology, takes the measure of these options by placing them, so to speak, on a theological scale. What are the theological issues this text raises? They include: God and testings, the relationship between sin and the environment, the origin of evil, human freedom, and the relationship between acts and consequences. To continue with the question of the origin of evil, within the canon are three "parallel" stories of what went wrong (Ezek. 28:1–10; 28:11–17; and Isa. 14:3–23). The closest parallel is Ezekiel 28:11–17, an oracle related to kingship myths of the ancient Near East. The motifs shared by Ezekiel 28:11–17 and Genesis 3 are readily listed: perfection, wisdom, beauty, Eden, garden, cherub, expulsion, and the notion of a fall (Ezek. 28:15–16). This parallel story can help answer a vexing question: "What really is the root of sin?" Genesis 3 indicates the answer might be "disobedience." According to the parallel accounts in Ezekiel, the answer seems to be "pride" (28:17; cf. 28:2). These parallel stories broaden the canonical definition of evil.

Another way of getting a handle on the topic of evil is to check a theological dictionary for its entry on *sin*.[22] The semantic field is large, but three of the most-used terms are *pesha*ᶜ, *ᶜawon*, and *ḥaṭa*ʾ. The first word, *pesha*ᶜ, has its secular home in the political sphere, describing a negative relationship between suzerain and vassal. *Pesha*ᶜ was once thought to mean "offense," in the sense of "outright rebellion," but it is now understood to mean any rift or breach within a relationship. Politically, disruption could be as extreme as an insurrection, but it could also be as subtle as the vassal secretly withholding what was due the suzerain. So the word *pesha*ᶜ may describe any relationship that is not in good repair, whether breached, fragmented, or tattered. Another term for sin is *ᶜawon* 'crookedness.' The imagery evoked is that of a straightedge placed alongside something that is curved, bent, or twisted. Perversity of whatever stripe fits into the cat-

22. For example, *NIDOTTE*. This dictionary, even though it discusses the Hebrew terms, is so well indexed that relevant articles are readily located without knowledge of Hebrew.

egory of *ʿawon*. The most frequent Hebrew term for sin is *haṭaʾ*, which means missing the mark. The everyday use of the word is instructive. A narrator reports that seven hundred left-handed stone slingers were excellent marksmen; they could aim at a hair and not miss (*haṭaʾ*) (Judg. 20:16). Religiously, the word describes behavior that is wide of the mark. The three major terms—*peshaʿ*, *ʿawon*, and *haṭaʾ*—frequently occur in clusters (Exod. 34:7; Lev. 16:21; Job 13:23; Ps. 32:5; Isa. 59:12).

None of these three words for sin, however, is employed in Genesis 3. Still, a profitable exercise is to overlay these three terms on the Eden story. Are all three appropriate in some way to describe what happened in Eden? How? Are some terms more adequate descriptors than others?

Granted, before us is a story, not an abstract essay on sin. The scriptural index in one of the books on Old Testament theology leads us to a summary of C. Westermann's theological analysis of sin. Westermann has not one story in view, but the four found in Genesis 1–11. Together they chronicle the corrosive nature of sin. Westermann summarizes the origin of evil as a break in the God-person relationship. He details the three stories after Genesis 3 as showing a break in other relationships: person-person; person-nature; and person-culture. But— and here is the gospel—while each infraction necessitates God's judgment, there is in each a word or action of grace. The chart serves as a pictorial interpretation of Genesis 1–11; a little reflection will then show what insights we can derive for Genesis 3.

A Theological Summary of Genesis 1–11

Incident	Nature of the sin	Divine threat	God's grace word
Adam and Eve (Genesis 3)	Against God	Death	A promise of offspring
Cain (Genesis 4)	Against man	Fugitive existence	A mark on Cain
Flood (Genesis 6–9)	Against natural order	Destruction	Deliverance of one family
Tower (Genesis 11)	Against culture	Dispersion	Election of Abraham

Source: Adapted from C. Westermann in Elmer A. Martens, *God's Design: Focus on Old Testament Theology*, 3d ed. (North Richland Hills, Tex.: Bibal, 1998), 27.

Interplay of Legal Texts, History of Religion, and Biblical Theology (Exodus 20)

The first five books of the OT canon are known as *torah*, a word whose root means "to teach." Terms such as ʿ*edoth* (decrees), *huqqim* (statutes), and *mishpatim* (ordinances), which are found in this literary bloc, point mostly to legal material. The mode is clearly didactic; the texts are intended to instruct. I select the Ten Commandments, identified in Scripture as "the Ten Words" (Deut. 4:13; 10:4), as candidates for our exegetical laboratory, in order to show how our two tools—history of religion and Old Testament theology—assist with interpretation.

In Search of Legal Codes: History of Religion

The "history of religion" tool allows us to trace the development of law codes, first in Israel, then in the ancient Near East, and, with a little stretching, to modern religions. The covenant code (Exod. 20:22–23:33) is said by some historians to precede the Ten Words, which some critical scholars date to the Deuteronomic reformers of the seventh century.[23] It is also claimed that, in the seventh century, reconstructionist historians assembled the Deuteronomic Code (Deuteronomy 12–26; 28). The cultic decalogue (Exod. 34:10–26) and the Holiness Code (Leviticus 17–26), both with their priestly concerns, are dated by critical scholars to the sixth century.[24] Other scholars who champion Moses as the author/editor of the Torah date all of these codes to his time (fifteenth or thirteenth century B.C.E.) or earlier.

More to the point may be the observation that, in the Book of Deuteronomy, both the Ten Words and the covenant code receive amplification. That is, a later generation, as represented in Deuteronomy, built upon an earlier code. W. Kaiser, drawing on Stephen A. Kaufman's work, charts the way in which the Ten Words receive legal commentary and expansion in Deuteronomy.[25] Dale Patrick has charted the passages in Deuteronomy that expand on the covenant code.[26] Moreover, echoes of the Ten Words appear in the works of the prophets more than five centuries after Moses. Hosea's indictment of the people—their swearing, lying, murder, stealing, and adultery—is made against the background of the Ten Words (4:1–3). Similarly, an echo of the Ten Words may be heard in Jeremiah's temple sermon, when he

23. Albertz, *History of Israelite Religion*, 1.205.
24. Fohrer, *History of Israelite Religion*, 314.
25. Walter C. Kaiser Jr., *Toward Old Testament Ethics* (Grand Rapids: Zondervan, 1983), 27–137.
26. Dale Patrick, *Old Testament Law* (Atlanta: John Knox, 1984), 97.

asks rhetorically: "Will you steal, murder, commit adultery, swear falsely . . . and then come and stand before me in this house . . . ? (Jer. 7:9–10; cf. Ps. 50:18–20). One perspective on the prophets is to see them working from the baseline of the covenant, including the Ten Words. In postexilic Israel, Torah comes to be identified with wisdom (Ecclus. 19:20; 24:23).

Turning to examine law codes in the ANE, we note that the law code of Hammurabi (eighteenth century) from Babylon antedates the Mosaic law code by several centuries. As with the Ten Words, there is a prologue given by Hammurabi, in which he cites a mandate from the gods Anum and Enlil, charging him to "promote the welfare of the people . . . cause justice to prevail in the land, and to destroy the wicked and the evil."[27] Comparing the two law codes highlights several significant differences, one of which has to do with motivations. For example, the second commandment prohibiting images of deities and the third about taking the Lord's name in vain are reinforced by the exhortation that God both punishes and rewards. In the ANE there are also "motive clauses," but none that refers to history or the will and promise of the deity. A major benefit of even cursory comparisons is noting what is distinctive, and therefore possibly significant, in the biblical account.

The inquiry could profitably be extended to modern religions. To the extent that the Ten Words embody an ethical code, this question is pertinent: what is the ethical content of Hinduism, Buddhism, or Islam? In what way, if at all, are the ethical requirements of those systems related to the Ultimate? For preachers especially, the usefulness of books summarizing modern faith systems other than Christianity is obvious.

Finding a Place to Stand: Old Testament Theology

Roaming within Israel's history and in the larger religious environment is an adventuresome process of gathering ideas. But how are we to pin down matters theologically as we make interpretive decisions? By asking three questions: (1) What theological questions does the text raise? (2) With what major theological realities does the text connect? and (3) How does the major topic of the text fit within a system of biblical theology?

So what theological questions does Exodus 20:1–21 raise? A crucial theological question centers on how this passage illumines God. For an answer we might note the significance of God's self-introduction: God is Israel's personal god and is characterized by completing a giant act of salvation (20:2). If this introduction paints a worship-friendly God,

27. *ANET* 164.

the closing lines of the text depict a deity of whom Israel was afraid (20:18–21). They were so afraid that they did not wish to continue the exercise, but pled with Moses to be a mediator. To this paradox about God—invitation to intimacy countered by a repelling awesomeness—can be added an observation about the details of the "laws." These laws, mostly in the negative, present a God who will not leave people ignorant. God is not a God of caprice—a point stressed by W. Eichrodt. One need not guess in what this God desires or delights. God offers to be known.

Our second question is, With what other theological topics does this text connect? Drawn from our wider theological knowledge, answers include creation, redemption (see preceding paragraph), covenant, community, justice. I focus briefly on covenant. Research into treaties of the ancient Near Eastern empires has shown how the requirements (stipulations) fit within the whole of the treaty. Stipulations were preceded by a historical prologue (as in the Ten Words; cf. Exod. 20:2) reviewing and updating the relationship between treaty maker and treaty recipient. The "legal" parts that followed did not so much establish a relationship as define the relationship. The stipulations specify what is entailed in maintaining (not establishing) a relationship. The prologue section of the treaty or covenant must be given full weight (Exod. 20:1–2). A God who has delivered a people addresses Israel. There is wisdom, therefore, in the statement: "To preach the ten commandments will require eleven sermons." An initial sermon devoted to the topic of covenant should set the stage. Unless the Ten Words are contextualized theologically within covenant, interpretation of them is likely to be skewed.

The third question is more expansive still. How does the theological subject matter of the text fit in the theological structure of the Old Testament? The interpreter may have developed his or her own theological grid and would answer accordingly. Even so, a look at the indices or sometimes at the table of contents of one or two texts on Old Testament theology leads soon to sections in which this question is vigorously and variously discussed. From the shelf I pull the volume by B. S. Childs and peruse chapters with the headings "Mosaic Traditions" (a subtopic of which is "Sinai, Law, and Covenant") and "Law and Gospel."[28] Granted that a good part of his discussion is occupied with the history-of-religion agenda, important theological perspectives about law are emphasized. The law is a means of life, and in that the psalmist rejoices (Ps. 119:77). Its life-giving function is reiterated by Ezekiel (chap. 18), by Jesus (Luke 10:25–28), as well as by Paul (Rom. 9:30–10:5). The law

28. Childs, *Biblical Theology of the Old and New Testaments*, 131–38; 532–65.

is a gift for a people's good (Rom. 7:7; 9:4). At the same time, there is an ominous side to the law. At Sinai, the people tremble (Exod. 20:18–21). Certain laws are there to "horrify Israel" (Ezek. 20:25–26), for broken laws pose a threat (Ps. 50:16–23). Fundamentally the law is an expression of the divine will. "The giving of the law was . . . a gracious gift for constituting her [Israel's] identity.[29] The promise and threat connected with the law may be difficult to sort out, but the imperative for obedience is basic. Even these few observations bring to Exodus 20 the beginning of a larger frame of theological reference. Like the frame for a work of art, if rightly chosen, greatly enhances the picture, the theological frame lends distinctiveness and power to the text.

The Interplay of Poetry, History of Religion, and Biblical Theology (Psalm 8)

In bringing Psalm 8, an exhibit from Hebrew poetry, into discussion, we reiterate the assumption that close-up work on the text has been done. The interpreter steps back, figuratively speaking, and asks, What is the significance of this text? Help can come through a diachronic survey, found in texts on the history of religion that outline ideas and religious patterns. Help can also come from theological reflection, and specifically from scholars (biblical theologians) who sort out where the weight of Scripture lies on the issue. We will discover that a minimum of help in this case comes from the history of religion, while biblical theology yields large insights.

Scanning the History of Religion(s) to Discern Form and Content

The use of the first tool—history of religion—comes into play at several points: in discerning the form and content of the text, and in understanding a component (the expression "Son of Man"). The literary form of Psalm 8 is that of hymn. An early biblical song has hymnic elements (Exodus 15), and, outside the Psalms, hymns and hymn fragments appear in the Book of Isaiah (e.g., Isaiah 12; 42:10–13) and in Amos (4:13; 9:5). The reason for praise in Exodus 15 and Isaiah 12 is Yahweh's intervention in history; the Amos fragments highlight creation. Psalm 8, while making a reference to created things, has a different emphasis.

The focus of the psalm is how to think of humans, especially in light of the vastness of the cosmos. The answer includes echoes of the creation account in Genesis, if not in vocabulary then surely in content. God has created the human species (Ps. 8:6 MT [5]; Gen. 1:27) and given

29. Ibid., 536.

it rule over other creatures (Ps. 8:7–9 MT [6–8]; Gen. 1:28). In the Bible, there is no sustained treatment of this philosophical question of creature and cosmos, but snatches in Israelite documents raise the question. In places, the question lurks in the background (cf. Ps. 144:3–4) and receives a very different answer than in Psalm 8 (see Job 7:17–18).

Moving to the expression "Son of Man," a history of Israelite religion calls attention to its use in Ezekiel, in which it refers to an earthling (3:1); to its occurrence in Daniel, in which it describes a heavenly figure (7:13); to the intertestamental material, in which an eschatological figure by this name is quite prominent (e.g., 1 Enoch 48:4); and to the NT, in which Jesus applies the title to himself (Mark 10:45). Wrapped around each reference are complex issues, which, depending on the interest of the interpreter, can be pursued.

When we move from Israel's history to world religions, and pose the question of how to think of humans, we hear a cacophony of answers. In Hinduism, the human person is caught in a cycle of reincarnations, although the possibility exists to be freed of the cycle and to be absorbed into the impersonal Brahman.[30] Written over human beings is the word *meaninglessness*. Jean-Paul Sartre, the twentieth-century existentialist, echoes that Hindu sentiment when he announces, "Man is the incommensurable idiot of the universe." Buddhists characterize humans as caught in the web of suffering, a condition that results from endless desires. Written over the individual is the word *pain*. Marxists reach to the economic context to describe humans. For Marxists, written over the individual is the word *struggle*.

The immediate value, for the interpreter of Psalm 8, of this hasty visit to other faiths is the confrontation with the singular answer the text gives. How different is the Bible's view on what it means to be human! Human beings are persons of dignity and responsibility. The psalm can celebrate the "glory" of being human; other religions tend, by comparison, to engender pessimism, even disparagement.

Focusing on Biblical Theology and Ideas of the Human

Such mixed signals send us to biblical theology to arrive at a more fixed idea. Theological reflection proceeds by asking questions and reaching for answers, as the Psalm itself wonderfully illustrates. One of the theological questions the psalm raises is, Why is God so interested in human beings? The psalm itself sharpens the question, given that the cosmos is God's domain. Wherein lies the glory of human beings? Some initial clues are in the text and in humans' position vis-à-vis God

30. David W. Shenk, *Global Gods: Exploring the Role of Religions in Modern Societies* (Scottdale, Pa.: Herald, 1995), 108, 113.

194 Interpreting the Old Testament

and nature. How is the glory of humans (Ps. 8:6 [5]) related to God's glory (Ps. 8:2–3 [1–2]? If persons are rulers—kings of sorts—what does that say about humans and God?

Or we may ask a question of theological systematization: in what category is the question about humans answered? Some would answer that the category is peculiarly Hebraic rather than Greek. To ask the question, "What are human beings?" could be understood as asking for *essence*. The Greeks, Aristotle in particular, stressed that definitions provide terms for a "thing" in its makeup, or essence. Attention was given to the properties that a "thing" had. Hence a table was wooden, hard, brown, round. But another way of getting at the definition is to ask, not for a "thing's" essence, or its properties, but for its function, or role. The question, What is a table? can be answered in terms of its function—a table is a raised platform on which smaller items can be placed. When the poet asks, "What are humans?" the answer does not form along the lines of essence, that is, along the lines of body, soul, and spirit. The answer comes in terms of relationships or functions. Humans are characterized by their mandate to rule over nature. They do so because, as creatures just below God in the hierarchy of things, they partake of God's mandate, which is to govern.

Another type of reflection involves asking about perspective. What else, other than dignity and a position of privilege, does the Bible assert about human beings? The question calls for an answer as broad-based as the canon itself. Included would be the distinction that the Bible observes throughout, namely that humans are not to be equated with deity (as in New Age thought), and that, for all their pristine dignity, humans are, since Eden, encumbered with sin. Both realities must be asserted: humans are made in the image of God and have an aura of glory; human beings are enmeshed in sin and bedraggled with shame. Although these two views are in tension, the word about human dignity is the first word. The Book of Hebrews, citing this text in reference to Jesus, will not let us forget that he embodied the Ideal, and that through his salvation he will one day bring that potential dignity to a glorious realization (Heb. 2:5–9). We know both the first and the last word about human beings: glory and dignity. By now the person preparing an exegetical paper or readying a sermon must make some choices from the overabundance of material.

The Interplay of Prophecy, History of Religion, and Biblical Theology (Jeremiah 7)

The Former Prophets (Joshua, Judges, Samuel, and Kings) along with the Latter Prophets (Isaiah, Jeremiah, Ezekiel, and the Twelve) constitute a large percentage of the Old Testament. After doing the basic research, the careful exegete will not rest until exploring larger questions raised about religion and theology.

To illustrate, we select Jeremiah's famous temple sermon, which contained two major warnings: (1) a warning not to be deceived by clichés about the temple, and (2) a warning about bad behavior. The sermon concluded with a historical reference to Shiloh and a threat of God's punitive action (Jer. 7:1–15). The sermon was so incendiary that Jeremiah's lynching was barely averted (see the parallel text in Jer. 26:1–24).

Learning about Worship Structures from the History of Religion

What does the history of religion contribute to this text? It contributes much data, but we limit ourselves to the sermon's reference to the temple: "Do not trust in these deceptive words: 'This is the temple of the Lord, the temple of the Lord, the temple of the Lord'" (7:4). Research on the temple, most readily available in a Bible dictionary, offers data about worship structures:

- the portable shrine, called a *tabernacle*, was in use at the time of Israel's wilderness wanderings (c. fifteenth or thirteenth century B.C.E.)
- the cult center at Shiloh flourished during the period of the judges, 1200–1000 B.C.E.
- the Solomonic temple (c. 950–587 B.C.E.) was the subject of Jeremiah's remark
- the temple, rebuilt following the exile (and completed in 516 B.C.E.), was expanded under Herod; it was destroyed by the Romans in 70 C.E.

The history of religion also chronicles the ideology associated with worship structures. One of these beliefs is that the deity resided in or was present in some way at the worship place. One of the names for the tabernacle, the portable shrine, is *mishkan*, from the root meaning "to tent, to dwell." David, who made arrangements for building the Jerusalem temple, argued that a house was appropriate for Yahweh (2 Samuel 7). The psalmist also holds to this ideology: "For the LORD has chosen Zion; he has desired it for his habitation: 'This is my resting place forever; here I will reside, for I have desired it'" (Ps. 132:13–14). Ezekiel describes his vision of a temple, concluding the report with the telling name, *Yahweh Shammah* ("Yahweh is there [present]") (Ezek. 48:35). Isaiah had earlier reached for this understanding of the temple in reassuring Hezekiah of safety at a time (701 B.C.E.) when Assyria threatened (Isa. 37:30–35 = 2 Kings 19:29–34).

Peoples surrounding Israel had a similar ideology about worship structures. The Bible itself gives one scenario. During Samuel's time, the Israelite ark, itself a symbol of God's presence, was captured and brought by the Philistines in Ashdod to "the house of Dagon." Dagon was a god of grain worshiped by the coastal people, the Philistines, who had constructed a building for their deity (1 Sam. 5:1–5). In Babylon, the ziggurat temple was the home of the god Marduk.

Such an understanding of the deity inhabiting a temple or shrine continues into modern times. In the Hindu religion, the shrines dotting the Indian landscape are stopping places for worshipers.[31] At the larger shrines along the roadside, an attendant or priest may be present. One priest explained that he "was taking care of his god." Before they begin worship at the shrine, Buddhists ring a bell to wake their god.

Checking Theological Coordinates to Understand Worship

The ideologies summarized above might be described, from another vantage point, as "theologies." Using biblical theology, we are prepared to establish some of the theological ideas behind worship. A good place to begin is to ask about pre-understandings. "What is problematic with the people's chant in Jeremiah 7:4, since the ideology of a present deity is affirmed in other Scriptures?" For an answer we look to other theological assertions about temples. Using word studies, we discover that while the tabernacle was called *mishkan* ("to dwell"), it was also called *miqdash* ("sanctuary," from the root *qds'* "to be holy"), a point echoed in Isaiah's experience at the temple (Isaiah 6). Moreover, worship, as insisted throughout Scripture, was premised on the interior purity and righteousness of the worshipers (Isa. 1:10–17; Ps. 24:3–4; Jer. 7:8–11; cf. John 2:13–17).

In a strikingly graphic vision, Ezekiel made clear that God could and would take leave of God's temple because of sin (i.e., idolatries) (Ezekiel 8–11). Invoking temple imagery, Paul admonishes Christians about moral purity (1 Cor. 6:15–19). Jeremiah, by referring to Shiloh, a worship center destroyed four hundred years earlier (1 Samuel 4), has history on his side when he insists that the existence of a temple is not a guarantee of a deity's presence. So, yes, a temple may bespeak the presence of the deity, but it does not guarantee it. The irony in the Jeremiah text is that the temple, which was to assist in giving access to

31. Paul Hiebert, *Konduru: Structure and Integration in a South India Village* (Minneapolis: University of Minnesota Press, 1971), 131.

God, had become, because of concentration on means rather than ends, a huge obstruction in connecting with God.

Again, theological statements appear contradictory. God dwells in the temple, but God dwells with the contrite (Isa. 57:15). The latter part of Isaiah, as some scholars have argued, represents stormy debates between those keen on continuing construction of the temple after the exile and those who took a more "spiritual" view. These scholars point to the assertion, "Heaven is my throne and the earth is my footstool; what is the house that you would build?" (Isa. 66:1), as illustrative of an argument from those opposed to building. So the answer to whether God "dwells" in the temple must be answered by, "Yes, possibly, but not only."

A related question is, How could the theology of God's presence at the temple, invoked by Isaiah as reason for reassurance, be disqualified 150 years later? The theology, espoused by Isaiah at the time of the Assyrian threat (Isa. 37:30–35), allowed people a place to cling when threatened 150 years later by a Babylonian invasion. Jeremiah audaciously rules such reasoning fallacious! Does this mean that a theology, once valid, can later become invalid? The surprising answer is yes. But the yes needs explanation, both from a full-sized temple theology of divine presence and an insistence that moral considerations must be taken into account.

We could ask a more general question: what *is* the full teaching about worship structures in both testaments? The interpreter now begins a time-consuming task and may look for shortcuts. Fortunately, shortcuts are available. The indices of a text on Old Testament or New Testament theology will help navigate this subject, as will articles in theological dictionaries. The larger theological assessment of the temple would entail other factors, among them that the temple indicates people's priorities, as Haggai argued (1:7–11); that it can represent a witness to Yahweh (Ezek. 37:26–28); and that it serves as a symbol for understanding the NT people of God (1 Cor. 3:16; Eph. 2:19–22). Not all of this more expansive temple theology bears directly on the exegesis of Jeremiah 7, but it does bear on the larger question about the meaning of religious structures. The great benefit of this exercise is to appreciate the individual text (here Jeremiah 7) within the theological context of the Bible.

These comments about the history of religion and theology give "bite" to the Jeremiah passage. One can almost hear behind Jeremiah's words the implied accusation that God's people have an understanding about temple that differs little, if at all, from that of pagan peoples. Moreover, Jeremiah is saying in essence that the theology operative in one situation (e.g., at the time of Isaiah) is not necessarily valid at a later time. Jeremiah warns that aids to worship can themselves become objects of undue veneration.

Acquiring the Tools

Where does one find information about the history of Israelite religion? The Bible is one source. Access to topics is given in concordances and/or in computer software. Information from concordances, along with other information, is brought together in Bible dictionaries (e.g., *The Illustrated Bible Dictionary*; *Anchor Bible Dictionary*). Most helpful are monographs on the history of Israelite religion dealing with such topics as kingship, sacrifice, and temple. Often these histories are written by critical scholars who follow a reconstructed chronology. Their revisionist positions are usually not compatible with evangelical persuasions, especially for Israel's earlier history; still, these histories of religion are important as source material. An already near-classic work is Rainer Albertz's two-volume *History of Israelite Religion in the Old Testament Period*. An older work, also in the critical reconstructionist mode, is G. Fohrer's, *History of Israelite Religion*. (For details, see notes 17 and 18 above.)

Histories of Israel usually deal with the political story of God's people, but they will sometimes address changes in religious ideology and practice. Again, given the variety of theories of chronology, along with a variety of target audiences, the resources are extensive, and the choice depends on the student's interests and competence.

For Old Testament theology, the exegete brings an important inbuilt component: the ability to reflect. Theology calls for a configuration of the data along the axis of meaning. The greater the mastery of the data, and the more astute the researcher in methodology, the more likely that the interpreter will generate helpful and accurate theological syntheses. Basic to this inductive process is asking questions. With experience comes the ability to ask significant and probing questions.

Learning to ask appropriate questions is facilitated by acquaintance with the scholarly works on Old Testament theology. These are numerous.[32] The classic volumes for the twentieth century are those by W. Eichrodt, *Theology of the Old Testament*, and G. von Rad, *Old Testament Theology*. Novices in the field will benefit from two works that established themselves in conservative circles in the last half of the twentieth century: W. C. Kaiser's *Toward an Old Testament Theology* and E. A. Martens's *God's Design*.[33] To these two is now to be added the work by

32. See resources in Martens, *Old Testament Theology* (cited in n. 6 above).
33. For Kaiser, see n. 5 above; E. A. Martens, *God's Design: A Focus on Old Testament Theology*, 3d ed. (North Richland Hills, Tex.: Bibal, 1998).

Paul House, *Old Testament Theology*, which, since it is organized according to Bible books, should be especially beneficial to the exegete.[34] Two other works, since they cover such a wide range of topics, can serve well: B. S. Childs, *Biblical Theology of the Old and New Testaments: Theological Reflection on the Christian Bible*, which is valuable because it includes a discussion of New Testament theology, and W. Brueggemann, *Theology of the Old Testament: Testimony, Dispute, Advocacy*.[35] Books on biblical theology should be read on a regular basis, or even skimmed, by anyone working with the biblical text. The preacher especially has reason to heed this advice so that the sermon will not advocate a truncated or misleading interpretation.

Both the history of Israelite religion and Old Testament theology are indispensable tools for the scholar and the preacher as they engage an isolated biblical text. Both open a wider world of concepts and ideas and, thus, not only help nuance the interpretation of a text, but also illuminate its current relevance.

34. Paul House, *Old Testament Theology* (Downers Grove, Ill.: InterVarsity, 1998).

35. For Childs, see n. 5 above; W. Brueggemann, *Theology of the Old Testament: Testimony, Dispute, Advocacy* (Minneapolis: Fortress, 1997).

seven

Ancient Near Eastern Studies

Richard S. Hess

Some years ago I presented a paper at a scholarly society that reviewed the history of the application of ancient Near Eastern studies to the interpretation of Genesis 1–11.[1] At the end of the presentation, a prominent Old Testament scholar asked, "Has anything been gained in our understanding of Genesis 1–11 by the study of the ancient Near Eastern context?" It is the purpose of this essay to argue that yes, there is benefit in such study, not only for Genesis 1–11 but also for the entire Old Testament.

The discipline of ancient Near Eastern studies and its application to the Bible is one area of exegesis that is either completely avoided by the interpreter or sometimes embraced with a great passion that leaves the class/congregation of the teacher/pastor bewildered as to its significance for their own lives. Nevertheless, there are few areas more significant for a proper interpretation of the biblical text than the ancient Near East. From the earliest application of the historical-grammatical

1. Subsequently this essay was published as "One Hundred Fifty Years of Comparative Studies on Genesis 1–11: An Overview," in *"I Studied Inscriptions from before the Flood": Ancient Near Eastern, Literary, and Linguistic Approaches to Genesis 1–11*, ed. R. S. Hess and D. T. Tsumura, Sources for Biblical and Theological Study 4 (Winona Lake, Ind.: Eisenbrauns, 1994), 3–26.

hermeneutic, the cultural context in which the Bible was written has remained an essential and substantive part of understanding the meaning and significance of the text. Although this area often appears limited to the horizon of ancient culture, with little of value for the modern age, its importance for understanding the original context is key in order to avoid misinterpreting and misapplying the message of the text today.

Principles of Interpretation

The subject is as vast as the scope of cultures. It encompasses the realms of geography, archaeology, linguistics, literary study, history, art, architecture, religion, and others. It is therefore difficult to posit a methodology for the comparative process. Most important is to become as familiar as possible with both the ancient Near Eastern material and the biblical text. When a comparison or contrast is made, its significance can be determined by the degree to which it is unique or, in the opposite direction, common throughout the ancient world. In order to provide perspective, it is appropriate to consider the surrounding cultures of Iran, Mesopotamia, Anatolia, Syria and Canaan, and Egypt, and then to focus on aspects of Israel itself. I will attempt to identify major tools and resources as well as to provide examples to guide use of the comparative method. This study will limit itself to works in English. It will exclude consideration of Israelite and Judean history, culture, and archaeology, which are discussed elsewhere in this volume.

Method is difficult to define for so wide an area as the ancient Near East. One of the most important observations, however, is to understand the people who received the revelation of God as very much part of the ancient world. In many ways, understanding aspects of culture in the ancient Near East can help the modern reader appreciate the way in which the "gospel" message of God's love for Israel was communicated. A few examples are noted briefly. Stories of a universal flood are found in both Mesopotamia and in the Bible (Genesis 6–9). These stories possess too many similarities to be coincidence. The details match and suggest that there is a relationship. However, that relationship is not necessarily one in which there was direct borrowing from one culture to another. Instead, it may imply a common origin for the stories. However, the biblical version advances beyond that of the Mesopotamian version insofar as it understands a single God who brings judgment on the world due to sin. In the Mesopotamian accounts, the flood is a form of population control or a means to silence the noise that humanity creates. Thus the Bible makes use of the flood account to explain the terrible effects of sin, the holiness of God, and the principle of divine judgment and grace in the salvation of Noah and his family.

Another example is the way in which the covenant form defines God's relationship to Israel in texts such as Deuteronomy and Joshua 24. This covenant form is identical to the treaty structure found in ancient Near Eastern treaties of the second millennium B.C.E. Both contain specific elements in a consistent order: prologue, historical review, stipulations, curses and blessings, and witnesses. These elements appear in the Hittite treaties of the second millennium B.C.E., in which each serves a specific purpose. Thus, the historical review describes the faithfulness of the overlord to the vassal. This parallels much of Deuteronomy 1–4, which describes God's presence with Israel in the wilderness and God's faithfulness toward them despite their rebellions. The purpose is the same—to motivate Israel as the vassal to obey the covenant given by its overlord, God. Thus the Bible takes over the treaty form and transforms it for its own purposes. This is an example of the use of contemporary media and their transformation to describe the ways of God with Israel.

Another example is the temple of Solomon. This temple has parallels in form and structure with North Syrian models of the same time. Indeed, even the building description has similarities with contemporary descriptions of Assyrian temple constructions. Here again the faith of Israel has transformed a form for its people. Given the association of such temple structures with the worship of deities, it is not surprising that God should use the same form to communicate to Israel the importance of worship. Of course there are distinctives, such as the absence of images and the focus of worship on a single deity. Both the distinctives and the similarities teach the people and provide us with valuable insights as to how God chose to communicate.

Many types of literature in the Old Testament have similarities with ancient Near Eastern literature. These include history, prophecy, poetry, and wisdom literature. For example, poetry in the Bible resembles that found at the thirteenth-century B.C.E. city of Ugarit, on the northern borders of Canaan. The poetical texts from Ugarit provide numerous similarities of structure and form in parallelisms, chiasms, word pairs, phrases, and whole structures. Psalm 29 is renowned as an example in which parallel expressions of praise to God can be found at Ugarit as praise to Baal. Here again the transformation of the poetry has taken place. The "modern music" of ancient Israel's day, with its lyrics, is brought into the service of the one true God in forms of praise and worship that remain to this day.

This brief survey of examples reflects ways in which an understanding of ancient Near Eastern culture can enrich and deepen the Bible reader's understanding and appreciation of the Old Testament. The ancient Near East does not prove the Bible's truth so much as it illuminates its message. Therefore, the use of this field as a means to better understand the Bible is important.

Most useful principles of interpretation reflect common sense. For example, one of the most important points when comparing the ancient Near East and the Bible is to be certain that there is something to compare.[2] In the mid-1970s, the discovery of an archive from third-millennium B.C.E. Ebla at Tell Mardikh excited great interest that this would shed light on the patriarchal period of the Bible. Then came the report that the names of the cities mentioned in Genesis 14 had been identified on a cuneiform tablet from that site. At last, proof of the Genesis account had been found, or so people thought. However, it gradually became clear that this report did not correlate with any cuneiform text, and the story was discredited. This is one famous example of problems with sources. It is essential to have access to the sources themselves or to reliable editions and publications of the same. Amazingly, this report continues to circulate more than two decades after it was dismissed. Despite the absence of published textual evidence, it continues to be cited as evidence for the accuracy of the Bible![3] This demonstrates the danger of accepting sensational revelations without checking the primary sources. A major purpose of the "General Resources" and "Area Resources" sections below is to provide a list of reliable resources for busy pastors and teachers who wish to learn about the subject, but who cannot take the time to learn the languages and to gain the archaeological training necessary to discern the true and the false for themselves.

This leads to a second principle—that it is important to be trained in the disciplines of the ancient Near East before using them for comparative purposes. Sometimes helpful presentations in secondary literature allow the interested reader to understand the materials discussed, but it is always important to have as thorough a background as possible in order to understand the context in which the discoveries are presented. Broader knowledge also allows for more control of the views

2. Simon B. Parker, *Stories in Scripture and Inscriptions: Comparative Studies on Narratives in Northwest Semitic Inscriptions and the Hebrew Bible* (Oxford: Oxford University Press, 1997), 6: "The less like the things being compared, the less valuable the comparison."

3. B. Wood, "Have Sodom and Gomorrah Been Found?" *Artifax: An Evangelical Quarterly of Biblical Archaeology* 13, no. 1 (winter 1999): 19.

and opinions of others. William Dever, a leader in the field of Syro-Palestinian archaeology, said that archaeology had "disproved" the Bible;
he used as his example the absence of evidence for occupation at Tell
Dhiban, east of the Dead Sea, during the period when, according to the
Book of Numbers, Israel would have been in this region. However,
while the Jordanian archaeological studies have not identified occupation at the site during the wilderness wandering, it remains a fact that
a contemporary itinerary of Ramesses II mentions this site (*tbn*) in a
list of place-names east of the Jordan River and in this region. Thus two
independent pieces of textual evidence, the Bible and a Ramesside
itinerary, attest to the existence of Dibon late in the second millennium B.C.E. The argument should therefore be reversed. It is not that
archaeology disproves the Bible in this case. Instead, the Bible and
other epigraphic evidence call into question the conclusions of Near
Eastern archaeology.[4] A broader knowledge of the evidence from the
ancient Near East, both material and epigraphic, can prevent erroneous conclusions.

A third principle of method in the study of the ancient Near East is
to use comparisons appropriate to the type of material being studied.
This is essential for an appropriate analysis. The Babel-and-Bible controversy of the late nineteenth and early twentieth centuries provides
an example in which the creation and flood myths from Babylon were
understood as sources for the accounts of Genesis 1–9. Behind this interpretation lay the assumption that the Babylonian culture was superior to that of ancient Israel, and, therefore, that the myths of Mesopotamia must have had logical priority to the texts of Genesis. The fallacy
was recognized, and common elements in the two accounts were attributed to common sources rather than to the priority of one culture
over another.[5]

Another example can be found in the discussion of *ṣelem* and *dĕmût*,
the two words often translated as "image" and "likeness" in the account
of humanity's creation in God's image (Gen. 1:26–28). The use of two
words, rather than one, led to speculation that they refer to two different
aspects of creation or even to two different editions of the same biblical

4. R. S. Hess, "Fallacies in the Study of Early Israel: An Onomastic Perspective," *Tyndale Bulletin* 45 (1994): 342–45; W. G. Dever, "How to Tell a Canaanite from an Israelite,"
in *The Rise of Ancient Israel: Symposium at the Smithsonian Institution, October 26, 1991,*
ed. H. Shanks et al. (Washington, D.C.: Biblical Archaeology Society, 1992), 32; K. A.
Kitchen, "The Egyptian Evidence on Ancient Jordan," in *Early Edom and Moab: The Beginning of the Iron Age in Southern Jordan,* ed. P. Bienkowski, Sheffield Archaeological
Monographs 7 (Sheffield: J. R. Collis, 1992), 27–29.
5. See the discussion of the flood stories in the second paragraph of "Principles of Interpretation" above. See also Hess, "One Hundred Fifty Years," pp. 6–11.

text.[6] This latter theory hypothesizes the division of the Pentateuch into several documents (or editions, according to some) written over several centuries. Thus one word was added to clarify the forgotten meaning of the other. Glosses of this sort exist in the ancient world, and there are many examples in the fourteenth-century B.C.E. Amarna correspondence originating from Palestine. However, the glosses that occur in the Amarna correspondence are added immediately after the word being defined, not in a separate parallel phrase as in Genesis 1. Thus the only basis for this sort of literary analysis was the speculation of the modern scholars who worked on this text. However, the 1979 discovery of a ninth-century B.C.E. Aramaic and Akkadian bilingual inscription from the Assyrian province of Gozan provided a stronger argument against separating *ṣelem* and *dĕmût* and assigning them to two different authors or editors. The Aramaic text describes the statue on which it is written by both cognate terms, *ṣlm* and *dmwt*. Further, these two terms are translated by the same word sign (NU) in the Akkadian text. Thus the words, *ṣelem* and *dĕmût*, were synonymous and contemporary in the West Semitic world of ancient Israel. Their appearance together in Genesis 1:26–28 creates a literary effect, reinforcing the point of the divine "image," by repeating the idea.[7] The problem with the passage has been a textual analysis that does not appreciate the literary nature of the texts and their ancient Near Eastern context.

Finally, some scholars have argued that the genealogies of Genesis 4 and 5, those of Cain and Seth, derive from the same genealogy because both preserve similar-sounding names. One scholar compared ancient Near Eastern king lists and observed similar names and a common origin for the king list of Hammurabi and that of Assyria.[8] However, it has been noted that other closely related ancient Near Eastern lists, genealogies of the *apkallu* (cultural heroes) and Sumerian king lists, also preserve similar-sounding names, but derive from separate origins. Therefore, the common origin of the genealogies of Genesis 4 and 5 from one list is not proven.[9] Indeed, the assumption that king lists can be compared with biblical genealogies must be treated with caution. The form and purpose of the king lists does not assume origins in a single family,

---

6. For example, James Barr, "The Image of God in the Book of Genesis—A Study of Terminology," *Bulletin of the John Rylands Library* 51 (1968–69): 11–26, esp. 24–25; John F. A. Sawyer, "The Meaning of בְּצֶלֶם אֱלֹהִים ('In the Image of God') in Genesis I–XI," *Journal of Theological Studies* 25 (1974): 418–26.

7. R. S. Hess, "Eden—A Well-Watered Place," *Bible Review* 7 (December 1991): 28–33.

8. J. M. Miller, "The Descendants of Cain: Notes on Genesis 4," *Zeitschrift für die alttestamentliche Wissenschaft* 86 (1974): 164–74.

9. J. J. Finkelstein, "The Antediluvian Kings: A University of California Tablet," *Journal of Cuneiform Studies* 17 (1963): 50 n. 41.

but instead serves to legitimate the monarch reigning at the time of composition. The form and purpose of the genealogies of Genesis 1–11 have no explicit relationship with kings, but are concerned with a single family.[10] In this case, the comparative enterprise must be handled with care.

The use one makes of the resources of the ancient Near East in interpreting the Old Testament often says more about one's presuppositions than about the data. This is unfortunate, because there is much of value to be gained from studying this material. As a final example, consider an archive such as that found at the site of Alalakh in northern Syria (modern Turkey). In fact, there were two main archives, one dating from around the eighteenth century B.C.E. and the other dating from three or four centuries later. When the texts in the archive were studied, they revealed many possible points of illumination for the student of the Bible. Parallels were found to Solomon's gift of towns to Hiram (1 Kings 11:11); to David's public identification of Solomon as his heir (1 Kings 1); to the extradition of fugitive slaves (1 Kings 2:29–40); to the story of David's rise to kingship; to betrothal gifts (Gen. 34:12); to inheritance by daughters (Numbers 27); to the killing of an animal at the time of treaty making (Genesis 15); and to similarities between a variety of terms.[11]

The making of a treaty by killing an animal was originally discussed by Wiseman, the first scholar to work on and publish the cuneiform tablets from Alalakh.[12] John Van Seters challenged this connection and rejected the comparison. However, much of Van Seters's argument is problematic because he does not clearly distinguish between two of the cuneiform texts that Wiseman cites.[13] In fact, the parallel between the killing of an animal to create the land grant of Alalakh Text 456 and the killing of animals by Abraham in Genesis 15, just before he receives the promise of the land of Canaan from God, remains cogent.[14]

10. See additional observations in R. S. Hess, "The Genealogies of Genesis 1–11 and Comparative Literature," *Biblica* 70 (1989): 241–54.

11. R. S. Hess, "Alalakh Studies and the Bible: Obstacle or Contribution?" *Scripture and Other Artifacts: Essays on the Bible and Archaeology in Honor of Philip J. King*, ed. M. D. Coogan, J. C. Exum, and L. E. Stager (Louisville: Westminster John Knox, 1994), 199–215.

12. Donald J. Wiseman, "Alalakh," in *Archaeology and Old Testament Study: Jubilee Volume of the Society for Old Testament Study, 1917–1967*, ed. D. W. Thomas (Oxford: Clarendon, 1967), 118–35; idem, "Alalakh," in *New Bible Dictionary*, ed. J. D. Douglas, 2d ed. (Leicester, England: InterVarsity, 1982), 23–24.

13. John Van Seters, *Abraham in History and Tradition* (New Haven: Yale University Press, 1975), 100–103.

14. R. S. Hess, "The Slaughter of the Animals in Genesis 15: Genesis 15:8–21 and Its Ancient Near Eastern Context," in *He Swore an Oath: Biblical Themes from Genesis 12–50*, ed. R. S. Hess, P. E. Satterthwaite, and G. J. Wenham (Cambridge: Tyndale House, 1993), 55–65.

On the other hand, the use of the term *Ḥapiru* at Alalakh bears no resemblance to the usage of this term elsewhere (at Ugarit and in Egypt, for
example) and even less to the often compared *Hebrew* of the Old Testament. At Alalakh, the *Ḥapiru* were well integrated into the society and able
to rise to positions of responsibility, whereas elsewhere they were outlaws
who had little to do with organized society, except to threaten it.[15]

All this shows that comparison between ancient Near Eastern
sources and the Old Testament must proceed case by case, with attention to detail and with an attempt to bring as wide a knowledge of the
culture and history as possible.

General Resources

Reference Works

The comparative method for the study of the Old Testament can be approached in two ways. One is to study the background and context of the
ancient Near East as a discipline in its own right, and then to apply this
background understanding to the study of the Bible. Many of the reference works and introductions to ancient cultures make use of this method.
Perhaps the best example is Jack Sasson's *Civilizations of the Ancient Near
East* (4 vols.; New York: Charles Scribner's Sons, 1995). The four volumes
of about 2,800 pages are divided into eleven parts: "Ancient Near East in
Western Thought"; "Environment"; "Population"; "Social Institutions";
"History and Culture" (comprising all of volume 2); "Economy and
Trade"; "Technology and Artistic Production"; "Religion and Science";
"Language, Writing, and Literature"; "Visual and Performing Arts"; and
"Retrospective Essays." Every part contains many subsections, each written by a specialist in the field concerned. More than any other series, these
volumes (and especially volume 2) should form the starting point for
someone wishing to read broadly in the historical, cultural background of
the ancient Near East. No such work is perfect, and in Sasson's work the
history of Israel tends to be written from a highly skeptical perspective,
without consideration of alternative views. Nevertheless, for a general introduction to the ancient Near East, this is the best resource available.[16]

15. Hess, "Alalakh Studies and the Bible," 205–8.
16. Before the appearance of this multivolume work, possibly the best general resource for understanding the history of the ancient Near East was the *Cambridge Ancient
History*, 3d. ed. (Cambridge: Cambridge University Press, 1975). Except for the discussion of Israel's history, this is now superseded by *Civilizations of the Ancient Near East*.
The many general histories of the ancient Near East might be included here. Of these,
one of the most recent and reliable is A. Kuhrt, *The Ancient Near East, c. 3000–330 B.C.*,
2 vols. (London: Routledge, 1995).

A second multivolume product similar in focus but very different in presentation is Eric Meyer's *The Oxford Encyclopedia of Archaeology in the Near East* (5 vols.; Oxford: Oxford University Press, 1997). This is an amazing achievement, of similar length (in pages) to Sasson's work. It also reflects the combined efforts of an international team of Orientalists. However, this work is arranged alphabetically. There are a variety of entries on subjects, groups, and peoples, but nearly half of the 1,100 entries concern specific sites. This work is an example of the second approach to studying the relationship between the Old Testament and the ancient Near East. In this work, the reader chooses a specific biblical text and attempts to discover what the discipline of ancient Near Eastern studies offers for its interpretation. This approach has direct relevance for the interpreter of the biblical text. While one can wade through many volumes of background information before coming across anything helpful, this is not the case when using such an encyclopedia. Immediate access to relevant information is available.

Is it preferable to use a method that goes directly to the relevant information for a biblical passage, rather than a method that systematically studies the ancient Near East? Perhaps, but this method can have its problems as well. There is a tendency for the writer of the particular article or section to influence the readers in their interpretation. If the reader does not have some general understanding of the history, culture, literature, and archaeology of the ancient Near East, the interpretation can more easily be directed by others. It can also lead to idiosyncratic interpretations that a knowledge of the wider historical and cultural contexts would rule out. For this reason, it is best to use both methods, reading broadly for background information and using specific guides for the interpretation of a particular passage.

Having mentioned two larger reference works, I refer to several others that are essential for the interpreter. In archaeology, there is Ephraim Stern's *New Encyclopedia of Archaeological Excavations in the Holy Land* (4 vols.; New York: Simon & Schuster; Jerusalem: Israel Exploration Society, 1992). This is an essential reference work for referring to any excavated site mentioned in the Bible, especially those in modern-day Israel and Jordan. Its 1,552 pages list the sites according to their modern name and also include regional surveys. Many of the articles are written by the excavators or those closely associated with excavations. There is an index to refer readers who know the biblical (or other) name of the site.

As important, if not more so, is David Noel Freedman's (et al.) *Anchor Bible Dictionary* (6 vols.; Garden City, N.Y.: Doubleday, 1992). Personal and place-names, objects, customs, and other items mentioned in the Bible are listed in alphabetical order and analyzed. The volumes contain scholarly articles, written by leaders in their fields. Although any study like this is bound to have unevenness, there is no comparable resource to provide survey articles on so many topics as well as bibliographies to direct the reader elsewhere.

In the area of general reference works, it is important to mention the one-volume Bible dictionaries as resources for the study of the ancient Near East. Of these, the best overall remains J. D. Douglas et al., eds., *The New Bible Dictionary* (3d ed.; Leicester, England, and Downers Grove, Ill.: InterVarsity, 1996). The new edition updates some articles and completely rewrites other entries (e.g., the entries on "Ebla," "Mari," "Sumer," and "Ugarit"). Before the appearance of the third edition of this evangelical dictionary, Matthews and Moyer evaluated the one-volume Bible dictionaries on the market for usefulness in biblical archaeology.[17] They preferred *Harper's Bible Dictionary* (San Francisco: Harper & Row, 1985).

Along with reference works that introduce the reader to ancient Near Eastern topics are compendia that provide collections of primary source materials, especially those that select materials with their relation to the Old Testament in mind. These come in two forms, translations of ancient Near Eastern inscriptions and photographs of monuments and artifacts. Of the ones available in English, the standard for many years has been the two volumes edited by James B. Pritchard, *Ancient Near Eastern Texts Relating to the Old Testament* (third edition with supplement; Princeton: Princeton University Press, 1969); and *The Ancient Near East in Pictures Relating to the Old Testament* (second edition with supplement; Princeton: Princeton University Press, 1969). Both of these volumes are indexed and provide an essential resource. Both have also been abridged in smaller paperback volumes.[18] Although Pritchard's *ANET* has long been the standard, it is being replaced by a larger and more comprehensive collection of ancient Near Eastern texts edited by William W. Hallo and K. Lawson Younger Jr., *The Context of Scripture* (Leiden: Brill). As of this writing, the first two of three projected volumes have appeared: *Canonical Compositions from the Biblical World* (1997) and *Monumental Inscriptions from the Biblical World* (2000). The final volume, *Archival Documents from the Biblical World*, should appear soon. The format of these texts allows for the translators to include an introduction discussing the background of the

17. V. H. Matthews and J. C. Moyer, "Archaeological Coverage in Recent One-Volume Bible Dictionaries," *Biblical Archaeologist* 55 (September 1992): 141–51.

18. *The Ancient Near East, vol. 1: An Anthology of Texts and Pictures* (Princeton: Princeton University Press, 1958); *The Ancient Near East, vol. 2: A New Anthology of Texts and Pictures* (Princeton: Princeton University Press, 1975). There have also been other smaller volumes of texts; for example, D. Winton Thomas, ed., *Documents from Old Testament Times* (New York: Harper & Row, Harper Torchbacks, 1961).

text, an up-to-date bibliography, and footnotes for all the problems, issues, and significant points in each translation. As with some study Bibles in which the translation is divided into two columns, a middle column lists significant biblical parallels or points of reference. It is hoped that an index of these biblical references will appear. If so, this will become one of the most important tools for Bible students seeking to understand biblical literature in the light of ancient Near Eastern literature.

Journals

General reference works such as those above allow the reader to obtain basic information about and interpretations of the ancient Near East and biblical studies. They do this in a systematic fashion. However, discoveries have been made and important studies written since the publication of these works. For these it is necessary to turn to journals and magazines that publish and interpret recently discovered texts and artifacts (or new interpretations of older ones) that have relevance to the Bible. For both pictures and texts, the single most important source is *Biblical Archaeology Review*, edited by Hershel Shanks and published by the Biblical Archaeology Society in Washington, D.C. Appearing six times a year, the magazine is famous for beautiful color photography and for articles reporting the latest discoveries and scholarly controversies. The articles are often written by the initial discoverers and publishers of the texts and artifacts. *BAR* attracts leading scholars in the areas that it seeks to address.

Since the majority of discoveries related to biblical interpretation occur in and around the modern state of Israel, it is no surprise that some of the most important publications about new finds should occur in Israeli journals. Three journals publish articles, in English, about new discoveries: *Eretz-Israel* (an annual), *Israel Exploration Journal*, and *Tel-Aviv*. Of these, the *Israel Exploration Journal* has published the largest number of recent inscriptional discoveries from Old Testament times, such as the Tel Dan stele, the Ekron dedicatory inscription from Tel Miqne, the Hazor cuneiform tablets, and the Beth Shan cuneiform cylinder.[19] The *Israel Exploration Journal* also publishes summaries of each season of excavation at sites throughout the land.

19. *Tel Dan*: A. Biran and J. Naveh, "An Aramaic Stele Fragment from Tel Dan," *IEJ* 43 (1993): 81–98; idem, "The Tel Dan Inscription: A New Fragment," *IEJ* 45 (1995): 1–18.

Tel Miqne: S. Gitin, T. Dothan, and J. Naveh, "A Royal Dedicatory Inscription from Ekron," *IEJ* 47 (1997): 1–16.

Tel Hazor: A. Ben-Tor, "The Hazor Tablet: Foreword," *IEJ* 42 (1992): 17–20; W. Horowitz, "The Cuneiform Tablets at Tel Hazor, 1996," *IEJ* 46 (1996): 268–69; W. Horowitz and A. Shaffer, "An Administrative Tablet from Hazor: A Preliminary Edition," *IEJ* 42 (1992): 21–33; idem, "A Fragment of a Letter from Hazor," *IEJ* 42 (1992): 165–66;

Various English-language journals also publish sources and reviews of ancient Near Eastern discoveries and discussions. There is the British Association for Near Eastern Archaeology, although not much of its work focuses on themes related to the Old Testament. The Palestine Exploration Society and its *Palestine Exploration Quarterly* more frequently touch on matters related to biblical studies. The same is true of the publications of the British Schools in Turkey (*Anatolian Studies*), Iraq (*Iraq*), and Amman and Jerusalem (*Levant*). In North America, the American Schools of Oriental Research (ASOR) dominates the scene with three scholarly publications: *Journal of Cuneiform Studies*, *Bulletin of the American Schools of Oriental Research*, and *Near Eastern Archaeology* (formerly *Biblical Archaeologist*). The latter two regularly contain studies related to biblical interpretation. The American Oriental Society's *Journal of the American Oriental Society* and the University of Chicago's *Journal of Near Eastern Studies* should also be mentioned. An important annual published by the Ugarit Seminar in Münster, Germany, is *Ugarit Forschungen*. Many of its articles are written in English. Its papers discussing second-millennium B.C.E. Syro-Palestinian texts and artifacts are unparalleled in quantity and diversity. The Pontifical Bible Institute in Rome publishes the Near Eastern studies journal *Orientalia*. Although some articles appear in English (as is true of other European Near Eastern studies journals), this journal is especially important for the annual index that appears with each volume. This is perhaps the most comprehensive index of journals, articles, and books on themes related to the ancient Near East. The indexes include authors, subjects, and texts.

Among evangelical groups, the Near East Archaeological Society (NEAS) publishes its *Bulletin of the Near East Archaeological Society* and the related *Archaeology and the Biblical World*. This latter publication, like *Near Eastern Archaeology* and *Biblical Archaeological Review*, uses photographs and other visual aids to illuminate the presentation. Mention should also be made of Australia's Institute of Archaeology, an evangelical group that publishes *Buried History*.

Both ASOR and NEAS provide online E-mail services announcing new discoveries and publications related to the ancient Near East and the Bible.

---

idem, "Additions and Corrections to 'An Administrative Tablet from Hazor: A Preliminary Edition,'" *IEJ* 42 (1993): 167.

Beth Shan: W. Horowitz, "An Inscribed Clay Cylinder from Amarna-Age Beth Shean," *IEJ* 46 (1996): 208–18.

Area Resources

Because of the enormity of this subject, this essay will consider broad regions and discuss some of the most important general resources for understanding the archaeology, history, and culture of the area as well as specific matters that may be related to the study and understanding of the Old Testament.

Several evangelical contributions to the comparative studies of the ancient Near East and the Old Testament should be noted. Important discussions of a variety of ancient Near Eastern peoples can be found in A. J. Hoerth, G. L. Mattingly, and E. M. Yamauchi, eds., *Peoples of the Old Testament World* (Grand Rapids: Baker, 1994). This is the most recent survey of various peoples mentioned in the Bible (Sumerians, Babylonians, Assyrians, Persians, Hittites, Canaanites and Amorites, Moabites, and Edomites). It updates the earlier work of D. J. Wiseman, ed., *Peoples of Old Testament Times* (Oxford: Clarendon, 1973; included also are Hebrews, Ethiopians, Arabs, and Hurrians). A valuable study of various ancient Near Eastern literatures and their use in understanding the corresponding types of biblical literature is J. Walton, *Ancient Israelite Literature in Its Cultural Context* (Grand Rapids: Zondervan, 1989). The provocative and engaging style of K. A. Kitchen, as well as his mastery of the ancient Near East, shines in his *Bible and Its World: The Bible and Archaeology Today* (Downers Grove, Ill.: InterVarsity, 1977).

Iran

The study of ancient Persia is well summarized in traditional texts such as A. T. Olmstead's *History of the Persian Empire* (Chicago: University of Chicago Press, 1948), which interprets and harmonizes the relevant textual sources; and in R. Ghirshman's *Iran* (Hammondsworth, England: Penguin, 1954). M. Dandamaev, *A Political History of the Achaemenid Empire* (trans. W. J. Vogelsang; Leiden: Brill, 1989), followed the approach of Olmstead. However, the most recent work is both more critical and useful as a resource for this field, including essays on cultural and socio-economic matters. That is P. Briant's *From Cyrus to Alexander: A History of the Persian Empire*, vols. 1–2 (trans. Peter T. Daniels; Winona Lake, Ind.: Eisenbrauns, 1999).

A direct relationship between the Old Testament and Persia is affirmed in Edwin Yamauchi's *Persia and the Bible* (Grand Rapids: Baker, 1996). This 580-page volume provides a comprehensive survey of Persian history and artifacts and their relationship to the biblical narratives set in the Persian period. Of special importance is Kenneth Hoglund's *Achaemenid Imperial Administration in Syria-Palestine and the Missions of Ezra and Nehemiah* (SBLDS 125; Atlanta: Scholars,

1992). Hoglund provides a synthesis of the archaeological and textual data needed to understand and interpret the mid–fifth century and the work of both Ezra and Nehemiah.

Mesopotamia

This is a huge topic with a focus on the cultures of Sumer, Assyria, and Babylon. For a review of the history and culture of these areas, consult the readable G. Roux, *Ancient Iraq* (2d ed.; Hammondsworth, England: Penguin, 1980); or the culturally informative work of A. Leo Oppenheim, *Ancient Mesopotamia: Portrait of a Dead Civilization* (rev. ed.; Chicago: University of Chicago Press, 1977). It is a delight to see the new edition of one of the most valuable historical overviews of both Mesopotamia and Egypt: William W. Hallo and William Kelly Simpson, *The Ancient Near East: A History* (rev. ed.; New York: Harcourt Brace Jovanovich, 1998). Along with these, Samuel Noah Kramer's *Sumerians: Their History, Culture, and Character* (Chicago: University of Chicago Press, 1963) remains an important introduction into this early era. A useful resource for the study of Assyriology is the *Reallexikon der Assyriologie* (Berlin: Walter de Gruyter). The work is still being published. Some of the more recent volumes have included articles written in English.

The series on the State Archives of Assyria, along with its supplement series, continues to be published by Helsinki University Press. Of special interest for Old Testament interpreters are volume 2 of the series, S. Parpola and K. Watanabe, *Neo-Assyrian Treaties and Loyalty Oaths* (Helsinki: Helsinki University Press, 1988), and volume 9, S. Parpola, *Assyrian Prophecies* (Helsinki: Helsinki University Press, 1998). The companion volume to the latter has also appeared: *References to Prophecy in Neo-Assyrian Sources* (State Archives of Assyria Studies 7; Helsinki: Helsinki University Press, 1998). Another important volume for understanding the final decade or two of Jerusalem's independence is D. J. Wiseman, *Chronicles of the Chaldean Kings (626–556 B.C.) in the British Museum* (London: Trustees of the British Museum, 1956); it remains an important review of Nebuchadnezzar and his campaigns against Jerusalem and elsewhere. See also Wiseman's later *Nebuchadrezzar and Babylon* (Schweich Lectures of the British Academy, 1983; Oxford: University Press for the British Academy, 1985).

Although many articles identify relationships between specific aspects of Mesopotamian and Israelite life and culture, few books are devoted to general surveys of the subject. I mention the works of K. van der Toorn: *Sin and Sanction in Israel and Mesopotamia: A Comparative Study* (Studia Semitica Neerlandica 22; Assen and Maastricht, Netherlands: Van Gorcum, 1985); and *Family Religion in Babylonia, Syria, and*

Israel: Continuity and Change in the Forms of Religious Life (Studies in the History and Culture of the Ancient Near East 7; Leiden: Brill, 1996). The former is a valuable comparative study of aspects of the Decalogue and other legal texts from the Old Testament. The latter is a comprehensive volume on religion, although permeated with critical reconstructions of the history of Israel.

Having examined Mesopotamia's impact during and after the monarchy in Israel, it is also important to remember the significant impact that this area of the world has had on the interpretation of Genesis 1–11. In this regard, consult the first half of the work edited by R. S. Hess and D. T. Tsumura, *"I Studied Inscriptions from before the Flood": Ancient Near Eastern, Literary, and Linguistic Approaches to Genesis 1–11* (Sources for Biblical and Theological Study 4; Winona Lake, Ind.: Eisenbrauns, 1994). The collection includes essays by some of the leading scholars in Assyriology and their comments on the relationship of various literary works (creation stories, flood accounts, and so on) to the Bible.

Anatolia

The study of the Hittite civilization has advanced since O. R. Gurney's *The Hittites* (Hammondsworth, England: Penguin, 1954); however, this book remains one of the best introductions to the subject. The relationship of these texts to the Old Testament has been investigated by H. A. Hoffner. His latest work, *The Laws of the Hittites: A Critical Edition* (Documenta et Monumenta Orientis Antiqui 23; Leiden: Brill, 1997), continues this tradition with numerous references to the biblical laws.

A special group centered between modern-day Turkey and Syria were the Hurrians. Their culture had many similarities with the Western Semitic cuneiform cultures of Alalakh, Emar, and Ugarit. There are numerous examples of Hurrian customs and personal names in the Old Testament, especially in Genesis and the Books of Joshua, Judges, and Samuel. However, less is known of their own kingdom of Mitanni because no Hurrian archive from this land has been located. Nevertheless, Gernot Wilhelm's volume, *The Hurrians* (trans. J. Barnes; London: Aris & Philips, 1989), presents a synthesis of much of what is known of this people's history and culture.

The single most important archive for Hurrian culture and influence is that of Nuzi. Much has been written about the contracts and other documents that reflect social customs similar to those in Genesis. Useful and balanced reflections on these texts are those of Martin J. Selman, "Comparative Customs and the Patriarchal Age," in *Essays on the Patriarchal Narratives*, ed. A. R. Millard and D. J. Wiseman (Winona Lake, Ind.: Eisenbrauns, 1980), 91–139; Barry L. Eichler, "Nuzi and the

Bible: A Retrospective," in *DUMU-E₂-DUB-BA-A: Studies in Honor of Åke W. Sjöberg*, ed. H. Behrens, D. Loding, and M. T. Roth (Occasional Publications of the Samuel Noah Kramer Fund 11; Philadelphia: University Museum, 1989), 107–19; and John Walton, "Personal Archives and Epics," in *Ancient Israelite Literature in Its Cultural Context* (Grand Rapids: Zondervan, 1989), 45–65.

Finally, mention should be made of peoples who populated this area and the surrounding area in the first millennium—civilizations such as the Urarteans and Cimmerians. For a survey of archaeological and textual evidence and these peoples' mention in the Old Testament, see E. Yamauchi, *Foes from the Northern Frontier: Invading Hordes from the Russian Steppes* (Baker Studies in Biblical Archaeology; Grand Rapids: Baker, 1992).

Syria and Canaan

The archaeological evidence from Syria and Canaan can be divided into two groups: the major city-states of the third and second millennia B.C.E. and their archives; and the states of the first millennium B.C.E. The city-state archives include those of Ebla, Mari, Alalakh, Emar, Ugarit, and Amarna. The first-millennium sources include inscriptional evidence from the capital of Gozan in the east, Damascus and the Aramaean states in the west, and the Phoenician evidence from the coastal cities of Sidon, Dor, and especially Tyre. Finally, mention should be made of the Philistine pentapolis along the southern coast of Canaan and the Transjordanian states of Moab, Ammon, and Edom.

When the excavations at Ebla began to reveal thousands of cuneiform texts from the mid–third millennium B.C.E., a great deal was made of supposed parallels. However, the evidence was not confirmed. Similarities that appear more certain include Eblaite titles *malikum* and *šapiṭum*, which resemble Hebrew *melek* 'king' and *šopeṭ* 'judge', and personal names or elements in those names also found in Genesis, such as Adam, Eve, Noah, Jabal, Jubal, and Haran.[20]

20. See W. G. Lambert, "The Treaty of Ebla," in *Ebla, 1975–1985: Dieci anni di studi linguistici e filologici*, ed. L. Cagni (Istituto Universitario Orientale Dipartimento di Studi Asiatici Series Minor 27; Naples: Istituto Universitario Orientale Dipartimento di Studi Asiatici, 1987), 353–64; A. R. Millard, "Ebla Personal Names and Personal Names of the First Millennium B.C. in Syria and Palestine," in *Eblaite Personal Names and Semitic Name-Giving: Papers of a Symposium Held in Rome, July 15–17, 1985*, ed. Alfonso Archi (Archivi Reali de Ebla Studi 1; Rome: Missione Archeologica Italiana in Siria, 1988), 159–64; R. S. Hess, *Studies in the Personal Names of Genesis 1–11* (Alter Orient und Altes Testament 234; Kevelaer, Germany: Butzon & Bercker; Neukirchen-Vluyn: Neukirchener, 1993).

Mari was a major center on the middle Euphrates River. Most of more than twenty thousand cuneiform tablets discovered there date from the generations immediately before its destruction in the mid–eighteenth century B.C.E. Like Ebla, there are many personal names and names of peoples that resemble those found in the Bible. Even more important have been the studies on prophetic texts and terms, covenant/treaty rituals, and social aspects of nomadic/urban symbiotic relationships that have been compared with prophetic roles and texts, covenant rituals, and patriarchal movements in Genesis and elsewhere in the Old Testament.[21]

To the west of Mari and north of Ugarit, some miles east of classical Antioch, lay the city of Alalakh. Archives from two separate periods illustrate life around the eighteenth century B.C.E. and the fifteenth century B.C.E. Again, many customs described are similar to those in Israel's early history, and personal names are also attested. In addition, administrative texts include resemblances in form and structure to place-name lists and other texts found in Joshua and the Books of Kings.[22]

The site of Emar is east of Alalakh and Ugarit. The c. thirteenth-century archive was found in a city that appears to have been resettled by a superpower such as the Hittite empire. In addition to observations regarding prophets and their roles, as well as personal names, the most significant similarities with the Bible appear in Emar texts that describe festivals with features similar to those in Exodus and Leviticus.[23]

Thousands of cuneiform tablets were found at the international metropolis of Ugarit, a Syrian coastal city that flourished in the second

21. See V. H. Matthews, *Pastoral Nomadism in the Mari Kingdom (ca. 1830–1760 B.C.)* (ASOR Dissertation Series 3; Cambridge, Mass.: American Schools of Oriental Research, 1978); G. D. Young, ed., *Mari in Retrospect: Fifty Years of Mari and Mari Studies* (Winona Lake, Ind.: Eisenbrauns, 1992); A. Malamat, *Mari and the Early Israelite Experience* (Schweich Lectures, 1984; Oxford: Oxford University Press, 1989); idem, "A Note on the Ritual of Treaty Making in Mari and the Bible," *IEJ* 45 (1995): 226–29; R. P. Gordon, "Where Have All the Prophets Gone? The 'Disappearing' Israelite Prophet against the Background of Ancient Near Eastern Prophecy," *Bulletin for Biblical Research* 5 (1995): 67–86.

22. See R. S. Hess, "Achan and Achor: Names and Wordplay in Joshua 7," *Hebrew Annual Review* 14 (1994): 89–98; idem, "Alalakh and the Bible"; idem, "Slaughter of the Animals"; idem, "A Typology of West Semitic Place-Name Lists with Special Reference to Joshua 13–21," *Biblical Archaeologist* 59 (September 1996): 160–70; idem, "The Form and Structure of the Solomonic District List in 1 Kings 4:7–19," in *Crossing Boundaries and Linking Horizons: Studies in Honor of Michael C. Astour*, ed. G. D. Young, M. W. Chavalas, and R. E. Averbeck (Bethesda, Md.: CDL, 1997), 279–92; idem, "West Semitic Texts and the Book of Joshua," *Bulletin for Biblical Research* 7 (1997): 63–76; idem, "The Late Bronze Age Alalakh Texts at the Australian Institute of Archaeology," *Buried History* 34 (March 1998): 4–9.

23. See D. E. Fleming, "More Help from Syria: Introducing Emar to Biblical Study," *Biblical Archaeologist* 58 (September 1995): 139–47.

millennium B.C.E. before it became uninhabited in the early twelfth century B.C.E. The biblical parallels are similar to those with the Alalakh and Nuzi texts. However, the most important contributions come from Ugarit's mythological and ritual texts.[24] Terms for sacrifices, gods and goddesses, divine epithets, and literary forms and structures are similar to those described and used in the Old Testament.[25] Though now dated, the three volumes of *Ras Shamra Parallels* (ed. Loren Fisher and Stan Rummel; Analecta Orientalia 49, 50, 51; Rome: Pontificium Institutum Biblicum, 1972, 1975, 1981) remain some of the most useful volumes in English (with full sets of indexes) for identifying parallels between Ugaritic and biblical texts.

The site of Amarna is not in Syria or Canaan, but in Egypt. For a generation in the fourteenth century B.C.E., this was the country's capital. Here was gathered international correspondence from other major powers throughout the ancient Near East and the eastern Mediterranean. Correspondence from princes and officials scattered throughout Canaan, from "biblical" cities such as Hazor, Megiddo, Ashkelon, Shechem, Gezer, and Jerusalem, was also sent to Amarna. The leaders of these cities affirmed their loyalty to the pharaoh and accused their enemies of being *Ḫapiru*, opposed to the pharaoh. Though written in Akkadian, these texts are influenced by Canaanite dialects that antedate the Hebrew of the Bible. In addition to the language, the personal names and rhetorical forms in these texts also reflect similarities to figures mentioned in Joshua and Judges, as well as to the persuasive style found in books such as the Psalms. The relationship of the *Ḫapiru* and Hebrews as well as the sociopolitical realities of the period preceding Israel's emergence in Canaan all serve to illuminate early biblical history and society.[26]

---

24. See J. C. L. Gibson, *Canaanite Myths and Legends* (Edinburgh: T. & T. Clark, 1977).

25. See G. D. Young, ed., *Ugarit in Retrospect: Fifty Years of Ugarit and Ugaritic* (Winona Lake, Ind.: Eisenbrauns, 1981); P. C. Craigie, *Ugarit and the Old Testament* (Grand Rapids: Eerdmans, 1983); M. S. Smith, *The Early History of God: Yahweh and the Other Deities in Ancient Israel* (San Francisco: Harper & Row, 1990); G. J. Brooke, A. H. W. Curtis, and J. F. Healey, eds., *Ugarit and the Bible: Proceedings of the International Symposium on Ugarit and the Bible, Manchester, September 1992* (Ugarit-Biblische Literatur 11; Münster: Ugarit-Verlag, 1994).

26. See W. L. Moran, *The Amarna Letters* (Baltimore: Johns Hopkins University Press, 1992); R. S. Hess, "Cultural Aspects of Onomastic Distribution in the Amarna Texts," *Ugarit Forschungen* 21 (1989): 209–16; idem, "Hebrew Psalms and Amarna Correspondence from Jerusalem: Some Comparisons and Implications," *Zeitschrift für die alttestamentliche Wissenschaft* 101 (1989): 249–65; idem, "Early Israel in Canaan: A Survey of Recent Evidence and Interpretations," *Palestine Exploration Quarterly* 126 (1993): 125–42; idem, "Hurrians and Other Inhabitants of Late Bronze Age Palestine," *Levant* 29 (1997): 153–56.

From the first millennium B.C.E. comes important comparative insight from as far east as the state of Gozan, a near-neighbor of Assyria. A bilingual inscription (in Aramaic and Assyrian) was discovered in Gozan that preserves insights for the study of Genesis.[27]

Farther west lay Aramean city-states and a center of that culture, Damascus. An important contribution to understanding their culture is W. T. Pitard's *Ancient Damascus: A Historical Study of the Syrian City-State from Earliest Times until Its Fall to the Assyrians in 732 B.C.E.* (Winona Lake, Ind.: Eisenbrauns, 1987). Although this is the best work on the subject, it was published before the discovery of the Aramaic Tel Dan stele, for which see W. M. Schniedewind, "Tel Dan Stela: New Light on Aramaic and Jehu's Revolt," *Bulletin of the American Schools of Oriental Research* 302 (1996): 75–90.

The Phoenician cities of Sidon, Tyre, and Dor remained influential into the first millennium B.C.E. The most useful volume reviewing the textual data is H. J. Katzenstein, *The History of Tyre: From the Beginning of the Second Millenium [sic] B.C.E. until the Fall of the Neo-Babylonian Empire in 538 B.C.E.* (Jerusalem: Schocken Institute for Jewish Research, 1973). Archaeological excavations at Dor are summarized by E. Stern, *Dor—Ruler of the Seas* (Jerusalem: Israel Exploration Society, 1994).

Farther south and close to the Mediterranean coast lay the Philistine cities and their culture. A product of migrations in the thirteenth and twelfth centuries B.C.E., this people and their culture have been the subject of intense archaeological investigation. A good summary of the work is S. Gitin, A. Mazar, and E. Stern, eds., *Mediterranean Peoples in Transition: Thirteenth to Early Tenth Centuries BCE* (Jerusalem: Israel Exploration Society, 1998). However, the clearest statement of this people and their relationship to biblical Israel can be found in a series of articles by L. E. Stager, "When Canaanites and Philistines Ruled Ashkelon," *Biblical Archaeology Review* 17 (March/April 1991): 24–37, 40–43; idem, "The Impact of the Sea Peoples in Canaan (1185–1050 BCE)," in *The Archaeology of Society in the Holy Land*, ed. T. E. Levy (Washington, D.C.: Facts on File, 1995); idem, "The Fury of Babylon: Ashkelon and the Archaeology of Destruction," *Biblical Archaeology Review* 22 (January/February 1996): 56–69, 76–77.

To the east and south of Israel could be found the kingdoms of Ammon, Moab, and Edom. Many of the general reference works discuss

27. See S. A. Kaufman, "Reflections on the Assyrian-Aramaic Bilingual from Tell Fakhariyeh," *Maarav* 3 (1982): 137–75; Hess, "Eden—A Well-Watered Place."

these states in sufficient detail and make comparisons with Israelite history and culture.[28]

In this geographical context, it is appropriate to consider the Arabs, and here I mention a useful summary of the textual evidence from the first millennium B.C.E.: I. Eph'al, *The Ancient Arabs: Nomads on the Borders of the Fertile Crescent, Ninth–Fifth Centuries B.C.* (Jerusalem: Magnes, 1984).

Egypt

Egypt is a world distinct from the rest of the ancient Near East in language, culture, ethnicity, history, and geographical location. For those wishing background to this fascinating culture, see B. G. Trigger, B. J. Kemp, D. O'Connor, and A. B. Lloyd, *Ancient Egypt: A Social History* (Cambridge: Cambridge University Press, 1983); and B. J. Kemp, *Ancient Egypt: Anatomy of a Civilization* (London: Routledge, 1991). See also William Simpson's contribution to the revised edition of *The Ancient Near East: A History* as discussed above. Of greater interest is the growing literature discussing the relationship of Egypt to the Old Testament. The skepticism of D. B. Redford, *Egypt, Canaan, and Israel in Ancient Times* (Princeton: Princeton University Press, 1992), is now balanced by a general survey of Egypt's influence in Israelite history, J. D. Currid, *Ancient Egypt and the Old Testament* (Grand Rapids: Baker, 1997), and a scholarly discussion of issues surrounding Joseph, Moses, and the exodus, J. K. Hoffmeier, *Israel in Egypt: The Evidence for the Authenticity of the Exodus Tradition* (Oxford: Oxford University Press, 1997). A variety of views can be found in the small volume edited by E. S. Ferichs and L. H. Lesko, *Exodus: The Egyptian Evidence* (Winona Lake, Ind.: Eisenbrauns, 1997).

---

28. Greater depth can be found in W. Aufrecht, *A Corpus of Ammonite Inscriptions*, Ancient Near Eastern Texts and Studies 4 (Lewiston, N.Y.: Edwin Mellon, 1989); A. Dearman, ed., *Studies in the Mesha Inscription and Moab*, Archaeology and Biblical Studies 2 (Atlanta: Scholars, 1989); P. Bienkowski, ed., *Early Edom and Moab: The Beginning of the Iron Age in Southern Jordan*, Sheffield Archaeological Monographs 7 (Sheffield: J. R. Collis, 1992); and D. V. Edelman, ed., *You Shall Not Abhor an Edomite for He Is Your Brother: Edom and Seir in History and Tradition*, Archaeology and Biblical Studies 3 (Atlanta: Scholars, 1995).

eight

Compositional History

Source, Form, and Redaction Criticism

PAUL EDWARD HUGHES

The compositional history of the Hebrew Bible is a complex matter, its stages involving too many players for an introductory essay to cover in detail. Instead of meticulously presenting a comprehensive historical reconstruction of people, events, and theories, I sketch the significant waves of innovation and influence. As an attempt to concretize this approach, the criticisms under consideration will be brought into focus with texts from Genesis and Exodus.

Historical Perspectives

From the outset, I direct the reader toward the many excellent historical overviews of the methodology of Old Testament study, particularly relating to the critical avenues that this essay covers. For an excellent set of studies, see the essays in *To Each Its Own Meaning: An Introduction to Biblical Criticisms and Their Application.*[1] David J. A.

---

1. Edited by Stephen R. Haynes and Steven L. McKenzie (Louisville: Westminster John Knox, 1993). Especially pertinent for the present chapter are "Source Criticism," by Pauline A. Viviano (29–51), "Form Criticism," by Martin J. Buss (69–85), "Redaction Criticism," by Gail Paterson Corrington (87–99), and "Canonical Criticism," by Mary C. Callaway (121–34).

221

Clines's "Methods in Old Testament Study"[2] contains some useful insights, and John Barton's *Reading the Old Testament: Method in Biblical Study* provides a wealth of information for any discussion of method,[3] as does John Goldingay's theologically sensitive *Approaches to Old Testament Interpretation*[4] and *Models for Interpretation of Scripture*.[5] Other standard historical descriptions can be found in Ronald Clements's *One Hundred Years of Old Testament Interpretation*,[6] Herbert Hahn's somewhat dated *The Old Testament in Modern Research*,[7] John H. Hayes and Carl R. Holladay's *Biblical Exegesis: A Beginner's Handbook*,[8] and the excellent collection of essays in *Old Testament Form Criticism*.[9]

Hermeneutical Orientations

A hermeneutical consideration regarding the role of the interpreter must be registered from the outset. Traditionally, particularly within more conservative circles, it has been assumed that the biblical interpreter is a neutral observer whose aim is to cull objective data through use of the historical-grammatical method. This means, in effect, that the goal of the interpreter (also referred to as the *hermeneut*) lies in understanding the biblical text in its grammatical (i.e., linguistic, syntactical, semantic) context, as well as in situating it within its historical (i.e., cultural, social, comparative) milieu. Through these lines of inquiry, the attempt is made to recover the intention of the historical author(s), which is assumed to embody the determinate meaning of the text. Such an approach, especially if assumed to provide fairly exhaustible meanings, probably makes more sense within New Testament studies, in which the historical-compositional parameters constitute a period merely of decades, compared to the Old Testament compositional period of several centuries—not to mention that for many of the OT books, identification of the author is not possible, never mind the attempt to isolate and discern the author's underlying intention.

Shifts in more recent hermeneutical thinking perceive meaning to lie not only in authorial intention, as the above position can be de-

2. Chapter in *Beginning Old Testament Study*, ed. John Rogerson (Philadelphia: Westminster, 1982), 26–43.
3. Revised and enlarged edition (Louisville: John Knox, 1996).
4. Rev. ed. (Downers Grove, Ill.: InterVarsity, 1990).
5. Grand Rapids: Eerdmans, 1995.
6. Philadelphia: Westminster, 1976, published in Britain as *A Century of Old Testament Study*. Clements's second chapter, "Interpreting the Pentateuch," is most helpful.
7. Philadelphia: Fortress, 1966.
8. Rev. ed. (Atlanta: John Knox, 1987).
9. San Antonio: Trinity University Press, 1974. See especially the fascinating and thorough essay by Martin J. Buss, "The Study of Forms" (1–56).

scribed. Instead, the communications act involving author, text, and reader—analogous to the biblical author, the sacred text of Scripture, and the interpreting canonical community—must be seen as a multi-faceted entity. Therefore, although meaning can be derived from the historical-grammatical recovery of an author's intention, if and where possible, to say that this hermeneutical approach is the sole means of obtaining interpretive results remains too narrow.[10] The transactions in the text itself, with its own literary structure, narratological devices,[11] and rhetorical features, contribute toward a broader set of meanings that function beyond the intention of the author.[12] Also, the reader—whether an individual interpreter or the collective community (as often emphasized by contemporary hermeneutical theorists)—is affected by a complex web of social, cultural, political, historical, and linguistic factors that not only influence the meaning, but also can prescribe what questions are asked in the first place, prior to the determination of meaning. Hermeneutical processes, therefore, are complex, and the meaning for the biblical text lies somewhere in a "trilectical" relationship among author, text, and reader.[13]

Another potential problem at the introductory level must be diffused. This relates to the conceptual assumptions lying beneath the linguistic term *criticism*. For many, the term has an unfortunate negative

10. For the classic critique of the perspective that reduces meaning to the author's intention alone, see W. K. Wimsatt, "The Intentional Fallacy," and Monroe C. Beardsley, "The Affective Fallacy," in *The Verbal Icon: Studies in the Meaning of Poetry* (London: Methuen, 1954), 3–18, 21–39.

11. The term *narratology* was coined by Tzvetan Todorov in his *Grammaire du Décaméron* (The Hague: Mouton, 1969), in which *narratologie* depicted a new science for discourses with narrative structure like stories, myth, and film. Wendell Harris (*Dictionary of Concepts in Literary Criticism and Theory* [New York: Greenwood, 1992], s.v. "narratology," 258) defines narratology as "the study or science of narrative structure, inclusive of all narratives, not only those regarded as 'literary.'" For further information, consult Gérard Genette, especially his *Narrative Discourse: An Essay in Method*, trans. Jane E. Lewin (Ithaca, N.Y.: Cornell University Press, 1980).

12. Some writers have distinguished between the similar terms *intention* and *intentionality* to represent the goal a speaker or author wishes to achieve (intention) and the goal a text achieves (intentionality), such as Rolf Knierim, "Old Testament Form Criticism Reconsidered," *Int* 27 (October 1973): 435–68.

13. For a helpful discussion, consult Randolph W. Tate, *Biblical Interpretation: An Integrated Approach*, rev. ed. (Peabody, Mass.: Hendrickson, 1997). Also, Mark G. Brett, "Four or Five Things to Do with Texts: A Taxonomy of Interpretative Interests," in *The Bible in Three Dimensions: Essays in Celebration of Forty Years of Biblical Studies in the University of Sheffield*, ed. David J. A. Clines, Stephen E. Fowl, and Stanley E. Porter, JSOTSup 87 (Sheffield: JSOT Press, 1990), 357–77, and, more broadly, his *Biblical Criticism in Crisis? The Impact of the Canonical Approach on Old Testament Studies* (Cambridge: Cambridge University Press, 1991). Note Adele Berlin's helpful corrective in "The Role of the Text in the Reading Process," *Semeia* 62 (1993): 143–47.

connotation as a faith-destroying force that seeks to tear the Bible apart in a scientific manner, often with humanistic and strictly naturalistic agendas. It would be wrong to deny that, at times, these effects have followed various critical methodologies, but the term needs to be understood more precisely as being synonymous with careful analysis, evaluation, and judgment.

With a text as complex as the Bible, confessed to be of both human and divine origin, exegetes must err on the side of interpretive caution, carefully unpacking vocabulary and grammatical terms, cultural means and assumptions, social and historical frameworks, literary genres, implicit rhetoric, and other related considerations in order to reproduce its message.

> God speaks through scripture, but its meanings function within the structures of ordinary human language. Criticism depends on a grasp of style, of the relation of part to whole, of expression to genre; it takes the biblical diction very seriously and moves from the detail of language to the larger overarching themes. Approached in this way, the Bible is sometimes found to have meanings other than those that traditional or superficial interpretations have suggested. Criticism is thus "critical," not in the sense that it "criticizes" the Bible (it often reveres it as the basic and holy text), but in the sense that it assumes freedom to derive from the Bible, seen in itself, meanings other than those that traditional religion has seen in it. Biblical criticism thus uncovers new questions about the Bible, even as it offers fresh answers in place of old solutions.[14]

Source Criticism

Historically, source criticism has often been described under the broader rubric of *higher criticism*; in contrast, *lower criticism* refers to working back through the recensions of the text's transmission in order to determine the most original text (also called *textual criticism*).[15] The categories of higher and lower criticism are now largely outdated, and source criticism is sometimes still referred to as *literary criticism*—as opposed to textual criticism—in Europe, after the German description *Literarkritik*. This description must not be confused with the narrative-

14. James Barr, "Modern Biblical Criticism," in *The Oxford Companion to the Bible*, ed. Bruce M. Metzger and Michael D. Coogan (New York: Oxford University Press, 1993), 318.

15. For excellent treatments of textual criticism and the Old Testament, see both Ernst Würthwein, *The Text of the Old Testament*, trans. Erroll F. Rhodes, 2d ed. (Grand Rapids: Eerdmans, 1995), and Emmanuel Tov, *Textual Criticism of the Hebrew Bible* (Philadelphia: Fortress, 1992).

based poetic analysis of texts usually referred to as literary or narrative criticism in the English-speaking world.

Source criticism is also a historical pursuit, although source critics attempt to delineate not the early text types and their transmission but the compositional sources that produced the present text. The terms of source criticism are often scientific and humanistic, and source critics rely heavily on objective certitude about their findings. This sentiment is characteristic of the Enlightenment consciousness inherited from the seventeenth and eighteenth centuries. Postmodern critics, who are more humble in relation to knowledge, suspicious of power structures that they see behind texts and their consented readings, and realistic about the subjective role of the reader in the interpretive act, attempt to deconstruct such certainty.[16]

Traditional source criticism began with assumptions about the composition of the Pentateuch, and it is usually traced to the German scholar Julius Wellhausen with his widely influential *Prolegomena to the History of Israel*.[17] Wellhausen was influenced by many others, particularly the work of Karl Heinrich Graf; the so-called Documentary Hypothesis that represents Wellhausen's position is often referred to as the Graf-Wellhausen Hypothesis.[18] Essentially, the Documentary Hypothesis assumes that the books of the Pentateuch were composed by different literary hands over a large period of time, and that careful scrutiny of these bib-

---

16. For a useful epistemological description of postmodernism and its implications for various fields, including biblical studies, see Terence J. Keegan, "Biblical Criticism and the Challenge of Postmodernism," *Biblical Interpretation: A Journal of Contemporary Approaches* 3 (March 1995): 1–14. A more popular yet excellent critique of Enlightenment hubris can be found in Rolf Rendtorff, "What We Miss by Taking the Bible Apart," *Bible Review* (February 1998): 42–44. See also his "The Paradigm Is Changing: Hopes— and Fears," *Biblical Interpretation* 1 (February 1993): 34–53.

17. Translated by J. Sutherland Black and Allan Menzies, with a preface by W. Robertson Smith (Edinburgh: Adam and Charles Black, 1885).

18. Actually, Graf was the first to publish this new Documentary Hypothesis in his *Die geschichtlichen Bücher des Alten Testaments: Zwei historisch-kritische Untersuchungen* (Leipzig: T.O. Weigel) of 1866. Both Wellhausen and Graf were preceded by others with source-critical interests. Jean Astruc (1684–1766), a French physician, published his findings in 1753 (*Conjectures sur les mémoires originaux dont il paroit que Moyse s'est servi, pour composer le livre de la Genèse* [Brussels: Fricx, 1753]), in which he noted evidence for pre-Mosaic sources, even though Astruc held to Mosaic authorship for the Pentateuch. He observed that "Elohim" and "Jehovah" appeared in separate stories in Genesis, and he classified all the passages using "Elohim" in a source labeled *A*; the passages that used "Jehovah" for deity were labeled source *B*. Astruc's views were adopted by the German scholar J. G. Eichhorn (*Einleitung in das Alte Testament* [Leipzig: Weidmanns, 1780–83]), who utilized Astruc's findings and added other criteria for source division like style and thought-content, and who eventually gave up on Mosaic authorship altogether. Some refer to Eichhorn as the father of higher criticism.

lical books in their present state reveals evidence of different literary sources, documents that could be identified and described.[19] Many other biblical books, like Isaiah, for example, were assumed to have underlying sources as well. B. Duhm, in his *Das Buch Jesaja*, drew distinctions among the eighth-century prophet Isaiah, represented largely in chapters 1–39, the exilic collection of Deutero-Isaiah (chapters 40–55), and the postexilic Trito-Isaiah, covering chapters 56–66.[20] As Rolf Rendtorff writes in a critique of source-critical assumptions,

> For him [Wellhausen], and for his adherents in the following decades, the question of the sources of the Pentateuch was indissolubly connected with their respective historical settings. Dividing sources and dating sources were two sides of the same coin. Dating meant, however, relating the sources to a certain point in Israel's history, in particular in the history of its religion.[21]

The rise of historical criticism in biblical and particularly in Old Testament study reflected the greater historical concern that characterized much of the nineteenth century. Influenced by historical positivists who asserted that historical reconstruction could be undertaken with certainty—subsumed under the confident dictum of the German historian Leopold von Ranke, *wie es eigentlich gewesen* ("as it actually happened")[22]—early historical critics like Wellhausen in Germany and William Robertson Smith in Great Britain[23] were concerned to recover

19. The Documentary Hypothesis represents the most popular form of source reconstruction for the Pentateuch. There are, however, other minority perspectives. The Fragmentary Hypothesis found advocates in scholars like W. M. L. de Wette, A. Geddes, and J. S. Vater. It argued that, instead of sources or documents, a series of disconnected fragments lay behind the legal sections of the Pentateuch in particular. The Supplementary Hypothesis was posed by the German scholar H. Ewald in 1823; it stated that the E ("Elohim") document represented the core of the Pentateuch, and that a compiler had supplemented material from other sources.

20. Göttinger Handkommentar zum Alten Testament III/1 (Göttingen: Vandenhoeck and Ruprecht, 1892; 5th ed., 1968).

21. Rendtorff, "The Paradigm Is Changing," 36.

22. The concept of *positivism* was established by the French philosopher and sociologist Auguste Comte (1798–1857). It represents a school of empiricism that rejected metaphysics and theology and that, instead, held to experimental investigation and observation as the true sources of substantial knowledge. Von Ranke's full statement, "Er will bloss zeigen, wie es eigentlich gewesen," can be found in his *Geschichten der romanischen und germanischen Volker von 1494 bis 1514*, in *Sämmtliche Werke* (Leipzig, 1874), 33.vii.

23. Robertson Smith published *The Old Testament in the Jewish Church* in 1881 and *The Prophets of Israel* in 1882, popular lecture series aimed at spreading the new findings of scholarship to the broadest possible audience.

historical truth through newer critical methods like source criticism in order to make historical knowledge a foundation for faith.[24] Questions about the nature and rise of Israelite religion were approached from the larger perspective of the historical development of Israel within its ancient Near Eastern milieu. In this period, too, archaeological findings emerged from Greece and Rome, and, closer to home, from Mesopotamia and Egypt.[25]

Various criteria were employed to discern from which literary source a given text had come, such as *divine names* (whether the name for the Israelite covenantal deity—the Tetragrammaton YHWH—was used,[26] or the more generic Elohim, translated "God"); *doublets* (obvious duplication and repetition of material in the biblical text); *linguistic distinction* (such as variation in vocabulary and literary style); and *divergent ideas* (contrasting authorial perspectives, usually with respect to idiosyncrasies stemming from governing theological persuasions). From these assumedly detectable differences, specific sources were distinguished, and a developmental theory of the history of Israelite religion was established.

The proposed sources of the classic Documentary Hypothesis were named according to the following characteristics. The *J source*, or Yahwistic source, received its name from the German term *Jahwist*, because in these texts, the term "Yahweh" was used to describe the Israelite deity. The Yahwistic document was assumed to have been written in Judah during the early monarchy, c. 961–922 B.C.E., within the Solomonic era. The *E source*, or Elohistic source—so called because the general term used for deity was "Elohim"—was thought to have been written in Ephraim, the largest tribal territory in the northern kingdom, later called Israel. This document was believed to have been composed between 900–850 B.C.E. Both literary sources, J and E, were combined into a single version after the fall of Israel to the Assyrians in 721 B.C.E., an event that ended two hundred years of the divided kingdom. The *Book of Deuteronomy* (referred to as D) was connected with the "book of the law" found dur-

24. For a detailed analysis of historical-critical influence in Sweden, see Rebecca G. S. Idestrom, *From Biblical Theology to Biblical Criticism: Old Testament Scholarship at Uppsala University, 1866–1922*, Coniectanea Biblica, Old Testament Series 47 (Stockholm: Almqvist and Wiksell International, 2000).

25. Scholars like James Barr, somewhat in contrast, have suggested that the ultimate basis of biblical criticism lies more in the linguistic and literary character of the Bible, rather than in historical agendas that are brought to it. See, for example, Barr, "Modern Biblical Criticism," 318–24 (esp. 318, 320).

26. Generally depicted as "Yahweh" in English theological and particularly Christian scholarship; see below.

ing the reign of Josiah, described in 2 Kings 22, and was seen to differ radically from the preceding pentateuchal books. Therefore, it was thought that Deuteronomy had been written in Jerusalem during the seventh century B.C.E. in connection with the optimism and religious reforms of Josiah's reign. Finally, the *priestly source*, abbreviated to P,[27] was dated during the Babylonian exile, sometime between 587–539 B.C.E., and it emphasized things like sacrificial duties, the Sabbath, circumcision, and other ritualistic aspects of the Israelite cult.[28]

What are some examples of source criticism at work? The stories of beginnings in the Hebrew Bible represent two separate accounts with differing features that have been placed together in the text we now have. Genesis 1:1–2:4a, various source critics have noted, utilizes the divine name Elohim and portrays a powerful deity who remains somewhat aloof in creating the world and its inhabitants. The section is highly structured, adopting a seven-day framework that hints at the priestly concern for ritual and sabbath. Genesis 2:4b–25 (extending to 4:26) provides a different picture. The personal name Yahweh (or Yahweh Elohim) is used for deity, who is portrayed as being more immanent. The narrative is developed with elements of a gripping story, and Yahweh actively, anthropomorphically enters the human scene. Based on aspects like consistency of style, vocabulary, and theological perspective, in correspondence with other texts from the Pentateuch, source critics conclude that Genesis 1:1–2:4a should be attributed to the priestly document (P), while 2:4b–25 is the work of the Yahwist.[29]

Source criticism, then, represents a historically governed methodological approach to the biblical text in its attempts to recover the compositional sources by identifying their constituent features, according

27. Wellhausen originally referred to the priestly code as Q, from *quattuor* (Latin "four"), reflecting his view of it as the book of the four covenants (*Vierbundesbuch*).

28. Note that the term *cultic*, as used here, does not refer to heterodox sectarianism, but is a "sociology of religions" term indicating the ritualistic elements of a religion, like sacrifice.

29. Further analysis of these sections can be found in Viviano, "Source Criticism," 36–41. Placing later P material before the J narrative has strong redaction-critical implications (see below). Dale Patrick and Allen Scult, in their *Rhetoric and Biblical Interpretation* (Bible and Literature Series 26 [Sheffield: Almond Press, 1990]), have argued, developing a discourse-centred theory of power in the rhetoric of Genesis 1–2, that the J material offers a vision of human power in the give-and-take of human and divine action; the priestly writer, they conclude, allows his text to function powerfully by creating distance from the audience (see the chapter titled, "Genesis and Power: An Analysis of the Biblical Story of Creation," 103–25). Patrick and Scult argue that P supplied a frame of reference for the reading of J, and they give many implications of this rhetorical strategy.

to the considerations expressed above. Although many scholars in several countries adopted the new findings of source-critical inquiry, not everyone, whether Christian or Jewish, was, or has been, able to accept their validity. For example, Peter Miscall has voiced his disenchantment with "the disintegrative methods of historical-criticism." At least part of his problem lies with the excessive subdivision of sources and erroneous assumptions about them.[30] Jewish commentator Umberto Cassuto writes:

> The commentaries written in our generation on any book of the Pentateuch are, in most instances, chiefly devoted to investigating the sources and to determining the process by which they have been fitted together. They annotate the documentary fragments that they discern in the book rather than the book itself. The great importance attached by exegetes to the question of the sources diverts their attention from the study of the work that has grown out of these documents. In their opinion, the study of the sources takes precedence over that of the book as we have it. To my mind, the reverse view is the more reasonable.[31]

Form Criticism

Old Testament form criticism in the modern period looks to Hermann Gunkel (1862–1932) as its founder. Gunkel was the son of a Lutheran pastor and began his career in New Testament studies before switching to the Old Testament. Gunkel had been influenced by the folklore studies of the brothers Grimm—Jakob and Wilhelm—who had collected German folk traditions and classified them according to their respective categories: fairy tale, myth, saga, and legend.[32] Although Gunkel's initial contribution attempted to unravel the problems associated with the genre of apocalyptic in relation to ancient

---

30. P. Miscall, "Biblical Narrative and Categories of the Fantastic," *Semeia* 60 (1992): 39–40. See also Rolf Rendtorff's "How to Approach Leviticus" (in *Proceedings of the Tenth World Congress of Jewish Studies*; Division A: The Bible and Its World [Jerusalem: World Union of Jewish Studies, 1990], 13–20) for an excellent critique of source-critical weaknesses and the implications for writing a commentary on Leviticus. Rendtorff surveys the prior agenda of the Biblischer Kommentar series under the founding editorship of Martin Noth and Gerhard von Rad and then outlines his own perspective on writing a commentary for the third book of the Pentateuch. Whereas the original series sought to divulge information relating to traditional critical interests, Rendtorff chose to tread his own path: "[I]t has become fully clear that I am no longer sailing in the framework of the old German fleet which is still dedicated to the old-fashioned *Literarkritik*" (20).

31. U. Cassuto, preface to *A Commentary on the Book of Exodus*, trans. Israel Abrahams (Jerusalem: Magnes, 1967), 1.

32. See Gene M. Tucker, *Form Criticism of the Old Testament*, ed. J. Coert Rylaarsdam, GBS (Philadelphia: Fortress, 1971), 5.

Near Eastern mythology,[33] his commentary on the Book of Genesis, with its separately published introduction, represents his approach.[34] His work embodied a major methodological shift in questioning the function of literature in the ancient world, placing him in the Religionsgeschichtliche Schule (referred to in English as the history-of-religions school), and his form-critical analysis of Genesis attempted to locate the material within its original sociological milieu, known as its *Sitz im Leben*. Gunkel's method was originally called *Literaturgeschichte* (literary history), or *Gattungsforschung* (genre research), but later came to be known as *Formgeschichte*—form criticism—indicating its interest in arriving at the earliest forms of the Old Testament traditions, and in attempting to understand their particular genres and settings in life.[35]

Gunkel sought to distinguish the material that reflected popular oral tradition (designated *Sagen*) from the material that embodied history proper.[36] He also endeavored to elucidate the literary function of the formerly oral *Sagen* and classified them according to historical, ethnographic, and etiological categories. While historical legends reflected historical occurrences and ethnographic legends described race and tribal relations, the etiological legends (transcribed as "aetiological" in non-North American scholarship) were subdivided further by Gunkel into four types. *Ethnological* legends explained the present relation of tribes. *Etymological* legends interpreted the origin and real meaning of names of races, mountains, and so on. *Ceremonial* legends accounted for the derivation of regulations related to religious ceremony, and *geological* legends explained the origin of a locality.[37]

Gunkel identified the constituent unit of the Genesis material as the individual legend, many of which had been combined into larger collections of legend cycles during their transmission. The individual leg-

33. *Schöpfung und Chaos in Urzeit und Endzeit: Eine religionsgeschichtliche Untersuchung über Gen 1 und Ap Joh 12, mit Beitragen von Heinrich Zimmern* (Göttingen: Vandenhoeck & Ruprecht, 1895).

34. *Genesis: Ubersetzt und erklart*, HKAT I/1 (Göttingen: Vandenhoeck & Ruprecht, 1901). The introduction was published as *Die Sagen der Genesis* (in the revised edition of 1910), reprinted in English as *The Legends of Genesis: The Biblical Saga and History*, trans. W. H. Carruth (New York: Schocken, 1964). All subsequent references are to this English edition.

35. David J. A. Clines has distinguished between *first-order* methods (with understanding as their chief intention) and *second-order* methods (not principally intended to interpret the biblical text), and places form criticism with source criticism in the latter category. See his "Methods in Old Testament Study," in idem, *Beginning Old Testament Study*, 27–28, 38, 41–42.

36. Gunkel, *Legends*, 2–4.

37. Ibid., 24–36.

ends shared formal affinities with other ancient Near Eastern literatures and were thought to have possessed a long oral history before
their later incorporation into the larger collections.[38] Although collection of legends had begun at the stage of oral tradition, they were written down later after the disappearance of storytellers. The writings of J
and E—who were compilers or maybe schools of narrators, but certainly not authors, according to Gunkel—depicted "codifications of
oral traditions."[39]

Hugo Gressmann (1877–1927) supplemented the contributions of
Gunkel on Genesis through his form-critical study of the narrative sections of Exodus.[40] Gressmann was concerned to demonstrate that the
narratives about Moses and the exodus from Egypt embodied Israelite
saga. In contrast to Wellhausen, Gressmann assigned an early date to
the Decalogue of Exodus 20, due to its lack of Canaanite influence, assuming it to be earlier than the prophets and to represent one of the
foundational traditions of Israelite religion. Wellhausen had conducted
a literary analysis of the Sinai pericope, and, like Graf, argued that the
collections of cultic laws were late and that the Israelite ceremonial
laws were postexilic, postdating the prophets; but, contrastingly, he
viewed the Decalogue as an eighth-century product. Sigmund Mowinckel (1884–1966), a student of Gunkel's, argued that an old tradition could be discerned behind the account of Yahweh's revelation at
Sinai.[41] Connected with his Psalm studies, wherein he discerned several enthronement psalms (47, 93, 95–99) that celebrated the New Year
Festival, which he compared with the Babylonian *Akitu* festival, Mowinckel claimed that the Decalogue had originally been formulated in
the cult, and that its narrative context had taken shape as a result of its
cultic transmission.

In 1934, Albrecht Alt (1883–1956) published a significant form-critical article that sought to reach back from the final form of the legal
codes to their origins in ancient Israelite history.[42] Alt recognized that
the Old Testament itself presented the codes as having come directly
from Yahweh in speeches to Moses on Mount Sinai, immediately preceding the Israelites' entry into Palestine and simultaneous with the

38. Ibid., 88–91.
39. Ibid., 42–45, 123–24, 130.
40. *Mose und seine Zeit: Ein Kommentar zu den Mose-Sagen*, FRLANT 18 (Göttingen,
1913).
41. S. Mowinckel, *Le Décalogue* (Paris: n.p., 1927).
42. A. Alt, *Die Ursprünge des Israelitischen Rechts* (Leipzig, 1934); English translation,
"The Origins of Israelite Law," in *Essays on Old Testament History and Religion*, trans.
R. A. Wilson (Oxford: Basil Blackwell, 1966), 79–132. Alt's volume has recently been re-
published by Sheffield Press.

covenant-union of the people under Yahweh through Moses. Against this final-form testimony, however, Alt accepted the literary-critical conclusions of his day—that the legal codes had originated at various points in the history of Israel. The Deuteronomic Code (Deuteronomy 12–26) evidenced the restoration *Zeitgeist* of the seventh century B.C.E., when literary works had been compiled and edited upon the ideological foundations of a new national and religious consciousness. The priestly writing, whether including the Holiness Code (Leviticus 17–26) or not, was dated as late as the sixth or fifth centuries. The Decalogue (Exod. 20:2–17) and book of the covenant (Exod. 20:23–23:33) were much more difficult to date, but reflected a different place of origin than that presented in their final form.

Alt concluded that none of the codes had been composed as single literary units. To support these conclusions, Alt compared the book of the covenant with the Holiness Code, and suggested that the repetition and contradiction evidenced therein "would certainly have been removed if the separate codes had been built up into a single work."[43] Other factors, like the Decalogue destroying the coherence of the story in which it appeared and the book of the covenant manifesting "passages of different origin set side by side with virtually no formal connection,"[44] convinced Alt that the extant law codes were the conflated products of later redactions. Alt concluded, on the basis of form-critical grounds, that there were two main types of legal material within the Israelite legal corpus—the *apodictic*, which was absolute and unique to Israel, and the *casuistic*, which represented conditional case law, found all over the ancient Near East, particularly in Mesopotamian legal collections.[45]

Since the research of Gunkel and his more immediate followers, further developments in form-critical methodology have included a refinement of the method's basic axioms along with the formation of the cognate discipline, tradition history. An offshoot of form criticism, tradition history primarily aims to trace the history of each literary type by examining stages of its oral transmission.[46] After the earliest stage is decisively reached, the changes it has undergone are analyzed to reconstruct the history of the form. Resembling genre analysis in form criticism proper, the process is governed by dominant assumptions, such as that all literary types have evolved from simple structures, with basic

43. Ibid., 82.
44. Ibid., 84.
45. Alt also believed that legal forms existed that fell between the two primary forms.
46. See, conveniently, Robert A. Di Vito, "Tradition-Historical Criticism," in Haynes and McKenzie, *To Each Its Own Meaning*, 53–67.

content, to complex structures manifesting advanced concepts and complicated sentences.

Historians of exegesis often tend to present a smooth continuity between form criticism and its methodological forebear, source criticism, but as Rendtorff and others have shown, both hold independent assumptions about the form and function of the narrative, and about the historical process that brought about the text's final form. Rendtorff states, "Gunkel's approach actually was incompatible with the idea of literary 'sources' or 'documents.'"[47] Wellhausen thought the source documents of the Documentary Hypothesis had been inscribed during the particular periods and within the specific geographic localities to which he had assigned them. Hermann Gunkel, however, as a form critic interested in oral history and tradition, assumed that these same documents betrayed a series of smaller constituents, whose literary composition reflected only a later phase of their life and whose oral history could be traced much further into the past.[48] Gunkel perceived the documents as collections of oral traditions, authored only in the sense that schools of narrators had promulgated them. Therefore, in 1934, Paul Humbert stated boldly, "Gunkel by his methodological effort to dissolve the larger contexts and to go back to the smaller circles of sagas and to the single sagas as the primary units, is responsible for the downfall of the documentary hypothesis."[49]

Because of an assumed methodological impasse arising out of form criticism, James Muilenburg proposed rhetorical analysis as a means forward during his 1968 presidential address to the annual meeting of the Society of Biblical Literature.[50] Identifying problems with the form-critical method, Muilenburg argued that attention should be paid to stylistics and aesthetic criticism, in order to understand the nature of Hebrew literary composition.[51] Whether rhetoric is assumed to have a

47. Rendtorff, "The Paradigm Is Changing," 38. Rendtorff cites the 1901 review of Gunkel's Genesis commentary by Friedrich Giesebrecht (*Deutsche Literaturzeitung* 22: 1861–66), who was surprised that Gunkel continued to separate sources.

48. Gunkel's perspective on the relationship between oral and written material can be seen, for example, in "Fundamental Problems of Hebrew Literary History," in *What Remains of the Old Testament and Other Essays*, trans. A. K. Dallas (London: George Allen & Unwin, 1928), 62, 64.

49. P. Humbert; "Die neuere Genesis-Forschung," *TRu* (n.s.) 6: 208, cited in Rendtorff, "The Paradigm Is Changing," 39.

50. Later published as J. Muilenburg, "Form Criticism and Beyond," *JBL* 88 (1969): 1–18.

51. Ibid., 7–8. Muilenburg said, "It is clear that they [pericopes of Hebrew literary composition] have been skillfully wrought in many different ways, often with consummate skill and artistry. It is also apparent that they have been influenced by conventional rhetorical practices" (18).

Greek background in Aristotle and Plato, or an ancient Near Eastern background, as Katz has argued from Canaanite, Hebrew, and Meso-potamian texts,[52] rhetorical criticism within biblical studies can assist a move toward methodological balance. General principles have been expounded by Martin Kessler in *Art and Meaning: Rhetoric in Biblical Literature*[53] and more specifically in the helpful volume by Dale Patrick and Allen Scult, *Rhetoric and Biblical Interpretation*.[54]

Prior to giving an example of form criticism at work from the bibli-cal text, I offer a brief review of the principal axioms of contemporary form-critical inquiry.[55] The initial step, determining the size of the form-critical unit, analyzes the structure of the passage.[56] Recognition of beginning and ending formulas, often clearly marked in the text, and formal characteristics like parallelism and symmetry are imperative to the form-critical study of poetry.[57] After this delineation of generic pa-rameters, the specific genre of the form-critical unit, as a second step, needs to be identified.[58] The third step involves reconstructing the *Sitz*

52. Ronald C. Katz, *The Structure of Ancient Arguments: Rhetoric and Its Near Eastern Origin* (New York: Shapolsky/Steimatzky, 1986).

53. Edited by David J. A. Clines, David M. Gunn, and Alan J. Hauser, JSOTSup (Shef-field: JSOT Press, 1982), 1–19.

54. See n. 29 above. Patrick and Scult's essays on Job (81–102) and Genesis 1–3 (103–25) offer the best example of the method proposed here, although their theoretical chap-ters are also very good, especially chap. 1, "Rhetorical Criticism and Biblical Exegesis," and chap. 2, "The Rhetorical Character of Biblical Narrative." See also Yehoshua Gitay, "Rhetorical Criticism," in Haynes and McKenzie, *To Each Its Own Meaning*, 135–49.

55. Note that the Forms of Old Testament Literature commentary series (FOTL) con-cerns itself specifically with form-critical matters.

56. Gerhard Lohfink, *The Bible: Now I Get it! A Form Criticism Handbook*, trans. Daniel Coogan (Garden City, N.Y.: Doubleday, 1979), 35–39; Tucker, *Form Criticism of the Old Testament*, 12–13.

57. Klaus Koch, *The Growth of the Biblical Tradition: The Form-Critical Method*, trans. S. M. Cupitt (London: Adam & Charles Black, 1969), 91–100. One significant issue with form-critical implications regards what constitutes Hebrew poetry as distinguished from prose, discussed by James L. Kugel, *The Idea of Biblical Poetry* (New Haven: Yale Univer-sity Press, 1981), 63, 69–70, passim. Kugel rejects the sharp distinction between poetry and prose based on the presence or absence of parallelism; this identification of parallel-ism with poetry and non-parallelism with prose is a Hellenistic imposition, thinks Kugel, undertaken by earlier scholars steeped in the study of Greek meter (71, 85–86). For help-ful manuals on the workings of Hebrew poetry, see Wilfred Watson, *Classical Hebrew Po-etry: A Guide to Its Techniques*, JSOTSup 26 (Sheffield: JSOT Press, 1987), and idem, *Traditional Techniques in Classical Hebrew Verse*, JSOTSup 170 (Sheffield: Sheffield Ac-ademic Press, 1994).

58. Koch, *Growth of the Biblical Tradition*, 13–16, 23–26, 53–54; Lohfink, *The Bible: Now I Get It!* 39–42; Tucker, *Form Criticism of the Old Testament*, 13–15. The virtually endless variety of methods for discerning literary types can be seen by briefly scanning O. Eissfeldt, "The Pre-literary Stage: The Smallest Units and Their Setting in Life," in *The Old Testament: An Introduction*, trans. Peter R. Ackroyd (New York: Harper & Row,

im Leben from which the literary form originated.[59] G. W. Anderson, outlining Gunkel's approach, highlights the predominant form-critical assumption that all literary types have evolved from simple to complex structures: "Gunkel held that it was the function of literary history to recognize and classify their forms (*Gattungen*), to relate each to its setting in life (*Sitz im Leben*), and to trace their historical development. This development leads from the simple, short literary unit, produced and preserved by the oral tradition of which the community is the custodian, on to the blending and interaction of different *Gattungen* in more sophisticated ages."[60] The sociological milieu in which the genre was produced may relate, for example, to the cult or royal court, to legal institutions, to specific family settings, or to general clan life. Critics of Gunkel's rigid relationship between genre formalities and *Sitz im Leben* have shown, however, that matters are not as fixed as Gunkel originally presupposed.[61] The fourth step seeks to determine the intention and function of the unit, reflecting Gunkel's concern to classify the generic traditions according to historical, ethnographic, and etiological categories.[62]

A useful exemplar of form-critical practice can be found in the birth story of Moses from Exodus 2:1–10. Generally assumed by source crit-

---

1965), 9–127. Note the various critiques of Gunkel's rigid view of genre and other related genre issues in Martin J. Buss, "The Study of Forms," in *Old Testament Form Criticism*, ed. John H. Hayes (San Antonio: Trinity University Press, 1974), 1–56, as well as idem, "The Idea of *Sitz im Leben*—History and Critique," *ZAW* 90 (1978): 157–70; see also William G. Doty, "The Concept of Genre in Literary Analysis," in *SBLSP*, ed. Lane C. McGaughy (Missoula, Mont.: Society of Biblical Literature, 1972), 2.413–48; Rolf Knierim, "Old Testament Form Criticism Reconsidered," *Int* 27 (October 1973): 435–68; Tremper Longman III, "Form Criticism, Recent Developments in Genre Theory, and the Evangelical," *WTJ* 47 (1985): 46–67; and Roy F. Melugin, "The Typical versus the Unique among the Hebrew Prophets," in *SBLSP*, ed. Lane C. McGaughy (Missoula, Mont.: Society of Biblical Literature, 1972), 2.331–41.

59. Koch, *Growth of the Biblical Tradition*, 26–28, 34–38; Lohfink, *The Bible: Now I Get It!* 45–60; Tucker, *Form Criticism of the Old Testament*, 15–16.

60. G. W. Anderson, *A Critical Introduction to the Old Testament*, Studies in Theology (London: Gerald Duckworth, 1959), 5.

61. See Douglas A. Knight, "The Understanding of *Sitz im Leben* in Form Criticism," in *SBLSP*, ed. Paul A. Achtemeier (Missoula, Mont.: Society of Biblical Literature, 1974), 1.105–25, and Burke O. Long, "Recent Field Studies in Oral Literature and the Question of *Sitz im Leben*," *Semeia* 5 (1976): 35–49.

62. Lohfink, *The Bible: Now I Get It!* 42–45; Tucker, *Form Criticism of the Old Testament*, 16–17. Klaus Koch represents a position that integrates form-critical and traditio-historical concerns, thus broadening the scope of inquiry to: (1) define the unit; (2) determine the literary type; (3) investigate the transmission history; (4) reconstruct the setting in life; and (5) trace the history of redaction.

---

ics to derive either from the work of the Yahwist (J)[63] or the Elohist (E),[64] the passage receives different treatment from form critics, who are more interested to get behind the later written documents to understand the oral traditions underlying them. With respect to this pericope, the two foci for our present purposes are the generic form of the episode and the closing etiological segment—along with the relationship it holds with the surrounding narrative.[65]

With respect to form, comparative ancient Near Eastern studies have discovered the fairly close relationship that the text holds with the legend of Sargon of Akkad, a Mesopotamian king of the third millennium B.C.E.[66] Supported by some thirty-two comparative accounts from the ancient Near Eastern and Greco-Roman worlds, which include the motif of an exposed child who later becomes a hero,[67] the form of the narrative must be considered very seriously. As Marshall McLuhan would say, "The medium *is* the message." So what might this mean for the passage's interpretation? It means at least that this story, described as heroic saga by George W. Coats,[68] depicts a character of utmost significance for the narrative that follows, and that close attention should be paid to him.[69]

As discussed above, Gunkel classified biblical materials according to various categories, one of which was *etiological;* etiological el-

---

63. J. P. Hyatt, *Exodus*, New Century Bible (London: Marshall, Morgan & Scott, 1971), 22, 61, 63, who describes it as a "straightforward, almost secular, narrative lacking in names . . . likely to come from the basic J source" (63). Also, Noth, *Exodus: A Commentary*, trans. J. S. Bowden, OTL (Philadelphia: Westminster, 1962), 25.

64. Childs, *The Book of Exodus: A Critical, Theological Commentary*, OTL (Philadelphia: Westminster, 1974), 7.

65. For a thoroughly detailed discussion of what follows, see my "Moses' Birth Story: A Biblical Matrix for Prophetic Messianism," in *Eschatology, Messianism, and the Dead Sea Scrolls*, ed. Craig A. Evans and Peter W. Flint, vol. 1 of *Studies in the Dead Sea Scrolls and Related Literature*, Martin G. Abegg Jr. and Peter W. Flint, general editors (Grand Rapids: Eerdmans, 1997), 10–22.

66. For the standard texts of the legend, see *ANET* 119. See also Walter Beyerlin, ed., *Near Eastern Religious Texts Relating to the Old Testament* (London: SCM, 1978), 98–99. These similarities have been discussed since Gressmann's *Mose und seine Zeit* (see n. 40 above).

67. As discussed in Donald B. Redford, "The Literary Motif of the Exposed Child," *Numen* 14 (1967): 209–28.

68. G. W. Coats, *Moses: Heroic Man, Man of God*, JSOTSup 57 (Sheffield: JSOT Press, 1988), 1–42 passim, 43–48.

69. Terence Fretheim describes the story as "a paradigm for Israel's experience of redemption" (40) in his discussion of the larger section that he considers to be replete with irony. See his "Exodus," in *Interpretation: A Bible Commentary for Teaching and Preaching* (Louisville: John Knox, 1991), esp. 31–37.

ements seek to explain the origin of specific phenomena or to legit-
imize certain practices at the pre-literary phase.[70] One type from
Gunkel's subdivision was the *etymological* legend, concerned with
the explanation of name origins. Exodus 2:10 contains an etymological etiology in the words of Pharaoh's daughter, who names the
child: "She called his name Moses, and she said, 'Because from the
waters he was drawn.'" This etiological explanation is somewhat
puzzling, not only because it presents an Egyptian woman of royalty
speaking Hebrew, but more particularly because of apparent discrepancies between the participial form of the verb used in the explanation itself ("was drawn" is passive) and the form that the name
embodies. *Mosheh*, the Hebrew word for Moses, is not passive, as in
"he was drawn out," but is active, thus reading "he *will* draw out"—
an appellative that foreshadows the great role that this hero will
have in bringing the descendants of Israel out of the waters (Exodus
14) and into the Promised Land.[71] Only by paying critical attention
to matters of form can these details be discerned, imbued as they are
with theological significance for one's reading. Moses is singled out
as one who will become the great deliverer of Yahweh's people out
of Egypt and who will become a paradigm for the messianic ministry of Jesus.[72]

Redaction Criticism

Redaction criticism grew directly out of form criticism, developing
especially after the Second World War. This approach, referred to as
Redaktionsgeschichte in German, attempts to understand how a particular tradition came to its present shape;[73] more specifically, this branch
of criticism wants to discern what editorial (i.e., redactional) decisions
were made with respect to selectivity and theological emphasis, as the
various sources were brought into a unified (or at least, coherent)

---

70. Analysis of the difficulties of etiology, particularly relating to history, can be
found in Burke O. Long, *The Problem of Etiological Narrative in the Old Testament*, BZAW
108 (Berlin: A. Töpelmann, 1968); Brevard S. Childs, "The Etiological Tale Re-exam-
ined," *VT* 24 (October 1974): 387–97; and R. Smend, "Tradition and History: A Complex
Relation," in *Tradition and Theology in the Old Testament*, ed. Douglas A. Knight (London: SPCK, 1977), esp. 57–60.

71. For various viewpoints on the complicated matter of the name, see my *Moses'
Birth Story*, 15–16. The theological conclusion I draw there is that, as with the name of
Jesus, name equals vocation. The paranomasis (wordplay involving a personal name) of
Exodus 2:10 reinforces this perspective.

72. See my "Moses' Birth Story," 12–13, 21–22.

73. The term *Redaktionsgeschichte* (redaction history) was first used by Willi Marxsen
in *Mark the Evangelist*, published in German in 1956.

whole.[74] The study of redaction assumes, on the one hand, that the biblical text has circulated in different forms at earlier stages, and this work reflects the historical aspect of redaction criticism. There are, on the other hand, literary and theological decisions that must be considered as well. The redaction critic asks why a redactor selected the materials he did, and for what purpose the units of tradition were placed alongside each other. In other words, what rhetorical and theological purposes does this newer literary configuration of traditions serve? The redactors were not merely collectors and assemblers of the traditions they handled, it is assumed, but creative literary and theological contributors. Questions surrounding redaction criticism are much like those in the historical discipline of historiography, considering issues of selectivity, pattern, point of view, and the like.[75]

Although redaction critics work from the final form of biblical books, they assume that these texts represent the latest stage of the books' formation, and that many editorial changes and textual renegotiations have taken place in order to bring the book to its present state. For example, in the documentary theory of pentateuchal origins, various redactions took place as the J and E sources were brought together, with the D material subsequently joined to the JE block; ultimately, the priestly material (P) was worked into the JED collection.

In a word, then, redaction criticism concerns the work of the editors who incorporated earlier traditions into the present text. As a redaction critic, one is concerned to identify those places where a redactor has edited an earlier text or tradition, observing introductions and conclusions to biblical books, transitional passages, words or phrases that do not seem to fit the framework, and so on, in attempts to understand the editors' literary and theological objectives. The notion of redactional *intention* is very important.

In order to illustrate the significance of redaction criticism and the potential theological implications of redactional choices, I will exam-

74. Much of the study of redaction has occurred in New Testament studies, particularly in attempts to figure out the historical and theological relationships among the Synoptic Gospels. For a primer by a key New Testament redaction critic, see Norman R. Perrin, *What Is Redaction Criticism?* Guides to Biblical Scholarship, New Testament Series (Philadelphia: Fortress, 1969).

75. Standard historical description of these matters is found in E. H. Carr, *What Is History?* (New York: Vintage, 1961), passim, and in R. G. Collingwood, *The Idea of History*, edited and with a preface by T. M. Knox (London: Oxford University Press, 1946), 86–133. For a useful compendium—especially for Old Testament studies—of ancient versus modern concepts of history and the role of religious and theological matters, see Robert C. Dentan, ed., *The Idea of History in the Ancient Near East* (New Haven: Yale University Press, 1955), esp. "The Twentieth-Century West and the Ancient Near East," by Paul Schubert, 313–53.

ine the Exodus chapters that relate the plagues, as Moses and Aaron contest the Egyptian pharaoh and his magicians in Exodus 7–11. From a source-critical perspective, it seems clear that the account of the ten plagues derives from two separate literary sources, J (or JE) and P.[76] Differentiated source material can be gleaned from analyzing features within the plagues cycle, like formal structure, explicit character description of Pharaoh, Yahweh, Moses/Aaron, and the magicians, outcome (including distinctions between Israel/Egypt), and governing images.[77] Although these descriptions of the plagues seem to represent differing provenance, they have been redacted for expressly theological purposes in a pattern of three conceptually cumulative triads.

Moshe Greenberg has argued that, in their present form, the plagues evidence structural balance that promotes the powerful rhetoric of Yahweh's supremacy in the divine contest between Yahweh and Pharaoh.[78] Greenberg observes that the plague narratives occur in three triplets, which escalate in their development and are finally completed by a tenth plague that lies outside the framework;[79] the first triplet contains plagues 1, 4, 7,[80] the second triplet contains plagues 2, 5, 8,[81] and the third triplet contains plagues 3, 6, and 9.[82] Three introductory formulas characterize the triplets: in the first triplet, God commissions Moses to warn Pharaoh by the Nile in the morning (7:15; 8:20; 9:13); in the second, God directs Moses to warn Pharaoh in his palace (8:1; 9:1; 10:1); and, in the third, God instructs Moses and Aaron to initiate the plague without warning (8:16; 9:8; 10:21).

76. Some have suggested the influence of D as well. For example, William Johnstone, "The Deuteronomistic Cycles of 'Signs' and 'Wonders' in Exodus 1–13," in *Understanding Poets and Prophets: Essays in Honour of George Wishart Anderson*, ed. A. Graeme Auld, JSOTSup 152 (Sheffield: JSOT Press, 1993), 166–85.

77. Many of these features are covered in my "A Literary Reading of the Exodus Story" (Ph.D. diss., University of Edinburgh, 1994), esp. in "Appendix Two: Discourse Structure of the Plagues," 235–57.

78. M. Greenberg, "The Redaction of the Plague Narrative in Exodus," in *Near Eastern Studies in Honor of William Foxwell Albright*, ed. Hans Goedicke (Baltimore and London: Johns Hopkins University Press, 1971), 243–52. In this study, Greenberg is interested in tracing the redaction of the story that, for him, consists of the two tradition complexes of JE and P, each with an original seven-part plague story and unique intention—JE conceiving the plagues as punishment and P perceiving them as demonstrations of God's power.

79. Death of the firstborn, Exodus 11:1–10; 12:29–42.

80. Water to blood, 7:14–24; insects, 8:20–32; hail, 9:13–35.

81. Frogs, 7:25–8:15; death of livestock, 9:1–7; locusts, 10:1–20.

82. Gnats, 8:16–19; boils, 9:8–12; darkness, 10:21–29.

More significant from a theological perspective, three distinctive motifs appear within these triplets. The first triplet of plagues illustrates *the superiority of God and his agents to the magicians of Egypt*, supported by the phrase "that you may know that I am Yahweh" (7:17); the second triplet shows *God's presence within Egypt*, evidenced by the plagues that separate Israel and the Egyptians (8:18f.; 9:4, 6) and supported by the phrase "that you may know that I am Yahweh in the midst of the land" (8:22); the third triplet demonstrates *the incomparability of God*, demonstrated by the intensity of the plagues and supported by the phrase "that you may know that there is none like me in all the earth" (9:14).[83] These plagues have been brought together and structured to emphasize Yahweh's cosmological rule in a context of oppression and injustice, reinforced by the concentric triads of cumulative rhetorical thrust.[84]

Mention should also be made of *canon criticism*. Unlike the types of criticism examined thus far which tend to fall in the diachronic category and which are interested largely in historical reconstruction, the canonical approach arose out of the biblical theology movement of the American postwar period.[85] This approach is most commonly associated with Brevard S. Childs and James A. Sanders, although each defines and utilizes canonical criticism in slightly different ways.[86] For Sanders, canonical criticism flows naturally from redaction criticism, in that, for him, the *process* by which the faith community arrived at the text's final form is emphasized.[87] For Childs, on the other hand, canonical criticism overlaps with literary criticism because of its primary interest in the *product*, the final form of the text and its theological shape.[88]

---

83. Greenberg, "Redaction of the Plague Narrative," 244–45.

84. Cassuto describes the plague narrative as having been "constructed with architectonic perfection" in his *Commentary on Exodus*, 93. His views on composition differ from those of Greenberg.

85. The term was devised by James Sanders in his *Torah and Canon* (Philadelphia: Fortress, 1972).

86. For further examples of this approach, see the essay by Craig C. Broyles "Traditions, Intertextuality, and Canon," in the present volume (chap. 5).

87. See James A. Sanders, *Canon and Community: A Guide to Canonical Criticism* (Philadelphia: Fortress, 1984); and *From Sacred Story to Sacred Text* (Philadelphia: Fortress, 1987).

88. Already intimated in his *Biblical Theology in Crisis* (Philadelphia: Westminster, 1970), a clear introduction to Childs's method can be found in his *Introduction to the Old Testament as Scripture* (Philadelphia: Fortress, 1979). His *Old Testament Theology in a Canonical Context* (Philadelphia: Fortress, 1985) explores the theological dimension of his method.

Contemporary Criticisms

Several new methodological strategies have been brought to the text of the Bible,[89] generally reflecting what is going on in the criticism of literature at large. A brief perusal of M. H. Abrams's *A Glossary of Literary Terms*, which discusses methodological types of the twentieth century, reveals such diverse approaches as archetypal criticism, deconstruction, feminist criticism, influence and the anxiety of influence, linguistics, Marxist criticism, phenomenology, psychological and psychoanalytic criticism, reader-response criticism, reception theory, Russian formalism, semiotics, speech-act theory, structuralist criticism, and stylistics.[90] There are too many contemporary theoretical applications to treat them with adequacy.

One general wave, however, has moved from diachronic study—the standard mode of historical-critical inquiry—to concerns that are much more synchronic.[91] Begun by people like David Robertson[92] and Robert Alter,[93] this new wave includes many interpreters who have sought to uncover the narrative intricacies of the Hebrew Bible without recourse nec-

89. The third section of Haynes and McKenzie's *To Each Its Own Meaning*, cited above, provides a useful compendium for what is going on currently in biblical studies. Entitled "Overturning the Tradition," the section includes essays on structural criticism, narrative criticism, reader-response criticism, poststructuralist criticism, and feminist criticism. *Biblical Interpretation: A Journal of Contemporary Approaches* and, to a lesser degree, *Journal for the Study of the Old Testament*, are both important channels for newer methodological readings. *Biblical Interpretation*'s mandate is to "provide both a forum for fresh interpretation of particular texts and a forum for theoretical debate."

90. See M. H. Abrams's excellent comprehensive essay, "Modern Theories of Literature and Criticism," in *A Glossary of Literary Terms*, 5th ed. (New York: Holt, Rinehart & Winston, 1988), 201–47. An excellent reader in current literary method is *Contemporary Literary Theory*, ed. G. Douglas Atkins and Laura Morrow (n.p.: University of Massachusetts Press, 1989).

91. The diachronic/synchronic distinction arose out of Ferdinand de Saussure's lectures at the University of Geneva between 1906 and 1911 (published in English as *Course in General Linguistics*, trans. Roy Harris, ed. Charles Bally and Albert Sechehaye with the collaboration of Albert Riedlinger [London: Duckworth, 1983]). For de Saussure, the father of modern linguistics, *diachronic* study, described as "evolutionary linguistics," set out to document historical changes that occurred in a language or languages over a period of time (81, 89–90, 98, 139), examining their origins, development, and history. *Synchronic* study, referred to as "static linguistics," attempted to investigate the linguistic phenomenon and not its diachronic development through the historical process (81, 89–90, 98–100). Within biblical studies, *diachronic* usually refers to methods that have historical reconstruction in mind, while *synchronic* refers to methods more concerned with the text in its final form.

92. *The Old Testament and the Literary Critic*, Guides to Biblical Scholarship (Philadelphia: Fortress, 1977).

93. *The Art of Biblical Narrative* (New York: Basic Books, 1981).

essarily to a particular historical reconstruction.[94] Robertson stated already in 1977 that the literary study of the Bible represented a major paradigm shift.[95] Synchronic concerns with discovering enplotment, characterization, narratological structure, and the like have opened fresh readings of biblical texts. The study of character types and characterization techniques, for example, has uncovered literary-theoretical details that can greatly enhance theological understanding. Although historical-critical issues may be suspended in pursuit of more explicitly literary aims, blind resort to precritical assumptions, or denial of historical referentiality that is replaced by an assumption of the Bible's self-referential status[96]— akin to the New Critics' idea of *autotelicism*[97]—must be avoided.[98]

94. See, for example, Shimon Bar-Efrat, *Narrative Art in the Bible*, JSOTSup 70, Bible and Literature Series 17 (Sheffield: Almond Press, 1989); Adele Berlin, *Poetics and Interpretation of Biblical Narrative* (Sheffield: Almond Press, 1983); David Gunn and Dana Nolan Fewell, *Narrative in the Hebrew Bible*, Oxford Bible Series (Oxford: Oxford University Press, 1993); Meir Sternberg, *The Poetics of Biblical Narrative: Ideological Literature and the Drama of Reading* (Bloomington: Indiana University Press, 1985).

95. To be precise, a *fourth* paradigm shift. The *first* paradigm change occurred when Jewish people began to read the diverse Hebrew writings as Scripture. The *second* occurred when Christians took over this canonical literature and read it as Scripture from a Christian perspective. The *third* paradigm shift is represented in the more recent enterprise of reading the Old Testament according to the strict parameters set by critical historiography (Robertson, *Old Testament and the Literary Critic*, 4).

96. Robertson, *Old Testament and the Literary Critic*, 5. A helpful discussion of *reference*, which considers both mimetic and "textual world" issues, appears in Wendell V. Harris, *Dictionary of Concepts in Literary Criticism and Theory*, Reference Sources for the Social Sciences and Humanities 12 (Westport, Conn.: Greenwood, 1992), s.v. "reference," 330–37.

97. *Autotelicism* distinguished literature and art as self-referential entities from works that referred to things and/or reality outside of themselves. The New Critics were a group of American writers in the 1930s and 1940s who opposed critical efforts associated with Romanticism and nineteenth-century Realism. The term was popularized by John Crowe Ransom's *The New Criticism* (1941), which ordered a new approach to the study of literature described as "ontological," against traditional criticism that was connected firmly with the intention of the writer, along with his or her biographical details and influences. Instead, the New Critics encouraged a close reading of the text as a self-contained work. See *The Cambridge Guide to Literature in English*, ed. Ian Ousby (Cambridge: Cambridge University Press, 1993), s.v. "new criticism," 674; *Bloomsbury Guide to English Literature*, ed. Marion Wynne-Davies (London: Bloomsbury, 1989), s.v. "new criticism," 744; *The Oxford Companion to English Literature*, ed. Margaret Drabble, 5th ed. (Oxford: Oxford University Press, 1985), s.v. "new criticism," 693; and the more exhaustive overview by John R. Willingham, "The New Criticism: Then and Now," in Atkins and Morrow, *Contemporary Literary Theory*, 24–41. For a helpful integration with biblical studies, see John Barton's *Reading the Old Testament: Method in Biblical Study*, cited above, and his chapter on "New Criticism."

98. Note the important qualifications of Brigid Curtin Frein, "Fundamentalism and Narrative Approaches to the Gospels," *Biblical Theology Bulletin* 22 (spring 1992): 12–18, and Mark Allen Powell, *What Is Narrative Criticism? A New Approach to the Bible*, Guides

Conclusion

In closing, it must be emphasized that a certain degree of method-ological pluralism is welcome; of course, Robert Alter's distinction be-tween "interpretive pluralism" and "interpretive anarchy" must be re-spected.[99] There is no methodological hierarchy, however, at the top of which stands *the* supreme and ultimate method. Instead, it must be ac-knowledged that "methods are a means to an end,"[100] that "a 'method' will only be coherent if it is guided by a clearly articulated question or goal."[101] As Walter Moberly writes, encouraging metacritical reflection in a discussion of approaches to pentateuchal issues,

> [T]he crucial question, which is prior to questions of method and sets the context for them, is that of purpose and goal. To put it simply, *how we use the Bible depends on why we use the Bible*. In practice, many of the dis-agreements about how are, in effect, disagreements about why, and fail-ure to recognize this leads to endless confusion.[102]

Theoretically, one must articulate and hold firm to foundations such as, for example, notions of biblical authority and inspiration within the hermeneutical pursuit. It is imperative to recognize, along with Ray-mond Hammer, that "the biblical message is addressed to the whole person and not simply to the intellect. Hence, to recognize the author-ity of the Bible is to respond to the imperatives made by the God of the Bible. For ultimately what is looked for is an encounter not with lan-

---

to Biblical Scholarship, New Testament Series (Philadelphia: Fortress, 1990), esp. 3. Both Frein and Powell emphasize that a literary approach is not automatically antihis-torical or opposed to diachronic exegesis, but merely that narrative critics move beyond historical criticism, considering each text open to multiple interpretations from a variety of hermeneutical strategies.

99. R. Alter, *The Pleasures of Reading in an Ideological Age* (New York: Simon and Schuster, 1989), 19. Mark Brett, in his monograph on Childs's canonical method, offers a useful distinction between hermeneutical *pluralism* (advocating a plurality of methods rel-ative to the goals of the interpreter), and hermeneutical *monism* (which assumes a com-monality of interpretive goals) (Brett, *Biblical Criticism in Crisis?* 41–42). Harris helpfully distinguishes between *variation* ("The principle that readers' interpretations and responses will necessarily vary within certain limits") and *limitation* ("The principle that no one set of theoretical assumptions or methodological approaches and no one critical vocabulary can adequately describe a text or exhaust its possible meanings or significances") (*Dictio-nary of Concepts in Literary Criticism and Theory*, s.v. "pluralism [literary critical]," 283).

100. Clines, "Methods in Old Testament Study," 27.

101. Brett, "Four or Five Things to Do with Texts," 357. Brett suggests that discussion of method requires an earlier discussion of what he terms "interpretative interests."

102. W. Moberly, *The Old Testament of the Old Testament* (Minneapolis: Fortress, 1992), 2, also 182.

guage but with a person."[103] By maintaining a similar perspective, one will avoid the peril of Julius Wellhausen, who lamented,

> I became a theologian because of my interest in the scientific study of the Bible. Gradually I realized that a professor of theology has at the same time the practical task of preparing the students for their ministry in the Protestant church. But I do not succeed in this practical task; notwithstanding all my restraint, I render the students incapable of their ministry. Thus my theological professorship weighs heavily upon my conscience.[104]

103. R. Hammer, "Authority of the Bible," in *The Oxford Companion to the Bible*, ed. Bruce M. Metzger and Michael D. Coogan (New York: Oxford University Press, 1993), 67f.

104. Letter of 1872, quoted in Rolf Rendtorff, "What We Miss by Taking the Bible Apart," 43. Consider also Helmut Thielicke's plea for humility and balance within theology in his classic *A Little Exercise for Young Theologians* (Grand Rapids: Eerdmans, 1962).

nine

Theology and the Old Testament

JONATHAN R. WILSON

When Jesus was walking on the road to Emmaus with two of his disciples after the resurrection, Luke tells us that "beginning with Moses and all the Prophets, [Jesus] explained to them what was said in all the Scriptures concerning himself" (24:27 NIV). When the Holy Spirit was given to the gathered disciples on the day of Pentecost, Peter declares "this is that which was spoken by the prophet Joel" (Acts 2:16 KJV; see Joel 2:28–32). When Paul writes to the church in Corinth about the events of Jesus' life, he says "that he died for our sins according to the scriptures, that he was buried, [and] that he was raised on the third day according to the scriptures" (1 Cor. 15:3–4). When Paul writes to the Galatians in defense of the gospel of grace, his argument turns on the story of Abraham (Galatians 3–4).

Clearly, for the early followers of Jesus Christ, the Scriptures consisted of the "Old Testament" and were indispensable to their understanding both of God's work in Jesus Christ and of their own lives as Christians. When they declared that Jesus of Nazareth is "the Christ" (the Greek term for the Hebrew "Messiah"), where did they get their understanding of "Christ"? When the early church was given the Holy Spirit, where did they first turn to understand that gift? When they called people to faith, where did they turn for an exemplar of faith? The answer to all of these questions is, of course, the Old Testament.

Today, however, the situation is often different. Christians are unfamiliar with the Old Testament. They may recall a few exciting and romantic stories from Sunday school. But if they are pressed to explain how the OT shapes their lives in Jesus Christ, they would have very little to say. But "ordinary" Christians are not the only ones unfamiliar with the OT. The work of theologians is often also distant from the OT. As theology and OT studies have developed in the modern world, they have become increasingly specialized, and the gap between them has grown. Theology has taken on a life of its own, so that many theologians seem simply to be talking to and about other theologians and have forgotten the Scriptures that gave rise to their work. If the NT is of secondary interest, the OT seems positively irrelevant to a lot of contemporary theology.

So the OT is missing from much of the life of the church and from theology. But there are encouraging signs. Particularly among Christian scholars, several voices have been promoting renewed attention to the relationship between theology and biblical studies. We are being encouraged to close the gap and to overcome the sharp "wall of separation" between the Bible and theology.

I add my voice to that growing number by giving some directions for the role of the OT in the work of theology. By so doing, I will also give some directions for how the OT should shape our lives as followers of Jesus Christ. If the OT was indispensable to those who wrote the NT, then it should also be indispensable to us today.

This task is enormous; it touches on many difficult and controversial questions. For example, what is the relationship between the OT and the NT? Is the OT promise and the NT fulfillment? How is the "old covenant" related to the "new covenant"? What is the relationship between the Israel of the OT and the church of the NT? What commands of the OT are still in force today? Should we distinguish among various types of laws and regulations in the OT, such as ceremonial, civil, and moral? These are profound and controversial questions that give us a sense of the complexities that we face. I cannot fully answer them here, although I will certainly indicate how we should wrestle with them.

In this chapter my goal is to provide a guide for how we may submit to the authority of the OT while we do our theological work. In other words, I will give directions for how the OT guides the formation of our convictions and our lives as Christians. This chapter will not complete the work that we have to do; it will simply give some directions for how to begin that work and how to continue it.

Because the gap between biblical studies and theology has grown so wide and because attention has only recently been turned to closing that gap, I cannot draw on any scholarly consensus in this chapter. Instead I add my own thinking to some of the groundbreaking work that is being done.[1] Therefore, I devote the first three parts of this chapter to clearing away some misconceptions, so that the field will be clear for my own proposal.

I begin by addressing some practical obstacles to our understanding of the OT. These practical obstacles may be cleared away by the kind of work and study described in the previous chapters. But even after these obstacles are cleared, there are still two obstacles to a healthy relationship between theology and the OT. These obstacles are theoretical. The first is our understanding of theology. If we are to relate theology and the OT, we must have some concept of what theology is. As I will show, this is not as straightforward as we may think. Therefore, in this section I lay out four understandings of the task or purpose of theology that may shape in specific ways our approach to the OT. I argue that an "imaginative-practical" approach best opens the relationship between theology and the OT. The second "theoretical" obstacle is the dominant way of understanding the relationship between OT scholarship and the work of theology. I argue that this understanding is faulty and misleads us at several points. Next, I propose another understanding of the relationship between OT scholarship and theology that is based on my argument about the purpose of theology. Finally, I consider how my proposal guides the formation of our convictions and our lives as followers of Jesus Christ.

Practical Obstacles

Scholars are usually preoccupied with the kinds of issues that concern them as scholars—the kinds of issues that we consider in the next two sections. But it is also important to acknowledge that there are practical issues that obstruct our approach to theology and the OT. In this section I identify three such issues.[2]

1. Some works that explicitly seek to close this gap are Stephen E. Fowl, *Engaging Scripture: A Model for Theological Interpretation* (Oxford: Blackwell, 1998); Kevin J. Vanhoozer, *Is There a Meaning in This Text? The Bible, the Reader, and the Morality of Literary Knowledge* (Grand Rapids: Zondervan, 1998); Nicholas Lash, *Theology on the Way to Emmaus* (London: SCM, 1986); Brevard S. Childs, *Biblical Theology of the Old and New Testaments: Theological Reflection on the Christian Bible* (Minneapolis: Fortress, 1992); Frances Watson, *Text, Church, and World: Biblical Interpretation in Theological Perspective* (Grand Rapids: Eerdmans, 1994); and idem, *Text and Truth: Redefining Biblical Theology* (Grand Rapids: Eerdmans, 1997).

2. In what follows I am drawing on the thoughtful and accessible discussion of Tremper Longman III, *Making Sense of the Old Testament: Three Crucial Questions* (Grand Rapids: Baker, 1998), 17–22. Longman identifies four obstacles. I discuss the first three here. The fourth, more theological in nature (the place of the OT in the history of redemption), will be addressed below.

The first practical obstacle is the *sheer size and diversity of the* OT. Because of this fact, we are often familiar only with snippets of OT text. We may remember a few stories from Sunday school, but we would be hard-pressed to place them in the context of the larger OT story. We may draw on them for encouragement at various points in our lives, but we would have difficulty identifying their significance for our theology. We may also remember a few texts, such as the Ten Commandments or Psalm 23, but again we would have difficulty describing their place in the work of God witnessed in the OT.

The second practical obstacle is the *antiquity of the* OT. Because the OT is "old," we have difficulty placing the OT and its accounts in historical context. When we add to this that the OT covers more than 1,500 years of history, from Abraham to the restoration from exile, the problem is compounded. Because we are unfamiliar with ancient history, we tend to "flatten out" our reading of the OT. That is, we tend to read it as contemporary literature. Certainly, the OT is God's word for us today, but it comes to us from long ago.

This leads us to the third practical obstacle: *cultural distance*. Because many of us have grown up with the Bible in our homes, and because we tend to select passages from the OT that are most accessible to us, a student's first encounter with the full text of the OT is often a strange and alienating experience. Students are simply not prepared for such a "cross-cultural experience." This culture shock can result in the OT quickly becoming a closed book for contemporary Christians.

The first step to overcoming these obstacles is simply a lot of hard work. We must find a translation of the OT that encourages and enables the reading of large portions of the text. We must become familiar with the history that it recites and the culture that it reflects. The second step is to recognize that God's redemption occurs within culture, not above it (wherever that might be). So the strangeness of the OT can be an aid to understanding God's work today, because it gives us some distance from our own familiar culture. An illustration may help here. Many students report that they really begin to understand how their native language works when they first study another language. In the same way, studying God's work in the OT may help us better understand God's work today. Since the OT was the Scripture of the earliest Christians and their guide to understanding God's work in Jesus Christ, then we who are followers of Jesus today should approach the OT with joy and with a willingness to do the hard work necessary for overcoming these practical obstacles.

Theoretical Obstacles I: Understanding Theology

In 1984, George Lindbeck identified three ways of understanding the nature of doctrine and the work of theology.[3] His proposal generated significant discussion and debate.[4] Although the details of his work have been questioned, his typology has proved to be helpful in thinking about the work of theology. In this section, I outline his types and add my own in order to guide our understanding of the relationship between theology and the OT.

This survey is important for two reasons. First, it will provide a basis for understanding how our conception of theology shapes our approach to the OT. As we work through these understandings of theology, I point out the differing ways that each may work with the OT. Second, the survey will allow me to establish an understanding of theology that guides my own proposals about the relationship between theology and the OT.

Lindbeck identifies three "theories of doctrine." The first two are descriptions of different ways that doctrine and theology have been understood. The third is Lindbeck's own proposal, which seeks to resolve the problems of the first two approaches. I will not try to give an exhaustive account of Lindbeck's argument. Instead, I draw insights from his analysis to accomplish my own task.

One approach to doctrine and theology seeks to identify and systematize the various propositional beliefs of Christianity. The task of theology, then, is to identify the essentials of Christian belief and to put them in an order that is logical and that shows their relationships to one another. These doctrines are mental concepts that mirror reality. Here the work of theology is primarily if not exclusively concerned with "cognitive assent," that is, with thinking. In this approach, doctrine and ethics are separated from one another. Doctrine is concerned with "what we believe," and ethics is concerned with "how we live." Ethics may follow from the doctrine, but it is not part of the doctrine, because doctrines are concerned with propositions.

On this understanding, theology might look to the OT for the beliefs that are still in force today. One obvious area would be the doctrine of God. Many of the "attributes" of God that we typically list in theology, such as omnipresence, omniscience, and omnipotence, are drawn from

---

3. George Lindbeck, *The Nature of Doctrine: Religion and Theology in a Postliberal Age* (Philadelphia: Westminster, 1984).

4. Bruce Marshall, ed., *Theology and Dialogue: Essays in Conversation with George Lindbeck* (Notre Dame, Ind.: University of Notre Dame Press, 1990), and Dennis Okholm and Timothy Phillips, eds., *The Nature of Confession: Evangelicals and Postliberals in Conversation* (Downers Grove, Ill.: InterVarsity, 1993).

the OT. Thus, theologians of this sort would look to OT scholars for identification of the central concepts of the OT and for a contextual and linguistic explanation of these concepts.

There are several things wrong with this conception of theology.
First, as Lindbeck argues, it treats doctrines like mental notions or concepts that line up with reality. We certainly want to say that Christian
beliefs are true and that they teach us about reality, but it is wrong
merely to identify them with mental concepts. In the OT, what Israel believed was not merely a matter of thinking, it was a way of living. In
Deuteronomy 6:4, we find the "Shema" of Israel: "Hear, O Israel: the
LORD our God, the LORD is one" (NIV). This is certainly a, perhaps the,
foundational belief of Israel. But it is immediately followed by the command to "love the LORD your God with all your heart and with all your
soul and with all your strength." Israel is further commanded to incorporate this belief in all of its living. Theology, for Israel, was not just
about ideas, it was about life. To regard doctrine and theology as primarily or exclusively concerned with mental assent to certain concepts
runs contrary to the OT.

The second problem with this "cognitive" approach to doctrine is
that it abstracts its work from the OT text. Once we have the concepts
that are central to the OT and their definitions, we really have no more
theological need for the OT. It becomes something like a can of food:
once we have removed the food, we no longer need the can. Many theologians who hold the understanding of theology that I am criticizing
would protest vehemently. And certainly many affirm the continuing
authority and spiritual vitality of the OT. But their *theology* has no further need of the OT once they have abstracted the propositions from it.

We can further explore this problem by considering how the OT itself
treats claims about God and commands from God. For the OT, statements about God's character and nature only make sense within a narrative. This does not mean that the literary genre is always narrative,
but that the story of Israel and God provides the context within which
confessions about God and the commands of God make sense. For example, the confession that the LORD is gracious and compassionate,
slow to anger and abounding in love and faithfulness (see Exod. 34:6),
is set within the story of God's liberation of Israel from Egypt and the
forgiveness of Israel's disobedience. The psalmist's confession of God's
mercy is rooted in his experience of God's forgiveness of sin. Similarly,
the commands of the OT are rooted in the story of God and Israel. The
Ten Commandments begin with the reminder of all that God has been
and is for Israel: "I am the LORD your God, who brought you out of
Egypt, out of the land of slavery" (Exod. 20:2 NIV). For the OT, then,

doctrines are not abstract concepts; rather, they are part of the story of God and Israel.

The third problem with this "cognitive" understanding of theology, closely related to the second, is that it removes theology from life. When we read theology and find it dry and abstract, we are probably encountering this approach to doctrine. Here doctrine becomes a self-contained system that seems to operate outside the messy realities of our lives. How far this is from the OT, in which profound thinking about God and the world is inextricably intertwined with the reality of human disobedience, suffering, the search for meaning, the judgment of God, the blessing of God.

Before we move to the second approach to theology identified by Lindbeck, I must make one important observation: my quarrel is not with concepts, propositions, or ideas as such; rather, my quarrel is with the distance between the biblical text and this "cognitive-propositional" understanding of doctrine and theology. As I have noted, the biblical text is full of concepts, propositions, and ideas, but they are treated very differently in the OT. Good questions to ask are: "Does the theology that I am reading drive me toward the Bible or away from it? Does it treat the Bible as dispensable or indispensable?" Consider how John Calvin's *Institutes of the Christian Religion* seeks to teach us how to read the Bible, or how John Wesley's theology is found primarily in sermons that are continually engaged with the Bible. Can we find the same, can we recover the same, for theology today? When I come to my own proposal for theology and the OT, I will seek to emulate these teachers from the past.

The second approach to doctrine and theology identified by Lindbeck regards doctrine as a way of expressing experience. On this understanding, the task of theology is to find symbols that effectively enable others to enter the same experience that we have had. Thus, the OT becomes a record of Israel's experiences, symbolized by various concepts and images. The work of OT scholars, then, is to identify the central experiences and symbols of the OT. The work of theology is to find new symbols that work for people today.

Having just considered the problems of a "cognitive-propositionalist" approach to doctrine, we may initially find this "experiential-expressivist" approach very attractive. After all, haven't we just seen that OT beliefs are rooted in Israel's experience of God? As Lindbeck identifies theological works that take this approach, however, several problems become evident.

First, for this approach, experience becomes the primary authority, and doctrines (symbols) become subordinate to the experience. Thus, my experience begins to define who God is and how God relates to the world. This approach neglects the persistent OT claim that in our fallen state we are wicked and self-deceived. The truth is found in God, not in us. Experience is not self-interpreting; we need God's Word to teach us how to understand our own experiences. For example, Israel's constant tendency in the OT is to interpret God's graciousness toward it as a sign of favoritism. As a result, they often presumed God's blessing in their disobedience. The exile was a painful corrective to their self-deception and idolatry. God chose them to be a witness to God's holiness and grace and to be a blessing to all peoples. God "favored" Israel so that all might come to know the holiness and love of God.

The second problem with this approach is that it makes dispensable the concepts and images of Scripture. In effect, it says, "If you find the biblical concepts and images ineffective, then discard them and find symbols that work for you." Certainly, the authors of Scripture constantly develop their understanding of God and find new images for God, but they do so under the guidance of the Holy Spirit. As our final rule of faith and practice, the Bible provides us with concepts and images, rooted in the OT in the story of Israel (and in the NT in the story of Jesus and the church), to which we submit our lives. The task of theology is not to replace the teaching of Scripture with something more effective but to make that teaching lively and powerful in our lives. The task of theology is to call us into the "biblical world," the world of God's holiness and grace that is present today—not away from it, into a world created by our own experiences and imagination.

Before we move to Lindbeck's own proposal, I must make one careful distinction. My criticisms of this "experiential-expressivist" approach are not meant to downplay the work of God in Israel's life or in our lives. Rather, my criticisms are meant to place theology in its proper relationship to this work. For Christians, the "principle of authority" is found not in our experience in and of itself but in the grace of God that we experience.[5]

Lindbeck labels his own approach "cultural-linguistic." On this understanding of doctrine, the task of theology is twofold. First, it is to initiate us into the community of faith. It is to create a "world" in which we live. In the OT, Israel represents a "culture" that organizes life through various practices and institutions that seek to reflect God's work of redemption. Second, theology is to teach us the language of that community of faith in God. This community teaches us, for exam-

---

5. See P. T. Forsyth, *The Principle of Authority in Relation to Certainty, Sanctity, and Society: An Essay in the Philosophy of Experimental Religion* (London: Hodder and Stoughton, 1912).

ple, that adultery is not to be described as freeing, fulfilling, and excit-ing; instead, it is to be described as sin, the breaking of covenant with God and spouse. In other words, reflecting one criticism of the experi-entialist approach, Lindbeck's approach assigns to theology the task of teaching us the language that interprets our experience.

Lindbeck's proposal is very attractive. It retains a concern for prop-ositions properly related to the story of the Bible. It restores experience of God's grace to its proper place. That is, it safeguards the very ele-ments of biblical revelation that the first two approaches to doctrine get wrong. Moreover, it drives us back to the Bible in our theological work.

Lindbeck's proposal is also attractive because it provides alterna-tives to some common and mistaken assumptions. For example, we often think of the work of hermeneutics as separating the culturally rel-ative from the theologically binding. But, in fact, there is no way to state something "theologically binding" apart from culture. We must always use a particular language—Hebrew, German, English—to do the work of hermeneutics, and language is always bound up with cul-ture. Hermeneutics does not somehow extract a timeless meaning from ancient texts, then restate that timeless meaning for contemporary cir-cumstances; rather, as I argue below, the task of biblical scholarship and theology is to enable us to become part of the story that begins in the OT.

Like Lindbeck's reconfiguring of the significance of culture, his "lin-guistic" emphasis corrects some of our mistaken assumptions. When Lindbeck calls for a linguistic understanding of doctrine, he does not mean that we must all learn Hebrew to be Christians, though some of us must. Nor is he making the mistake that James Barr exposes in *Se-mantics of Biblical Language*.[6] Rather, he is saying that doctrine is the language by which the community of faith identifies the "world" in which we are called to live as God's people.[7]

Lindbeck's account is instructive and illuminating. Nevertheless, I want to propose another understanding of doctrine and the work of theology that I will call "imaginative-practical." Since culture and lan-guage shape the world we see and the way we live in it, my "imagina-tive-practical" proposal is not so much a replacement for Lindbeck's as a restatement that brings to the fore the strengths of his proposal. As I

6. James Barr, *Semantics of Biblical Language* (London: Oxford University Press, 1961).
7. I am indebted to Craig Broyles for raising the questions I have addressed in the pre-vious two paragraphs. But he is not responsible for the way I have answered them.

argue below, it also has the advantage of more closely reflecting biblical emphases.

The imaginative part of my proposal is not a call to imagine what God is like or to imagine that God is present where God is absent. Rather, it is a call to be so disciplined by the biblical narrative that we "see past" the way the world and our sinful hearts teach us to see, in order to see God and the world as they are truly revealed in the Bible. Thus, "imaginative" might also be called "visual." I prefer "imaginative" because it reminds us of the illusory ways of seeing to which we are often captive.

The practical part of my proposal reminds us that Christianity is a way of living, not just a way of thinking. This emphasis teaches us that what we believe cannot be separated from how we live. Ethics is not incidental to doctrine. The way we live is not "added on" to what we believe; it is bound up in what we believe. Even that is too weak: what we believe *is* the way we are to live. To believe in God revealed in the Bible is to live in a particular way. This "practical" aspect of doctrine, then, is meant to reflect the conviction that theology is for life.

Together, "imaginative" and "practical" do two things. First, they reflect the constant biblical emphasis on seeing and hearing. The biblical authors are continually concerned with discerning God's work in the world. The prophets exemplify this when they discern God's blessing and judgment in the midst of political and military events. At the same time, the prophets and others in the OT call upon the people of God to "hear" God in such a way that we obey God's voice—in the Bible, true hearing results in the practice of God's will. Second, "imaginative" and "practical," taken together, are mutually reinforcing. We live in the world that we see, and we see the world according to the way that we live in it. For example, seeing forgiveness embodied enables us to practice forgiveness. Similarly, practicing forgiveness enables us to see it more clearly. So we need both the imaginative work and the practical work of doctrine in order to retain the biblical emphasis on seeing and hearing and to be faithful in our own lives.

I have engaged in this lengthy consideration of the nature of doctrine and the purposes of theology to show how various conceptions of theology shape approaches to the OT. I have also introduced my own proposal for the nature of doctrine and the work of theology. But to be persuasive I need to detail how my imaginative-practical approach relates the OT and theology. Before I give that account, however, I must clear one further obstacle to a proper relationship between theology and the OT.

Theoretical Obstacles II: Understanding the Relationship between Theology and Biblical Studies

For many decades, one approach has dominated our understanding of the relationship between biblical studies and theology. This approach has been so dominant that it simply seems intuitively right. We have not imagined that there are other possibilities. Because it has become part of "the air that we breathe," because it seems so natural and obviously right, any challenge appears wrongheaded. Nevertheless, I think that this dominant approach is wrong in its account of the relationship between OT studies (and biblical studies more generally) and theology. Because it is dominant and because it is wrong, I must show its errors in order to clear the ground for my own proposal.

The dominant understanding of the relationship between OT studies and theology may be roughly characterized by the phrase, "what it meant-what it means."[8] The task of biblical scholarship is to tell us what the Bible or some portion of the Bible meant; the task of theological scholarship is to tell us what the Bible means. Biblical scholarship is a descriptive, historical task; theology is a normative task. This account is attractive. It seems to acknowledge the linguistic and cultural gap between us and the original text. Biblical scholars are those who learn the ancient languages and culture in order to discern the original meaning of the text. Theologians take the results of biblical scholarship and seek to make it relevant and meaningful for today. As we have seen, this theological work depends, at least in part, on one's view of the nature of doctrine.

Although this view may seem natural and obvious, a closer examination exposes a number of problems. Some of these problems are relatively easy to identify, others concern hotly debated issues in contemporary scholarship.[9] In this chapter I am concerned with three problems that relate most directly to the relationship between theology and the OT.

One problem with this approach is that it creates what we might call a "relay method" of biblical interpretation.[10] Using the what it meant-what it means scheme, we could picture the first leg of biblical inter-

---

8. The classic statement of this formula is Krister Stendahl, "Biblical Theology, Contemporary," in *Interpreter's Dictionary of the Bible* (New York: Abingdon, 1962), 1:418–31.

9. For a fuller consideration of these problems, see Ben C. Ollenburger, "What Krister Stendahl Meant—A Normative Critique of Descriptive Biblical Theology," *Horizons in Biblical Theology* 8 (1986): 61–98, and Fowl, *Engaging Scripture*, 13–21.

10. The image is taken from Nicholas Lash, *Theology on the Way to Emmaus* (London: SCM, 1986), 79. His entire chapter is relevant to our discussion; see "What Might Martyrdom Mean?" 75–92.

pretation being run by the biblical scholars, whose job is to discover what the text meant. Having accomplished this, they hand the baton (what the text meant) to the theologians, whose job is to discover what the text means. They then hand this baton to pastors, perhaps ethicists, who apply this meaning to the lives of Christians. Even if we change the image a bit and imagine the same person running every leg of the relay, we still need to be cautious of the image, as I argue below.

Although this image may seem overdone, it fairly reflects a pervasive picture of biblical interpretation and application. Once we have this picture in place, we can see several problems. One problem is that it places biblical scholars at a distance from the church. They are not to concern themselves with normative Christian convictions; theirs is a descriptive, historical discipline. In effect they are to say, "It is true that Christians once claimed X, but don't ask me if X itself is true. That's for the theologians to consider." At the same time that this relay method places biblical scholars at a distance from the church, it places theologians at a distance from the Bible. Theologians can only run their leg of the relay once biblical scholars have determined what the text meant. Given disagreements among biblical scholars, we can well imagine five runners arriving at the handoff point and the poor theologian not knowing which baton to take.[11] One can equally imagine a pastor confused by the arrival of several theologian-runners at the handoff point.

In contrast to this relay method, we need a practice of interpretation that calls biblical scholars to be concerned with (normative) theology as they interpret Scripture and that calls theologians to be concerned with Scripture as they teach doctrine. Moreover, we need a picture of the relationship between biblical scholars and theologians, and of biblical scholarship and theology, that regards the relationship as ongoing. The biblical scholar does not retire to the infield after handing off a baton, and the theologian does not leave the biblical scholar behind when doing theology. Rather, they should be constantly "meddling" in one another's work.[12]

A second problem with the what it meant–what it means scheme is that it treats the Bible as a container of meaning. As I noted above, if the Bible merely contains meaning that we can extract, then once the

11. I well remember when I first began preaching how I agonized over interpretive disagreements as I prepared my sermons. I will return to the problem of multiple interpretations below.

12. This is an appropriate point to acknowledge my debt to my colleagues in biblical studies—Karen Jobes, Bruce Fisk, and Tremper Longman—for "meddling" with an earlier version of this chapter. Their questions, comments, and criticisms have improved it, even where they may disagree with me.

meaning is extracted, we no longer need the container. In this instance, we might picture the biblical scholar as a gold miner with a panful of dirt and sludge. Sluicing away the sludge leaves the gold nuggets of what the text meant. These are passed to the theologian, who refines and purifies the nuggets into what the text means, which are then passed to the pastor for fashioning into jewels of application. Although the very notion of "meaning" is problematic, we may note that the meaning of a text is not something that exists independently of the text.[13]

One common way of applying the what it meant-what it means scheme is to think that the Bible contains a cultural husk and a theological kernel. On this view, our job is to peel away what is culturally relative, leaving only what is theologically binding. As I noted earlier, we must realize that there is no way for us to convey meaning apart from culture. We simply cannot discern acultural meaning in a text. "Meaning" always depends on a cultural context simply to have meaning. The easiest way to see this is to recognize that we use a particular language to convey meaning—Hebrew, Greek, Latin, English, Japanese, and so on. And language is always shaped by a particular culture. When we think that we have peeled away the cultural husk of the OT to discern the theological kernel, we are simply obscuring the new cultural husk that gives meaning to our claims. Indeed, this shows us that we should not even think of cultural husks or culturally relative elements in the text. Rather, we must develop an approach to the OT and theology that takes cultural differences seriously while also honoring the necessity of culture.

Running through these criticisms is a larger problem that I noted briefly: the what it meant-what it means method separates the work of biblical scholars and theologians. Indeed, there is good historical evidence that it was meant to do precisely that, in order to free biblical interpretation from the authority of the church. Of course, all this did was place the Bible under another authority, the authority of the academy and the guild of professional biblical scholars.[14] This separation of the two disciplines and their increasing specialization means that the distance between the Bible and theology has also been increasing.

13. For a good introduction to the problems of meaning, see Jeffrey Stout, "What Is the Meaning of a Text?" *New Literary History* 14 (1982): 1–12. See also Fowl's discussion in *Engaging Scripture*, 56–58, and Vanhoozer, *Is There a Meaning in This Text?*

14. Stephen E. Fowl, "The Ethics of Interpretation, or What's Left Over after the Elimination of Meaning," in *The Bible in Three Dimensions*, ed. D. J. Clines, S. E. Fowl, and S. E. Porter (Sheffield: Sheffield Academic Press, 1990), 379–98. I should also note that theology is not exempt from this same captivity to the academy and to professional guilds.

What we need, then, is an understanding of the relationship between biblical scholarship and theology that closes this gap. We also need courageous biblical scholars and theologians who resist the "discipline" that their professional guilds impose on them in subtle and not-so-subtle ways.

To begin this process, I propose, as a replacement for the "what it meant-what it means" approach, a "this is that" approach.[15] The phrase "this is that" is taken from Peter's sermon on the day of Pentecost (Acts 2:16 KJV). It reflects that Peter's imagination was so formed by the OT that he recognized what was happening at Pentecost as that which was spoken by the prophet Joel. "This is that" calls biblical scholars to be so formed by the Bible—by the biblical world, we might say—that they see that world present today. This scheme calls theologians to see our present situation through the eyes of Scripture so that they see God working today. This leads us back to my call for an imaginative-practical view of the nature of doctrine and the work of theology.

This Is That: Imaginative-Practical Theology and the Old Testament

"Imaginative" theology transforms our vision of God, the world, and ourselves. It exposes the illusions by which we are held captive, so that we can see truly. "Practical" theology transforms the way we live. It reminds us that a proper interpretation of the text is not another text, but a life rooted in seeing and hearing God through the Scriptures. Theology calls us to "perform the Scriptures."[16]

The relationship between theology and the OT is vital in two senses—it is necessary and it is lively. It is necessary because the OT is the God-inspired revelation of truth. It is lively, because the OT, by its age and cultural difference, displaces us from our familiar world, our familiar ways of seeing and living. This displacement helps make it possible for God to break into our world, to expose our illusions, and to call us to a new life.

This way of thinking guides our theological study of the OT. The OT scholar's knowledge of ancient languages and cultures is for the purpose of entering into—indwelling—the world of the OT, and for re-creating it in such a way that others, including theologians, can indwell it.

15. I have been thinking along these lines for many years, ever since learning that *This Is That* was the British title of the book by F. F. Bruce, which was published in North America as *The New Testament Development of Old Testament Themes* (Grand Rapids: Eerdmans, 1968). More recently, see the development of "this is that" in James Wm. McClendon, *Systematic Theology: Doctrine*, vol. 2 (Nashville: Abingdon, 1994), 44–46, 408–9.

16. Lash, *Theology on the Way to Emmaus*, 37–46.

Thus, we see the OT work of God and hear the OT voice of God today. We recognize that "this is that." Theologians are those whom the church has set aside to dwell in the world that OT study has re-created. From this place, they are to tell us what they see. If we want to draw a clearer line between OT exegesis and theology, we may say that OT exegesis is an exercise in seeing "that"—what God has done in the past—and theology is an exercise in seeing "this"—what God is doing today. When we bring OT study and theology together in mutual encouragement and correction, then we see "this is that."

This way of construing the relationship between theology and the OT binds them inextricably. They are no longer in a relay race. Instead, we may picture our study of the OT and our theologizing as a kind of "group project." They are in constant dialogue with one another, and their tasks overlap. As OT studies re-creates the world of God's working and speaking in the OT, theologians must constantly be asking OT scholars, "Is this what you mean? Would you agree that this work of God today is that work of God in the OT?" At the same time, OT scholars—whose special assignment is the study of the OT—must constantly be asking theologians, "What concerns the church today? What in our present situation requires a response from the church?" Both must also engage in mutual examination and correction. For example, OT scholars must say, "This is what God was concerned about in the Old Testament. Are we concerned with this today?" And theologians must say, "These are the ways that our culture has shaped us. Are you importing them into the text?"

This work requires both courage and humility on the part of OT scholars and theologians. It requires courage because it violates the long-dominant view of scholarship, which emphasizes increasing specialization and the separation of disciplines. Theologians and OT scholars who adopt this proposal will be doing work that has not traditionally been understood as "real scholarship." This work also requires humility, because it calls scholars to abandon safe and secure specialization and to expose themselves to new sources of criticism. Theologians must humbly submit to the correction of OT scholars, and OT scholars must submit to theologians. This practice of humble submission helps prevent bad interpretations that lead to unfaithfulness. The Bible has often been used to justify all manner of evil in God's name. By constantly examining one another and acknowledging the significance of gifts other than our own, we are guided in the path of truth rather than error.

This sketch is rooted in the conviction that the Holy Spirit gives different gifts in the church. Some have gifts that call them to OT scholarship, others have gifts that call them to theology. To these we must add many other gifts. Some in the church are gifted in their sensitivity to injustice and force OT scholars and theologians to attend to the biblical call to justice. Others are gifted in works of mercy and call us to pay attention to God's work of mercy. Still others may be administratively gifted in making sure that everyone's voice is heard, and most of all that we discern the guidance of the Holy Spirit.[17]

This proposal presents an enormous challenge to our desire for control. In scholarship, we want to master our subject matter; in this proposal, we are called to submit to our subject matter. Certainly, OT scholars must learn the languages, content, and cultures of the text, but they do so not to exercise control over it, but to submit to it by entering its world. Likewise, theologians must learn the history of theology, but they do so to submit to the ways that previous believers have seen and heard God.

At the same time that this proposal closes the gap between OT studies and theology, it guides us as Christians in our faithfulness to the OT. "This is that" reminds us that the OT is fulfilled in Jesus Christ. "Fulfilled" means that the OT is filled with meaning, not that it is superseded or set aside. With the earliest followers of Jesus, we turn to the OT Scriptures to understand God's work in Jesus. We understand Jesus of Nazareth as the Messiah only when we understand how he fills messianic hope full of meaning. We understand the church as the people of God today only when we understand Israel as the people of God in the OT. We must not extract concepts and principles from the OT that we then interpret for today. We must submit ourselves to the eyes and ears of the OT so that we see and hear God now as God's people did then.

Imaginative-practical theology also guides our struggle with multiple interpretations of the text. For those who recognize the authority of the Bible and seek to submit to it, one source of great frustration is the variety of interpretations. We seem to be caught in a situation in which a text can mean whatever one wants it to mean. In reaction, we seek *the* meaning of a text. If we recognize that the purpose of Bible study is to shape our vision and to guide our hearing, then we may be able to recognize that the text prohibits some interpretations without its meaning being exhausted by one interpretation.[18]

17. For a similar account, see John Howard Yoder, "The Hermeneutics of Peoplehood," in *The Priestly Kingdom: Social Ethics as Gospel* (Notre Dame, Ind.: University of Notre Dame Press, 1984), 15–45.

18. The issues here are very complex. For further helpful discussion, see Fowl, *Engaging Scripture*, 32–61, and Vanhoozer, *Is There a Meaning in This Text?* 98–147, 416–21.

If the purpose of Scripture is to shape our vision and guide our hearing, then we may see the purpose of multiple interpretations. No one scene can be captured by a single photograph. No one's personality is exhausted by a single portrait. In the same way, our vision is not formed by a single meaning of a text. A text may call us to look at something from several different angles, and multiple interpretations enable that. However, we may say that a picture does not capture a scene or that a portrait does not look anything like the person it purports to represent. We may also say that one portrait captures more of the subject's personality than any other portrait. Likewise, we may say that some interpretations of a text do not represent the text at all. And we may say that one particular interpretation forms our vision and guides our hearing better than others.

If we are to learn that "this is that," then we may also be able to rejoice in the inexhaustible meaning of the Bible. In the NT, Psalm 22 becomes a significant guide to understanding the death of Jesus. But Psalm 22 did not languish without meaning until the coming of Jesus. It had meaning for the psalmist when he wrote it and for Israel when they included it in their worship and in the Book of Psalms. Moreover, it has meaning for us today. "This is that" teaches us that biblical texts are inexhaustible in their meaning for God's people.

As we engage in an imaginative-practical theological approach to OT studies and learn this is that, we are dependent on the Holy Spirit.[19] This dependence runs counter to much biblical study and theology. Our usual way of approaching these disciplines is to construct a methodology that has the practical effect of excluding the work of the Spirit or at least making it very difficult for the Spirit to guide us.

Here imaginative-practical theology becomes very practical, because we begin to ask about the character of students of the Bible and theology, not about their methodology.[20] Is our study of the Bible and our theology rooted in a life of worship? Are our lives centered in the community of faithful and gifted people? Does our study of the Bible and our theology arise from a life of prayer? These questions and concerns may strike us as oddly out of place in a guide to OT exegesis. We are used to concerns about literary genre, cultural and historical contexts, and hermeneutical method. Those skills are necessary to the continuing faithfulness of the church. But there is also a long and honored history in the church, much neglected today, of insisting that students

19. Vanhoozer, *Is There a Meaning in This Text?* 407–31; Fowl, *Engaging Scripture*, 97–127.

20. Vanhoozer, *Is There a Meaning in This Text?* 431–41; Fowl, *Engaging Scripture*, 62–96.

of the Bible be first and foremost praying people. The people who wrote the Bible were people of prayer and worship, who found their lives in the community of faith. If we are to see and hear as they did, then we must live as they lived.

Therefore, our understanding of theology and the OT leads us in the end to recognize that the first step toward OT exegesis is to become a people of prayer. Prayer is not something to add to other skills; it is the foundation and the sustenance for faithful study of the OT. In prayer we enter into friendship with God.[21] This friendship transforms us by purifying our seeing and sharpening our hearing so that we see and hear God and our ancestors in the faith. Today we may often view prayer as a kind of "home shopping network" for people of faith—in prayer we dial God's number to place an order with God. But this consumer mentality is far from Christian prayer. In Christian prayer we first listen to God so that our vision of God, the world, and ourselves is changed. Then we are in a position for our lives to be joined with God and to ask God to bring about what God intends for our time and place. This prayer, then, is joined closely with Bible study and theology that helps us to see and to hear God. Prayer is integral to imaginative-practical theology.

Finally, we can focus this discussion on the difficult question of the "cultural situatedness" of the Bible and theology. All along I have been providing ways of taking seriously the differences between the cultures of the OT and today's cultures. Certainly, the cultures of the OT are different from our own; we do not dress as they did or worship as they did. However, we are wrong if we think that our study of the OT is for the purpose of distinguishing the culturally relative from the theologically universal. OT exegesis does not equip us to identify and peel away the cultural husks of the OT; rather, it enables us to enter the cultures of the OT so that we see and hear God's work in those times and places. Theology does not seek to discern acultural theological concepts; rather, it seeks to let us see that same work of God and hear that same voice of God in the midst of our own culture. Theology and OT studies do not help us separate the work of God from culture; they help us discern the work of God in culture. When OT studies and theology are in constant lively conversation with one another and with other gifts in the church, then we are able to see past the *illusions* of a particular social setting so that we see God at work, judging and redeeming in that particular setting. We are able to hear God's

---

21. James M. Houston, *The Transforming Power of Prayer: Deepening Your Friendship with God* (Colorado Springs, Colo.: NavPress, 1998).

voice piercing the noise of our lives and our age, so that we practice what God calls us to do as God's people.

This Is That: Two Examples of Imaginative-Practical Theology and the Old Testament

If we are to live as God's people today, as Israel was called to live in the OT, then there is much for us to learn from Israel. For our own situation as the people of God in Western European culture, one lesson stands out.

In the OT, Israel, as God's people, was blessed by God. But that blessing was not for themselves, it was for all people. When God calls Abraham (Genesis 15), God promises to bless him, but God also promises that in him all the nations of the earth will be blessed. Israel's wealth and strength were not for its own enjoyment, but for the purpose of fulfilling its mission of making God's holiness and love known among all people. When the people of Israel presumed on God's blessing and used their wealth for their own purposes, God judged them, destroying the northern kingdom and exiling the southern kingdom, leaving only a remnant through which to bless the nations. This blessing for all people came through Abraham when Jesus Christ was born as Abraham's seed and as the Savior of all peoples, Jew and Gentile.

Today, the church needs to see that we are the people of God. To us have been entrusted, at least for a time, the blessings of Israel. Like Israel, we need to recognize that those blessings are not for us to build stone mansions, lush vineyards, beautiful beds, or to indulge in fine dining (Amos 5–6). Rather, those blessings are given for the fulfillment of our mission, to make known to all peoples the blessing of God through Abraham's seed, Jesus Christ. If, like Israel, we presume upon God's call and blessing, we will also be judged as Israel was judged.

As my final example, I recount the most memorable theology lecture I have heard. It was given by Dr. Thomas Langford in the required theology course at Duke Divinity School. I was a graduate student there and Dr. Langford's teaching assistant.

In his lecture, Dr. Langford retold the story of Jacob so that we could see Jacob as a cheat, a liar, a greedy man, a con man, and a coward. His retelling was masterful. When he described Jacob's first encounter with Rachel, Jacob's future wife, Dr. Langford recounted how the text says that Jacob saw Rachel . . . and the sheep (Gen. 29:10). We all laughed, because we could see Jacob's character—his greed—subtly identified by the text. After Dr. Langford had established Jacob's character, he then went on to describe God's choice of Jacob. What God would choose such a man to be the father of the twelve tribes of Israel?

The answer, of course, is that only a God of grace and mercy would choose Jacob. But Dr. Langford was not finished. Sweeping his eyes across the lecture hall, he paused, gathered our attention, and then concluded: "And the truth is that everyone of us is Jacob. We are all liars, cheats, cowards. We are all chosen only by the grace and mercy of God." This is that. Grace and mercy are not concepts to be manipulated by theologians. They are realities known by Jacob, by God's people in the OT, and by God's people today. They are gifts to be received. As we receive them, our vision is transformed and our lives are changed.

Scripture Index

Subject Index